Mantle of the Sufi Kings

The rise and establishment of Safavid rule in Iran is a clear and momentous event in the wider history of the Middle East and Islamic world. In this study, Hani Khafipour explores how loyalty, social cohesion, and power dynamics found in Sufi thought underpinned the Safavid community's sources of social power and determination. Once in power, the Safavid state's patronage of art, literature, and architecture turned Iran into a flourishing empire of culture, influencing neighboring empires including the Ottomans and Mughals. Examining the origin and evolution of the Safavid order, *Mantle of the Sufi Kings* offers fresh insights into how religious and sociopolitical forces merged to create a powerful Shiʿi empire, with Iran remaining the only Shiʿi nation in the world today. This study provides a bold new interpretation of Iran's early modern history, with important implications for the contemporary religio-political discourse in the Middle East.

Hani Khafipour is a faculty member in the Department of History at the State University of New York at Buffalo, focusing on medieval and early modern Iran, Islamic political thought, and Sufism. His edited volume, *Empires of the Near East and India: Source Studies of the Safavid, Ottoman, and Mughal Literate Communities* (2019), won the American Historical Association's J. Franklin Jameson Award in 2021.

Cambridge Studies in Islamic Civilization

Other titles in the series are listed at the back of the book.

Mantle of the Sufi Kings

Political Sufism and the Rise of Early Modern Iran

HANI KHAFIPOUR

State University of New York at Buffalo

CAMBRIDGE
UNIVERSITY PRESS

CAMBRIDGE
UNIVERSITY PRESS

Shaftesbury Road, Cambridge CB2 8EA, United Kingdom

One Liberty Plaza, 20th Floor, New York, NY 10006, USA

477 Williamstown Road, Port Melbourne, VIC 3207, Australia

314–321, 3rd Floor, Plot 3, Splendor Forum, Jasola District Centre, New Delhi – 110025, India

103 Penang Road, #05–06/07, Visioncrest Commercial, Singapore 238467

Cambridge University Press is part of Cambridge University Press & Assessment, a department of the University of Cambridge.

We share the University's mission to contribute to society through the pursuit of education, learning and research at the highest international levels of excellence.

www.cambridge.org
Information on this title: www.cambridge.org/9781009663526

DOI: 10.1017/9781009663533

When citing this work, please include a reference to the DOI 10.1017/9781009663533

First published 2026

A catalogue record for this publication is available from the British Library

A Cataloging-in-Publication data record for this book is available from the Library of Congress

ISBN 978-1-009-66352-6 Hardback

To my grandparents,
Jebriyeh Salemi-fayyeh and Rahim Vatanzadeh.
Words fail to describe their love and my gratitude.

Contents

Figures and Maps

FIGURES

MAPS

Acknowledgments

This book has been a companion by my side for many years, written in various dwellings, and shaped by the insights of numerous scholars. Expressing gratitude adequately proves challenging.

I extend my deepest thanks to my inspiring teachers: Michael Bitter, John E. Woods, Fred Donner, Saeed Ghahremani, and the late professors Heshmat Moayyad, Iraj Afshar, Franklin D. Lewis, and Cornell Fleischer. Additionally, my understanding has been enriched by the works of eminent scholars whom I only met through their books and insights.

I am profoundly grateful to the institutions whose resources and support were indispensable in crafting this work. The Regenstein Library and the Oriental Institute at the University of Chicago provided unparalleled access to scholarly materials, enriching every chapter with depth and detail. The intellectual environment fostered by colleagues and friends there over several years was precious.

The University of Tehran Library, Majlis Library, and the University of Isfahan Library, along with their scholarly communities, provided essential materials and research support that deeply engaged me in fundamental questions concerning the rise of the Safavids. Across borders, the Süleymaniye Kütüphanesi and Topkapı Sarayı Müzesi in Türkiye, and the Georgian National Museum in Tbilisi, offered indispensable resources for exploring the early Safavid sources.

The Medieval Institute at the University of Notre Dame and the Leibniz-Institut für Europäische Geschichte in Mainz provided serene spaces for writing and research. The extensive collections of the Cambridge University Library, along with the resources and intellectual communities at Columbia University Library and Harvard University, provided invaluable insights and support throughout the research process. Each of these institutions played a crucial role in realizing this project, and their contributions are deeply appreciated. I wish to thank Azad Sadr and Emran El-Badawi, whose enduring friendship has meant so much. And to my siblings, Sara and Soheyl, for their boundless love.

With deepest gratitude, I honor my dear aunt Ameneh Vatanzadeh; my children—Soroush, Sosheyant, and Anahita—whose laughter and presence kept my spirit whole; and my immortal beloved, Alexandra Zirkle, whose love was the quiet hymn that carried me through the long, solitary nights of writing. Without their light, my solitary voyages through the shadows of the past to write this book would have been far darker.

Transliteration and Dates

TRANSLITERATION

The system of transliteration used in this book follows a simplified version of the one adopted by the *International Journal of Middle Eastern Studies.*

DATES

Dates are indicated first by the *hijrī* (AH), followed by the Gregorian Common Era (CE), year.

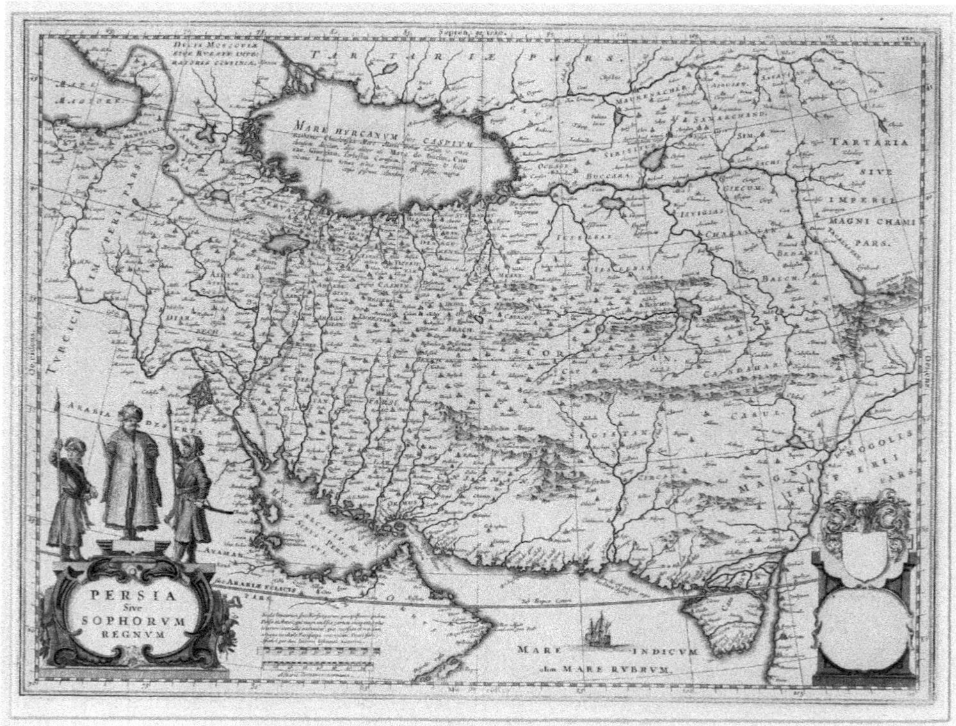

MAP 0.1 A seventeenth-century Dutch map of Safavid Iran. This detailed map of Persia was created by the Dutch cartographer Willem Janszoon Blaeu (1571–1638), who became the official cartographer for the Dutch East India Company (Vereenigde Oost-Indische Compagnie) in 1633. The map was included in Blaeu's celebrated *Theatrum Orbis Terrarum sive Atlas Novus* and published in 1635 in Amsterdam. It illustrates the Safavid Empire at its height, encompassing regions that now include parts of Turkmenistan, Afghanistan, the Caspian Sea, the Caucasus (Armenia, Azerbaijan, Georgia), as well as Oman, Bahrain, Kuwait, and the Persian Gulf.

Introduction

The principle animating this book was a cornerstone in a controversial case that nearly cost the forty-fifth president of the United States his office. The seemingly universal principles of loyalty and patronage were brought to light in one of the most anticipated hearings in recent years involving the newly elected president, Donald Trump, and the director of the Federal Bureau of Investigation (FBI), James Comey. President Trump had fired Comey on May 9, 2017, a decision many in Washington suspected was due to Comey's refusal to bury the FBI's investigation into Trump's connections to Russian interference that helped him clench the presidential victory. Comey's testimony months later revealed how loyalty was at the heart of the matter.

In the Senate Intelligence Committee's hearing into his dismissal, Comey recounted that a few days before his termination, on January 27, 2017, Trump invited him to dinner during which he threatened Comey's job. One thing Trump said stuck out acutely in Comey's memory of the evening: "I need loyalty. I expect loyalty." Comey interpreted Trump's demand and in fact the whole invitation to dinner as a means to compel him to ask Trump to allow him to keep his job in order to create a patronage relationship. Senator Mark Warner paused and asked Comey about that point during the hearing:

COMEY: The dinner was an effort to build a relationship – in fact he asked specifically of loyalty in the context of asking me to stay.

WARNER: That was just a few days before you were fired.

COMEY: The next Friday I have dinner, and the president begins by wanting to talk about my job. And so I'm sitting there thinking, wait a minute, three times . . . you've asked me to stay or talked about me staying. . . . but my common sense told me what's going on here is, he's looking to get something in exchange for granting my request to stay in the job.

WARNER: This [*sic*] constant requests, again, quoting you, him saying that he – you explained your independence he came back to I need loyalty, I expect loyalty. Have you ever had any of those kind of requests from anyone else you ever worked for in the government?

COMEY: No. [And that is] what made me uneasy. I'm at that point the director of the FBI. The reason that congress created a ten year term is so that the director is not feeling as if they're serving at – with political loyalty owed to any particular person.[1]

Trump eventually walked away unscathed from allegations that he had colluded with Russian intelligence services, and Comey went on to write a bestseller about his experience, which he titled, *A Higher Loyalty*. The book was later made into a television miniseries.

As hinted earlier, this quintessentially modern political scandal points to seemingly universal political power dynamics that would not have been out of place in preindustrial societies, in the early modern Eurasian states such as the Safavid state of Iran, the setting of this book. Trump attempted to generate a patronage relationship with Comey, offering job security in exchange for Comey's personal loyalty and service as a "client" in this case, to quash the investigation that threatened his election victory.

Comey found Trump's overtures censorious – even criminal. Sectors of the American public were likewise stunned. Comey upheld his loyalty to state institutions and balked at offering loyalty to an individual and placing himself under a patron's obligation. For Comey, loyalty meant a duty to the state and its institutions, not to an individual.

But Comey's visceral abhorrence of Trump's understanding of loyalty and patronage has another side that is equally legitimate. Indeed patron-client relationships have long organized political life. Comey's position is a relatively recent invention, one that slowly gained prominence as the standard configuration of political loyalty at the time of the formation of nation-states, and later as the paradigm of nationalism in the twentieth century, spreading to the Global South during the colonial and the

[1] Ryan Teague Beckwith, "Read the Transcript of James Comey's Testimony," *Time*, June 8, 2017, https://time.com/4810345/james-comey-testimony-real-time-transcript/.

postcolonial years. Prior to this transformation, patronage-client relationships were endemic to the structuring of political life among early modern Eurasian dynasties. In early modern Iran, the focus of this book, for example, patron-client relationships were the pulse that sustained state politics and the creation of loyalty and maintenance of patronage underpinned it all. As I hope to make clear in what follows, loyalty and patronage were a vital feature of Safavid political life because of the ways they fueled group cohesion – the central pillar of their political and military power.

The inkling for writing this book began some twenty years ago when I became fascinated with the Safavids during graduate work at the University of Chicago. What lured me was the puzzle of why this Sufi community succeeded as a political order when so many others had failed. What were the long-term processes involved in the transformation of a Sufi order into a regional military power capable of perpetuating its religiopolitical institutions? Even in the loose way in which I phrased the questions, the book is an attempt to answer this initial curiosity. It does not intend to provide a host of historical causes that gave rise to the Safavids, but to give account to the ideological sources of power as a way toward building up to a multicausal explanation. I have tried to be mindful of positivist and determinist traps while presenting my explanations. The Safavids might have vanished from the political landscape had it not been for other socioeconomic and ecological factors that converged in the later middle period not discussed here. My emphasis in studying the Safavids' ascent to sovereignty has been on the ideological dimension of power and material inducements as they pertained to patronage activities and gift exchange, and trust that economic and social historians would enrich my findings with insights of their own.

This book recounts how loyalty, patronage, and the monopoly on the sources of ideological power sustained the Safavid community's sense of cohesion long term. The substructure of the Safavids' rise to power is a particularly rich context for such an exploration because the Safavid Sufi order by the mid-ninth/fifteenth century had become a hybrid political organization with considerable military capability. The nature of their group cohesion steeped in Sufi tradition thus provides a critical piece of the puzzle in deciphering their ascent to power at the turn of the sixteenth century.

To make sense of this patronage-fueled political structure I explain the ideas, relationships, and organizational capacities entailed in generating ties of loyalty that sustained political relationship, hardening ties, and shaping group solidarity against the backdrop of continual war and systemic political instability.

Understanding the inescapable dynamics of political power ensconced in patronage, loyalty, and group cohesion are not just keys to decoding the Safavids' long-term success, but also to shedding light on the historical context of present-day political crises that precisely challenge the concepts of loyalty and clientelism. As the ex-president Trump impressed upon the former FBI director with three powerful words his demand as his patron: "I expect loyalty." However much Comey wished modern conceptions of political loyalty be based on ethics and impartiality, and not be personal, his belief couldn't be further from that of Trump who conceived of loyalty as deeply personal with ethical elasticity.

Modern political loyalty can masquerade as ethically framed and impersonal, yet the "patron's" demand for loyalty of his "client" in exchange for patronage as Comey faced hundreds of years later shows the persistence of this human challenge. Instances of favoritism, coercion, unlawful protection of powerful clients, and accusation of financial corruption in power politics across the contemporary world can be traced to the challenges posed by the misconceptions of patronage and the obligations of loyalty.

The court societies of the early modern world were interwoven with networks of patrons and clients, and the Safavid dynasty of Iran offers a fascinating case of the cultivation of loyalty as a central pillar of statecraft. Section I.1 provides an overview on the historiography of the Safavid ascent to power.

I.1 CONTEMPORARY PERCEPTIONS OF THE SAFAVID ASCENT TO POWER

The Safavid dynastic climb to power in what is roughly modern-day Iran during the opening of the tenth/sixteenth century was a watershed in global history. The Safavids were a Sunni Sufi order founded in the mid-eighth/fourteenth century that achieved the unimaginable: the establishment of a resilient Shiʿi state in the heart of West Asia – and they succeeded in expanding and propagating its structures of religiopolitical domination until the present day. They are the reason why Iran is the only Shiʿi country in the world today and helped shape Iran's current geopolitical relations with Lebanon, Syria, and Iraq rooted in the Safavid support of Shiʿi communities and patronage of holy pilgrimage sites beyond their heartland.

The Safavid dynasty bequeathed to today's Iran exquisite art, architecture, philosophy, music, and a defined protected territory. Their patronage of the arts is the underpinning of Iran's contemporary cultural reawakening in religious as well as secular arts as seen in the works of Shoja Azari, Siamak Filizadeh, Hamid Rahmanian, and others, who by using Safavid-era leitmotifs have created a reformulation of Iran's artistic authenticity as well as an avenue for critiquing power and political domination.[2]

When one examines the origins of the Safavids to understand how generations of loosely affiliated Sufi communities in eighth/fourteenth-century northwestern Iran, devoted to Islamic mysticism and spiritual transcendence, over a span of two centuries transformed into one of the most powerful and vibrant states of the early modern era, fortunately one finds several pieces of the puzzle already assembled. Safavid historians in and outside of Iran do not generally disagree on the reasons for the Safavids' ascent to power and would concur that a host of factors contributed to their success. Their analysis is one of emphasis and not of fundamental disagreements as one finds in the early historiography of the Ottoman rise to power. These views have included emphasis on the "power vacuum" of the late ninth/fifteenth century created by the decline of the Aqquyunlu and Timurid dynasties that had ruled greater Iran for nearly a century. Another overlapping explanation was the *ghāzī* (holy warrior) origins of the dynasty, similar to that offered to explain the Ottoman success, which suggests that the early Safavids gained vital military and psychological benefits from campaigns against the Christian territories in the Caucasus, in Georgia and Armenia, in the late ninth/fifteenth century. Others have stressed the unfaltering support of the Shiʿi-leaning Turcoman warrior tribes of eastern Anatolia and northwestern Iran. This camp considers the "charismatic leadership" of the founder of the dynasty, Shah Ismail, central in their rise to power as speculation of his hallowed aura in the eyes of his followers linked him to a host of messianic and eschatological anticipations.[3]

[2] Hani Khafipour, "Echoes of the Safavid Past," in *In the Fields of Empty Days: The Intersection of Past and Present in Iranian Art*, ed. Linda Komaroff (Los Angeles: Los Angeles County Museum of Art, 2018), 66–80. See the works of Azari, Filizadeh, and Rahmanian explored in Komaroff's *In the Fields of Empty Days*.

[3] A comprehensive literature review of Safavid historiography and bibliography has been provided by Andrew J. Newman in *Safavid Iran: Rebirth of a Persian Empire* (I.B. Taruris, 2006), 1–13, 248–65, as well as recent doctoral dissertations available in online databases. Below is a short list of some of the relevant research important to the subjects discussed in this book in alphabetical order. The list is not meant to be exhaustive but serves as an

Yet, researchers are hard pressed when attempting to explain what enabled the Safavid community to withstand recurrent setbacks and elimination of their leadership when they militarized in the second half of the ninth/fifteenth century. What's more elusive to research is how they managed to have the depth to replenish their political-military ranks and ideological resources, and not only recuperate but to harden, expand, and ultimately develop the competence to defeat forces larger and better equipped than themselves. Scholars faced with this problem often point to the Safavid exceptional group cohesion as a vital advantage and an established fact to explain their long-term success, then quickly move on. This book pauses, instead, to consider the nature of this cohesion, and sheds light on the processes involved in its development and preservation

introductory guide for further research. Primary sources are not listed here and can be consulted in the Bibliography. Rula Jurdi Abisaab, *Converting Persia: Religion and Power in the Safavid Empire* (London: I.B. Tauris, 2015); Adel Allouche, *The Origins and Development of the Ottoman-Safavid Conflict* (Berlin: Schwarz, 1983); Ali Anooshahr, "The Rise of the Safavids according to Their Old Veterans: Amini Haravi's Futuhat-e Shahi," *Iranian Studies* 48, no. 2 (2015): 249–67; Said A. Arjomand, *The Shadow of God and the Hidden Imam: Religion, Political Order, and Societal Change in Shi'ite Iran from the Beginnings to 1890* (University of Chicago Press, 1984); Willem M. Floor, *Safavid Government Institutions* (Costa Mesa: Mazda Publishers, 2001); Masashi Haneda, *Le Châh et les Qizilbāš le Systeme Militaire Safavide* (Berlin: Schwarz, 1987); Rasūl Jaʿfariyān, *Sīyāsat va Farhang-i Rūzgār-i Safavī* (Tehran: Nashr-i ʿIlm, 1388); Rasūl Jaʿfariyān, *Tārīkh-i Tashayyuʿ dar Īrān: Az Āghāz tā Pāyān-i Qarn-i Nuhum-i Hijrī*, 2 vols. (Tehran: Nashr-i ʿIlm, 1395); Ayfer Karakaya-Stump, "Who Really Were the Kizilbash? A Rethinking of the Kizilbash Movement in Light of New Sources and Research," in *The Safavid World*, ed. Rudi Matthee (London: Routledge, 2021), 37–55; Rudi Matthee, "Loyalty, Betrayal, and Retribution: Biktash Khan, Ya'qub Khan, and Shah 'Abbas I's Strategy in Establishing Control over Kirman, Yazd and Fars," in *Ferdowsi, the Mongols and the History of Iran: Art, Literature and Culture from Early Islam to Qajar Persia*, ed. Robert Hillenbrand, A. C. S. Peacock, and Firuza Abdullaeva (London: I.B. Tauris, 2013), 184–200; Kazuo Morimoto, "The Earliest ʿAlīd Genealogy for the Safavids: New Evidence for the Pre-Dynastic Claim to Sayyid Status," *Iranian Studies* 43, no. 4 (2010): 447–69; Murtazā Mudarrisī Chahārdahī, "Tashkīlāt-i Tarīqāt-i Safaviyyah," *Nashrīyah-i Anjuman-i Āsār-i Millī*, no. 2, 2535/1976; Amīr Rajabī, *Sharh-i Safā: Zindagī va Taʿālīm-i ʿIrfānī-i Shaykh Safī al-Dīn Ardabīlī* (Tehran: Shirkat-i Intishārāt-i Sūrah-i Mihr, 1397); Kāmil Mustafā Shaybī, *Tashayyuʿ va Tasavvuf tā Āghāz-i Sadah-i Davāzdahum-i Hijrī*, trans. ʿAlī Rizā Zakāvatī Qarāgūzlū (Tehran: Amīr Kabīr, 1387); Mansūr Sifat'gul, *Sākhtār-i Nahād va Andīshah-i Dīnī dar Īrān-i ʿAsr-i Safavī: Tārīkh-i Tahavvulāt-i Dīnī-i Īrān dar Sadah'hā-yi Dahum tā Davāzdahum-i Hijrī-i Qamarī* (Tehran: Muʾassasah Khadamāt-i Farhangī-i Rasā, 1381); Faruk Sümer, *Safevî Devletinin Kuruluşu ve Gelişmesinde Anadolu Türklerinin Rolü* (Ankara: Güven Matbaası, 1976); Zeki Velidi Togan, "Sur l'origine des Safavides," in *Mélanges Louis Massignon*, vol. 3 (Damascus: Institut Français de Damas, 1957), 345–57; Rıza Yıldırım, "Shīʾitisation of the Futuwwa Tradition in the Fifteenth Century," *British Journal of Middle Eastern Studies* 40, no. 1 (2013): 53–70; ʿAbd al-Husayn Zarrīn'kūb, *Justujū dar Tasavvūf-i Īrān* (Tehran: Amīr Kabīr, 1385).

in a politicalized Sufi order undergoing militarization. I've tried to understand this community's relative ideological advantages and incremental alterations in the nature of their political ties from their early days in the mid-eighth/fourteenth century to their assumption of power in the first half of the tenth/sixteenth century. Sufi orders were susceptible to militarization. They possessed the internal ideological structures and organizational capability to facilitate acquisition and maintenance of power. Equally overlooked in the historiography is the semicentennial reign of Tahmasb I (d. Qazvin, 984/1576), Ismail's son and the second Safavid shah. Shah Ismail (d. near Tabriz, 930/1524) seized power and the throne by the sword, but it was Tahmasb who guarded and developed the Safavid state, as I aim to show in Chapters 4–6.

The Safavid Sufi community was an exceptional case that managed to militarize, survive violent clashes, and gradually rose to the level of sovereignty by the mid-tenth/sixteenth century. In essence, this is a study in political Sufism in the early modern era.

Sufism, or Islamic mysticism, is often interpreted as an inner spiritual journey under the supervision of a Sufi guide or guides (i.e., *shaykh* or *pīr*) aimed at eventual union with the Creator, God. This journey usually spans a lifetime, during which the disciple must confront their base human instincts, their animalistic desires that hinder their "spiritual flight." To successfully embark on the Sufi path, the disciple must fully submit to the sheikh's mentorship and commit to a series of progressively intense spiritual and physical practices. These practices aim to cleanse, or rather empty, the aspirant's inner vessel that is filled with worldly cravings and fill it instead with yearning for union with the Divine or the Beloved. For instance, while some of their practices involve physical austerity such as fasting, seclusion, and silence, celibacy is not emphasized as a Sufi virtue. The disciple progresses through various stages on the path toward this envisioned union. This is further discussed in Chapter 2.

Sufism, as an Islamic tradition of seeking transcendence, is distinct in world religions, but has strong connections to mysticism found in Judaism, Christianity, and Hinduism, making its values and belief system appear universal and timeless.

From the onset, like early Christianity, an ascetic branch emerged within Islam rooted in imitation of the Prophet Muhammad's humble lifestyle, members of his household (*ahl-i al-bayt*), and many of his companions (*sahāba*). The term "Sufi," believed to refer to "wool-wearers," is itself a symbol of poverty and detachment from worldly affairs. This perspective stood in sharp contrast to the increasingly luxurious and opulent lifestyle of the early Muslim caliphs and their cadre of religiopolitical authorities in, for instance, the Ummayyid (661–750 CE) and ʿAbbasid courts (750–1258 CE). This was an affront to many Sufi sheikhs who viewed this trend as imitations of the Persian and Byzantine imperial courts that the Prophet warned against – a clear deviation from the Revealed Path. Other sheikhs, on the other hand, found reason to accommodate the flawed caliphs and tried to influence and tame their cruelty and iniquities (see Chapter 2).

While sometimes Sufi practices and interpretations of the Qurʾan appeared at odds with Islamic law (*sharīʿah*), which made them vulnerable to charges of religious deviation, others maintained a balance between outward adherence to Islamic law and inner devotion. These Sufis avoided public spiritual pretension, while movements like the Malamatiyya deliberately concealed their orthodoxy, performing good deeds in private and seeking public contempt to guard against "spiritual pride." Their aim was to counter popular perception that asceticism was a source of spiritual superiority.

A persistent challenge in writing about Sufism is the predominance of secondary literature that is sympathetic to Sufi history and thought. This bias often leads to a narrow examination of its history and broader sociopolitical context. A prevalent and enduring myth is the portrayal of Sufis as apolitical, pacifistic practitioners of the greater jihad (the spiritual struggle against the carnal self), in contrast to the lesser jihad of physical warfare against external foes. Yet, the historical records demonstrate that Sufi communities frequently engaged in politics, uprisings, and war. Despite this evidence, the militant aspect of Sufism is often downplayed in favor of spiritual dimensions, portraying only a narrow view of their historical reality.

The foundational principles of Sufism harbor immense potential for creating social and political movements. Historians of colonialism are no strangers to the powers of group cohesion forged in politicalized Sufi communities. Some of the most formidable resistance movements, for instance, fighting against the brutal British, French, and Italian colonial occupations in West Asia and North Africa during the nineteenth and early twentieth century were Sufi groups.

Throughout the book I've maintained that the key to unlocking the cryptic transformation of the Safavids from a Sufi order into a powerful political-military organization lies in decoding their sources of social power that produced their solidarity, not as an issue of paramountcy in their rise to power but as one that made other political achievements possible – without group solidarity, durable ties of loyalty, and patronage to sustain it long term, there could be no viable political organization. Patronage relationships among the political elite are favorable to cohesion-building and advantages them over the general population, who often lack intensive organizational capabilities, thus enabling their political domination.

In decoding political power relations, some of the book's arguments connect with findings in historical sociology, in works of Michael Mann, for instance, and certain theories of power as proposed by Steven Lukes, Dennis H. Wrong, Talcott Parsons, and others. My emphasis on the ideological aspect of power as central to fostering group cohesion should not diminish the impact of the other sources of social power that are interrelated in essential ways. What is meant by ideological power here is derived from three interconnected postulations: (a) since humans cannot fully understand their world through sense perception, they require categories of meaning, and as Weberians have long argued, collective and distributive power can be exercised by a group who control and shape that meaning; (b) a shared understanding of how people should behave *morally* in relation to each other if they wish for a prolonged social cooperation, akin to Durkheimian speculation that a group that can stimulate mutual trust among its members may be rewarded by heightened sense of cohesion and collective power; and (c) the importance of ritual practice, suggesting that a distinctive category of power is conveyed through communal rites, songs, dance, and prayers that binds people. These three broad categories constitute only a partial sketch of how organizations such as the Safavids exercised power as they are intertwined with the economic and military power dynamics.[4]

In their writings, Safavid political actors reveal the manners in which they understood and preserved their ties to one another and to their

[4] I'm grateful to Michael Mann for our conversations in Los Angeles regarding theories of power and politics. His model of the four sources of social power (i.e., the ideological, economic, military, and political) attempts to offer a broad explanation of power dynamics in human societies and helped shape my understanding of power. Michael Mann, *The Sources of Social Power* (Cambridge University Press, 2012). One of Lukes' theories, the "three faces of power," proposes that power is exercised in three ways: decision-making power, non-decision-making power, and ideological power. Steven Lukes, *Power: A Radical View* (London: Palgrave Macmillan, 2005). See also Dennis H. Wrong, *Power: Its Forms, Bases, and Uses* (University of Chicago Press, 1988); Talcott Parsons, *Politics and Social Structure* (New York: The Free Press, 1969); Talcott Parsons, "Power and Social System," in *Power: Readings in Social and Political Theory*, ed. Steven Lukes (New York University Press, 1986), 94–144.

leadership. My approach has been to study this community's self-descriptions in explaining their religiopolitical ties. Their political relationships, as conveyed in the sources, though possessing a particular internal logic in the early modern world, are comprehensible without use of contemporary technical social-scientific language. When necessary, however, I have provided the pertinent explanation in the footnotes so as not to burden the narrative.

The book is divided into two halves, echoing the history of the Safavids' insurrection; the first half (Chapters 1–3) is devoted to the embryotic phase during the eighth/fourteenth and ninth/fifteenth centuries, while the second half (Chapters 4–6) accounts for the alteration and the consolidation of their sociopolitical gains once the "Sufi warriors" attained substantial military and economic power in the first half of the tenth/sixteenth century. The following is a theoretical sketch of the basic elements of cohesion, loyalty, and patronage necessary for better understanding of the Safavid rise and hold on power explored in subsequent chapters. This is followed by a brief discussion on the three "domains of power" to which the Safavid court had to reorient itself in order to negotiate its sources of social power.

I.2 ON GROUP COHESION

Outwardly, the Safavids like other medieval Sufi orders developed distinctive markers of collective identity that created forms of exclusivity which invariably affected their sense of cohesion in relation to their peer groups. These markers were manifested in articles of clothing, headwear, and distinct communal rituals and mystical practices. Beneath the surface, however, lay a vast realm of interconnected relationships and competing loyalties that created and fostered their cohesion.

As noted earlier, decoding the rise of the Safavids through the study of their sociopolitical ties has not attracted the attention it deserves. This may be due to the dearth of interdisciplinary approaches to the study of Iran's early modern society and politics. The Safavid case in the discipline of history is by no means unique in that respect. As one sociologist in another field laments, "While there is an abundance of Durkheimian-influenced literature that focuses on the cultural aspects of group ties in the traditional and modern worlds and Marxist-inspired analyses that study the economic foundations of class and professional solidarity, there is a pronounced lack of studies that explore the origins and historical dynamics of group cohesion." Examining cohesion within a discipline-specific context against the backdrop of interdisciplinary findings and historical case is needed to focus the methodological approach.[5]

What further entangles exploring the Safavid case of cohesion is the fact that the Safavids had their origins as a Sufi order long before they became political and militarized. They thus exhibit a distinctive set of spiritual variables and power dynamics in their interactions that informed the ways they understood their social ties. But before we can delve into the Sufi dimensions of group solidarity, it is necessary first to discuss the views of the eighth/fourteenth-century North African scholar Ibn Khaldun (d. 808/1406) of Tunis, a contemporary of the early Safavids and considered to be the greatest of Muslim historians, who explored the subject of cohesion in a social-scientific manner. His distinctive approach and consistent analytical method for the study of society has earned him the recognition as the father of sociology.

Ibn Khaldun theorized about social cohesion within a broader context of his cyclical theory of history and the rise and fall of dynastic power. In his monumental work, *al-Muqaddimah*, he posits that the variegated interactions between sedentary and nomadic populations were key in understanding the development of political power and the gradual rise of civilization. The sedentary society, he posits, produces goods and services for the population while the nomadic "outsider" groups generate military power by which they conquer towns and cities. They achieve this due to the nature of their existence; a life of scarcity in inhospitable environments where violent conflicts among tribes are common forcing them to develop strong military skills. The organizational needs of a military force demand the forging of strong ties of loyalty. The sum of all these elements leads to a "sense" of group solidarity, which he termed *ʿasabīyya*.

The sedentary populations, on the other hand, live in safety and abundance, and whose love of luxury and ease leads them to lose their commitments and loyalty to one another and thus eroding their *ʿasabīyya*.

[5] Siniša Malešević, "Where Does Group Solidarity Come From? Gellner and Ibn Khaldun Revisited," *Thesis Eleven* 128, no. 1 (2015): 85–99. See furthermore Malešević's other contributions such as Siniša Malešević and Mark Haugaard, eds., *Making Sense of Collectivity: Ethnicity Nationalism and Globalisation* (London: Pluto Press, 2002); Siniša Malešević and Mark Haugaard, eds., *Ernest Gellner and Contemporary Social Thought* (Cambridge University Press, 2007); Siniša Malešević, *The Sociology of War and Violence* (Cambridge University Press, 2010); Siniša Malešević, *The Rise of Organised Brutality: A Historical Sociology of Violence* (Cambridge University Press, 2017).

Over time, they decline and fall to subjugation to another nomadic warrior tribe over the horizon whose *ʿasabīyya* remains intact. Once in power, the conquerors in turn, due to their lack of knowledge of running a state, enlist members of the previous elite and gradually get absorbed in the sedentary culture and within a few generations settle into a life of contentment, and thus sacrifice their group solidarity. And the cycle continues, he asserts. Ibn Khaldun wanted to stress that this dynamic between the sedentary and nomadic population is the pulse of historical transformations for human societies. This link between rise and fall of dynastic power is clear in the early Mongol imperial ideology a century prior to Ibn Khaldun's time that discouraged its nomadic elite from residing in palaces and constructing permanent settlements.[6]

According to Lacoste, "*ʿasabīyya* does not therefore mean social solidarity in general, but rather a very specific form of social organisation which allows a tribal aristocracy to control the forces of military democracy."[7] *ʿAsabīyya*, viewed from this angle, does not only create group solidarity, but also enables a dynamic in which the political and military elite can establish their legitimacy through some kind of revered lineage and sacred ideology, and coalesce around a political goal. Thus, empowered with relative cohesion vis-à-vis the general population that lacks unity, the elite impose and perpetuate their political domination. All the while, as Ibn Khaldun would assert, they sow the seeds of their own demise as their solidarity gradually breaks down due to the changes in their environment, from one of war and chaos, to one of safety and ease.

[6] Ibn Khaldun, *The Muqaddimah: An Introduction to History*, trans. Franz Rosenthal (Princeton University Press, 1967); Charles Issawi, *An Arab Philosophy of History* (London: John Murray, 1950); Ernest Gellner, "From Ibn Khaldūn to Karl Marx," *Political Quarterly* 32 (1961): 385–92; ʿAbd al-Rahmān Badawī, *Muʾallafāt Ibn Khaldūn* (Cairo, 1962); Muhammad Mahmoud Rabīʿ, *The Political Theory of Ibn Khaldūn* (Leiden: Brill, 1967); Muhsin Mahdi, *Ibn Khaldūn's Philosophy of History* (University of Chicago Press, 1971); Aziz al-Azmeh, *Ibn Khaldūn in Modern Scholarship: A Study in Orientalism* (London: Third World Centre, 1981); Yves Lacoste, *Ibn Khaldūn: The Birth of History and the Past of the Third World*, trans. David Macy (London: Verso, 1984); Abderahmane Lakhassi, "Ibn Khaldūn," in *History of Islamic Philosophy*, ed. Seyyed Hossein Nasr and Oliver Leaman (London: Routledge, 1996), 350–64; Róbert Simon, *Ibn Khaldūn: History as Science and the Patrimonial Empire*, trans. Klára Pogátsa (Budapest: Akadémiai Kiadó, 2002); Fuad Baali, *The Science of Human Social Organization: Conflicting Views on Ibn Khaldun's (1332–1406) Ilm al-Umran* (Lewiston, NY: Edwin Mellen Press, 2005); Allen Fromherz, *Ibn Khaldun: Life and Times* (Edinburgh University Press, 2010); Farid Alatas, *Ibn Khaldun* (Oxford University Press, 2013); Stephen Dale, *The Orange Trees of Marrakesh: Ibn Khaldun and the Science of Man* (Cambridge, MA: Harvard University Press, 2015).

[7] Lacoste, *Ibn Khaldūn*, 108.

Though Ibn Khaldun theorized about the Berber tribes of North Africa, his findings have long been recognized to be relevant to other groups. He would have been confirmed if he had observed the ascent and eventual fall of the Safavids, from a powerful tribal military confederation in the late ninth/fifteenth century with intense cohesion, to their overthrow by a stronger Afghan tribal confederation two centuries later. The Safavid chronicles at the time of their decline, especially during the siege of their capital at Isfahan and its eventual fall in the autumn of 1134/1722, are replete with accounts of insubordination and treachery among the military elite.

Ibn Khaldun's theory of group solidarity has its bases in the Islamic ethics that human beings are social creatures who by their nature are in a constant state of struggle with each other. Humans are at a disadvantage for they are forgetful creatures, prone to disobedience and thus succumb to ingratitude to their Creator's benefaction (i.e., divine patronage), and so they suffer. They require continuous reminders – hence the command to pray five times a day at distinct intervals. The idea of forging social cohesion, therefore, necessitates face-to-face interactions to resolve conflicts, communicate, and sometimes cooperate for a common good – necessary elements for the creation of clientelistic relationship in politics. To put it into perspective, in the modern industrial world where such personal dynamics are lacking, as Ernest Gellner has suggested, for example, solidarity is forged through concepts of nationalism, cultural homogeneity, and belief in social cooperation for economic benefit. From this point, Gellner can make the case that solidarity is the crucial factor that preserves social order.[8]

Though still undeveloped, the research into group solidarity has progressed to a point that clear patterns can be observed, leading one prominent specialist to assert that

> all small-scale groupings exposed to adverse conditions tend to develop intense esprit de corps: from platoons of soldiers on the battlefields, to clandestine organizations of conspirators, revolutionary activists, terrorist cells, perpetuators of genocidal projects, to members of close-knit social movements. In all of these

[8] Ernest Gellner, *Nations and Nationalism* (Oxford: Blackwell, 1983); Ernest Gellner, *Plough, Sword and the Book: The Structure of Human History* (London: Collins Harvill, 1988); Ernest Gellner, *Nationalism* (London: Phoenix, 1997); Ernest Gellner, *Muslim Society* (Cambridge University Press, 1981); Siniša Malešević, *The Sociology of War and Violence* (Cambridge University Press, 2010); Siniša Malešević, "Nationalism, War and Social Cohesion," *Ethnic and Racial Studies* 34, no. 1 (2011): 142–61.

> cases it is the emotional commitment, moral obligation and similarity of lifestyles that transforms a functional/operational unit into something much more: an almost sacred community where individual members are willing to sacrifice for each other.[9]

Would the Safavid venture at creating a viable political system be better understood against the backdrop of this universalist social-scientific appraisal of cohesion? Perhaps. But the equation is far from complete, as cohesion, loyalty, and patronage are inseparably linked, as I hope to show in this book.

I.3 ON LOYALTY

Loyalty is a phenomenon so fundamental, so common in our day-to-day interactions, that we seldom pause to ponder its far-reaching implications. One hears of it in songs, reads about it in countless legends and folklore, and watches its dramas unfold with intensity onstage and onscreen, as we saw with former president Trump and FBI director Mr. Comey. Political loyalties, romantic loyalties, religious loyalties, business and professional loyalties, in every corner where cooperation among humans is necessary to accomplish a task, one finds some kind of relational loyalty at work. So ubiquitous in the human consciousness that we cannot pinpoint its origins, though research has shown that it was well-defined among homo sapiens as they navigated their social relations for survival.[10]

No doubt, a myriad of circumstances creates the need to develop bonds of loyalty and to find ways to preserve them. In political-military organizations where stakes were high and death loomed large, the value and function of loyalty was amplified, revealing its inner workings and its centrality for the organization's collective survival. What lent loyalty its import in a political system, as I've tried to show in the case of the Safavids, was its role in the forging of group cohesion.

In addition to poets and litterateurs, most of our knowledge about the nature of loyalty in our time has come from psychiatrists, sociologists, and

[9] Malešević, "Group Solidarity," 9. See also the works cited therein.

[10] Jonathan Turner, *Face to Face: Toward a Sociological Theory of Interpersonal Behavior* (Stanford University Press, 2002); Jonathan Turner, *Human Emotions: A Sociological Theory* (London: Routledge, 2007); Alexandra Maryanski, "African Ape Social Networks: A Blueprint for Reconstructing Early Hominid Social Structure," in *The Archaeology of Human Ancestry: Power, Sex and Tradition*, ed. James Steele and Stephen Shennan (London: Routledge, 1995), 67–90.

political theorists who encountered it in their fields, to heal patients in psychotherapy, and in social sciences to make sense, for example, of social phenomenon such as tribalism, notions of identity, and nationalism.[11] Josiah Royce with the publication of his treatise *The Philosophy of Loyalty* in the first decade of the twentieth century laid the groundwork for modern research in the Anglophone world on loyalty, which later expanded to include occupational ethics deemed integral to the functioning of modern economies.[12]

Given its expanse, definitions of loyalty vary from one field to another with areas of overlap and intersection across eras and regions. And given its seemingly universal nature, a description comprehensive enough that could offer a point of departure for our discussions is one commonly used in the field of moral philosophy, that loyalty "can be characterized as a practical disposition to persist in an intrinsically valued (though not necessarily valuable) associational attachment, where that involves a potentially costly commitment to secure or at least not to jeopardize the interests or well-being of the object of loyalty."[13] This conceptualization of loyalty

[11] Harold Guetzkow, *Multiple Loyalties* (Princeton University Press, 1955); Morton Grodzins, *The Loyal and the Disloyal: Social Boundaries of Patriotism and Treason* (University of Chicago Press, 1956); Albert O. Hirschman, *Exit, Voice, and Loyalty: Response to Decline in Firms, Organizations and States* (Harvard University Press, 1970); Iván Böszörményi-Nagy and Geraldine M. Spark, *Invisible Loyalties: Reciprocity in Intergenerational Family Therapy* (New York: Brunner-Mazel, 1973); Katharine Doob Sakenfeld, *Faithfulness in Action: Loyalty in Biblical Perspective* (Philadelphia: Fortress Press, 1985); Bozena Zdaniuk and John M. Levine, "Group Loyalty: Impact of Members' Identification and Contributions," *Journal of Experimental Social Psychology* 37, no. 6 (2001): 502–9; James Connor, *The Sociology of Loyalty* (Dordrecht: Springer, 2007).

[12] Josiah Royce, *The Philosophy of Loyalty* (New York: Macmillan, 1908); Andrew Oldenquist, "Loyalties," *Journal of Philosophy* 79, no. 4 (1982): 173–93; Marcia Baron, *The Moral Status of Loyalty* (Dubuque, IO: Kendall/Hunt, 1984); Alasdair MacIntyre, *Is Patriotism a Virtue?* (Lawrence: University of Kansas Press, 1984); Alan Gewirth, "Ethical Universalism and Particularism," *Journal of Philosophy* 85, no. 6 (1988): 283–302; George P. Fletcher, *Loyalty: An Essay on the Morality of Relationships* (New York: Oxford University Press, 1993); A. T. Nuyen, "The Value of Loyalty," *Philosophical Papers*, 28 no. 1 (1999): 25–36; Simon Keller, *The Limits of Loyalty* (Cambridge University Press, 2007); Eric Felten, *Loyalty: The Vexing Virtue* (New York: Simon & Schuster, 2012); Jukka Varelius, "Is Whistle-Blowing Compatible with Employee Loyalty?," *Journal of Business Ethics*, 85 no. 2 (2009): 263–75; Stephen Coleman, "The Problems of Duty and Loyalty," *Journal of Military Ethics* 8, no. 2 (2009): 105–15; John Kleinig, *Loyalty and Loyalties: The Contours of a Problematic Virtue* (Oxford University Press, 2014); Brian Schrag, "The Moral Significance of Employee Loyalty," *Business Ethics Quarterly* 11, no. 1 (2001): 41–66.

[13] John Kleinig, "Loyalty," *Stanford Encyclopedia of Philosophy* (Summer 2022 Edition), ed. Edward N. Zalta, https://plato.stanford.edu/archives/sum2022/entries/loyalty/.

accedes that human beings inter alia are moral agents though they may engage in "immoral" behavior. Loyalty is thus viewed as a kind of virtue, though some deny this depending on their theoretical framing of virtue. R. E. Ewin, for instance, argued against admittance of loyalty into the pantheon of virtues and explained that if loyalty congeals and is placed in an immoral context (e.g., a loyal CIA agent torturning Iraqi POWs in the notorious Abu Ghraib prison), it forces its practitioner to suspend their innate sense of morality or good judgment. He argues that "the worth of any particular loyalty is thus reducible to judgments about the worth of the associations to which loyalty is given ... and is not due to loyalty in general being a virtue."[14]

Ewin's challenge to loyalty as a virtue and its inherent worth raises a fundamental question: Does loyalty have any value independent of the associational object to which it is coupled or is its value linked solely with the object of loyalty? Proponents of loyalty as a virtue, on the other hand, argue that loyalty is virtuous or vicious depending on what is done *out* of loyalty. Others posit that loyalty is always virtuous, although *can* be superseded when connected with immoral comportment.

The value of loyalty, irrespective of arguments for or against its inherent worth as a virtue, lay in the capacity it created for its members to "persist" and to justify immorality or sacrifice in associations that required sustained cooperation, where in lieu of service, some kind of material and psychological benefit was exchanged. In such a milieu, to be loyal was expected and its raison d'être self-evident. It was at times when an offense of disloyalty had occurred – when men pondered its philosophical dimensions – that without loyalty a group's chances of survival were severely diminished.

Medieval and early modern Muslim and Christian political thinkers did not question loyalty's merits along Ewin's critique. They primarily viewed it as a virtue (*fazīlah*) within the Islamic tradition and debated the distinctions between "substantive" and "executive" virtues (e.g., the substantive virtues as compassion, generosity, and kindness, whereas the executive virtues may include courage, integrity, and industriousness), both with clear moral implications for development and preservation of ties. Loyalty to the king expressed in obedience was not only virtuous but also endorsed by the Qurʾan and the sayings of the Prophet. Similarly, in the

[14] R. E. Erwin, "Loyalty and Virtues," *Philosophical Quarterly* 42, no. 169 (1992): 403–19; R. E. Erwin, "Loyalties, and Why Loyalty Should Be Ignored," *Criminal Justice Ethics* 12, no. 1 (1993): 36–42.

early modern European political parlance, the etymology of "loyalty," linked to the Latin *lex, legis* with connotations of obligation and law, reveals its connection to group cohesion. In Old French, for instance, we see it as *loial*, denoting allegiance, and in the early modern English courts, the term became synonymous with *homage*.

In Safavid Iran, for instance, loyalty in the political context was expressed with such terms as *yak-jahatī* (steadfastness), *dawlat-khvāhī* (faith in Safavid sovereignty or in the heavens' "turn of fortune"), and more importantly *ikhlās* (purity of intention), a spiritual concept that had the effect of encoding political loyalty with spiritual and moral value. Medieval and early modern scholars viewed *ikhlās* in a variety of ways as reflected in its wide usage in works of ethics, exegesis, politics, and Sufism, the latter of which specifically impacted how the Safavids conceptualized political loyalty. It is difficult to produce a singular English equivalent that would encapsulate its multiple meanings, but in the context of Iran's political theology, "devotional loyalty" may come close.[15]

One inescapable truth about loyalty in the political realm is its fragility. Conscious how fickle they could be in their commitments to one another while knowing the consequences of disloyalty, political men struggled to create assurances to preserve their ties in a political system that favored

[15] For early definitions of *ikhlās* and other important philological information, see, for example, Muhammad b. Ahmad al-Azharī, *Tahzīb al-Lugha*, vol. 7, ed. ʿAlī al-Najjār and ʿAbd al-Salām Sarhān (Cairo: Dār al-Qawmiyya al-ʿArabiyya li-l-Tibāʿa, 1384–87), 137–40. For its various usage in commentaries and ethics literature, see, for example, Rashīd al-Dīn Ahmad b. Ahmad Maybudī, *Kashf al-Asrār wa-ʿUddat al-Abrār, Maʿrūf bi-Tafsīr-i Khvājah ʿAbd Allāh Ansārī*, 10 vols., ed. ʿAlī Asghar Hikmat (Tehran: Intishārāt-i Dānishgāh-i Tehran, 1331–39); Nasīr al-Dīn Muhammad al-Tūsī, *Awsāf al-Ashrāf*, scrib. Muhammad Husayn ʿImād al-Kuttāb (Tehran: Daftar-i Nashr-i Farhang-i Islāmī, 1368), 22; Husayn Vāʿiz Kāshifī, *Akhlāq-i Muhsinī*, MS, Cambridge University Library, add 748, fols. 7v–8r. For its usage in Sufi literature, see, for instance, ʿAbd al-Karīm b. Hawāzin Qushayrī, *Tarjumah-i Risālah-i Qushayriyyah*, ed. and trans. Badīʿ al-Zamān Furūzānfar (Tehran: Bungāh-i Tarjumah va Nashr-i Kitāb, 1345), 322–27; Abu ʾl-Qasim al-Qushayri, *Al-Qushayri's Epistle on Sufism: Al-Risala al-qushayriyya fi ʿilm al-tasawwuf*, trans. Alexander D. Knysh (Reading, UK: Garnet Publishing, 2007), 220–26; Najm al-Dīn Kubrā, *Fawāʾih al-Jamāl wa Fawātih al-Jalāl*, trans. Muhammad Bāqir Sāʿidī Khurāsānī, ed. Husayn Haydarkhānī Mushtāq ʿAlī (Tehran: Marvī, 1407), 93; Nūr al-Dīn ʿAbd al-Rahmān b. Muhammad Isfarāyinī, *Kāshif al-Asrār: bi-Inzimām-i Pāsukh bih Chand Pursish. Risālah dar Ravish-i Sulūk va Khalvat'nishīnī*, ed. Hermann Landolt (Tehran: Intishārāt-i Muʾassasah-i Mutāliʿāt-i Islāmī, Dānishgāh-i Makgīl, Shuʿbah-i Tehran, bā Hamkārī-i Markaz-i Bayn al-Milalī-i Guftugū-yi Tamaddunhā, 1383), 4, 63, 97; Qutb al-Dīn Muzaffar b. Ardashīr al-ʿAbbādī, *al-Tasfiyah fī Ahwāl al-Mutasawwifah: Sūfī-nāmah*, ed. Ghulāmhusayn Yūsufī (Tehran: Intishārāt-i Bunyād-i Farhang-i Īrān, 1347), 101.

opportunism with little regard to ethics, especially at times of upheaval. The concept of *bayʿa* in Arabic (Pers. *paymān*), meaning a "mutual pledge" made between a leader and his followers, was an attempt to remedy the incessant problem of disloyalty in the medieval courts. The ritual of *bayʿa* has thus been evoked throughout the preindustrial Islamic world down to the present in various forms and settings.[16]

The meaning of *bayʿa* as oath of allegiance gained its legitimacy in the Islamic political culture from the Prophet Muhammad's usage, notably in the "second pledge at al-ʿAqaba," where he sought to ensure the cooperation of the people of Medina (Yathrib) in his struggle to protect the early Muslim community from the Meccan tribal confederacy. The term is often associated with the ruler seeking loyalty and submission of his subjects, be they members of the religious and political elite or commoners.

The fracturing of the ʿAbbasid Empire in the fifth/eleventh century and the restructuring of its political system overlapped with the rise of the Buyids of Iran, which demanded the creation of stronger assurances of loyalties and allegiances and contributed to the institutionalization of the *bayʿa* across the medieval Islamic courts.[17] In the later middle period, military commanders as well as Sufi sheikhs not necessarily associated with the ruling courts evoked the term to elicit loyalty. For the early Safavids, however, expressing a "political oath of allegiance" was implicit in the membership to the Sufi order. Safavid political men's self-identification as "disciples" of their sheikh, their Safavid shah, had understood their loyalty and allegiance embedded in Sufi order code of association and rites, likely the reason why the term is rarely used in this context.

[16] Eric J. Hanne, "Ritual and Reality: The *Bayʿa* Process in Eleventh- and Twelfth-Century Islamic Courts," in *Court Ceremonies and Rituals of Power in Byzantium and the Medieval Mediterranean*, ed. Alexander Beihammer, Stavroula Constantinou, and Maria G. Parani (Leiden: Brill, 2013), 141–57; Bettina Dennerlein, "Legitimate Bounds and Bound Legitimacy: The Act of Allegiance to the Ruler (*Baiʿa*) in 19th Century Morocco," *Die Welt des Islams* 41, no. 3 (2001): 287–310; Andrew Marsham, "The Architecture of Allegiance in Early Islamic Late Antiquity: The Accession of Muʿāwiya in Jerusalem, ca. 661 CE," in *Court Ceremonies and Rituals of Power*, 87–112; Elie Podeh, "The *Bayʿa*: Modern Political Uses of Islamic Ritual in the Arab World," *Die Welt des Islams* 50, no. 1 (2010): 117–52; Paula Sanders, *Ritual, Politics and the City in Fatimid Cairo* (Albany: State University of New York Press, 1994); Andrew Marsham, *Rituals of Islamic Monarchy: Accession and Succession in the First Muslim Empire* (Edinburgh University Press, 2009).

[17] Roy Mottahedeh, *Loyalty and Leadership in an Early Islamic Society* (Princeton University Press, 1980); Sanders, *Ritual, Politics and the City*, 63; Ella Landau-Tasseron, *The Religious Foundations of Political Allegiance: A Study of Bay'a in Pre-Modern Islam* (Washington, DC: Hudson Institute, 2010), 1–5, 20–30.

Roy Mottahedeh, drawing attention to the importance of ties of loyalty during the decline of the ʿAbbasid political power, explains that

> in the Near East of the tenth and eleventh century, deliberately acquired obligations created the positive and predictable loyalties that shaped society. Such loyalties were not "positive" because they were good, or "predictable" because men always lived up to them. Acquired loyalties were "positive" in that they were used as a basis for cooperation ... and "predicable" because, thanks to their somewhat formal nature, men who accepted them knew in considerable detail just what commitments such loyalties were believed to imply.[18]

He points to the famed army rebellion of 317/929 against their patron the ʿAbbasid caliph al-Muqtadir (d. 320/932) in which the caliph reminds the rebels of the obligation of gratitude (*shukr al-niʿmah*), which they must honor in the form of an oath of allegiance in lieu of all the benefits (*niʿmah*) of his patronage that they enjoyed.

The Safavid elite too exercised similar dynamics of allegiance in their political dealings as the Buyids, but often in an inhibitive manner, to deter disloyalty and the severance of ties. Furthermore, they had inherited their sacred political theology through Sufi dialectic of power, from the master-disciple dynamics, and the moral world of Sufi thoughts and practices prior to their militarization. The societal impact of organized political Sufism had not emerged as a force during the Buyid period. Their Sufi heritage had shaped their understanding of social ties and offered them ideological resources and a sacred history to contextualize their ties.

Mottahedeh further argues that the force of the "obligation of loyalty" emanated from the deep reverence accorded to the early days of the Muslim community under Muhammad's leadership, and in the primal covenant between humankind and their Creator as revealed in such verses as Qurʾan 7:172–73. Thus, the oath to create and preserve political ties in the Islamic political theology was largely understood as sacred and within a covenantal framework: God created humanity and all which benefit humankind; in exchange for such beneficence (*niʿmah*), humankind owes the Creator the obligation of gratitude (*shukr al-niʿmah*) and obedience (*tāʿah*). This morally colored formula extended to the caliph and provided the legitimacy for the ruler to elicit loyalty and obedience from his subjects. The Safavids followed a similar model.[19]

[18] Mottahedeh, *Loyalty and Leadership*, 40.
[19] Ibid., 42–46.

The Mongol invasions of the eastern and central Islamic lands and the collapse of what had remained of the ʿAbbasid political hegemony during the first half of the seventh/thirteenth century transformed the Islamic principles of kingship and legitimations. The devastation of the Islamic civilizational edifice symbolized in the fall of Baghdad in 656/1258 not only forced Muslim political thinkers to grapple with the imposition of the Genghisid bloodline as the basis for legitimation, thus rejecting the fundamental principles of Islamic kingship, but also pressured the society to search for alternative political associations. The rise of politicized Sufi orders in the aftermath of the Mongol invasions was in a concrete sense a response to the societal needs for an alternative political and military answer. Yet, the creation of ties of loyalty and how to prevent their severance among these newcomers in the political arena remained the leading challenge to their survival and the longevity of their organizations.

The Safavid order, for instance, once it became political and militarized, also ran into this problem. One way the early Safavid political men attempted to restrain disloyalty among themselves was to enshrine their patronage ties, interactions, and even the phenomenon of loyalty itself within spiritual codes as we noted earlier with *ikhlās*. Moreover, they used sacrosanct concepts to define their patronage ties, such as *shukr al-niʿmah*, deconstructed as "honoring the obligation of gratitude that one incurs in exchange for the benefits received." If studied closely, this concept reveals how moral codes were interwoven in attempts to create political loyalty and cohesion – the subject of Section I.4.

I.4 ON THE OBLIGATION OF GRATITUDE

Gratitude is a complex social relational phenomenon. On the fundamental level, gratitude can be defined as the appropriate response of a beneficiary to a benefactor for the benefits received, whether such a benefactor be divine, human, sentient, or even insentient. It is a subject of analyses in moral philosophy, normative and applied ethics, and political philosophy; the latter has direct bearing on our discussion here. Yet different views exist regarding the nature of gratitude and how it operates in various spheres of human activity, in politics, religion, and everyday life. Once more, because of the universal nature of this concept, a philosophical classification might be justified, which suggests that the phenomenon could be considered a virtue. Medieval and early modern political thinkers who were interested in moral philosophy in Islamic and Christian traditions did in fact perceive its social value as a virtue. Like loyalty, obligation of gratitude as a virtue was shaped by the deontic view, that one has a "duty" to honor one's obligation of gratitude. What this implied in political interactions was that gratitude was perceived as obligatory, that it is *binding*. It is a response that *must* be performed so as not to transgress the governing moral code commonly agreed upon. Failing to honor one's "moral duty" prima facie was thus viewed as *immoral* and carried some degree of negative social, spiritual, and sometimes a grave political cost.

To further illustrate the interwoven connection between loyalty, patronage, and gratitude, we can look at President Donald Trump once more, following his reelection in 2024. One of his most significant foreign policy challenges was the Russian invasion of Ukraine. Throughout his campaign, Trump had pledged to end the war, and upon taking office, he wasted no time signaling his willingness to engage with Russia and negotiate a peace agreement. This approach stood in stark contrast to his predecessor, Joe Biden, whom he criticized for his support of "forever wars" and whose popularity had plummeted due to his "ironclad" support of Israel's invasion in Palestine and Lebanon, and Israel's indiscriminate killing of civilians in Gaza and southern Lebanon leading some to dub him "Genocide Joe." Trump hosted the Ukrainian President Volodymyr Zelenskyy on February 28, 2025, at the White House, after initially excluding him from negotiations with Russia. During the press briefing, Trump and Vice President JD Vance repeatedly accused Zelenskyy of ingratitude. As Trump remarked in one exchange:

TRUMP: You're gambling with World War III. And what you're doing is very disrespectful to the country, this country that's backed you far more than a lot of people said they should have.

VANCE: Have you said thank you once?

ZELENSKYY: A lot of times. Even today.

VANCE: No, in this entire meeting. You went to Pennsylvania and campaigned for the opposition in October.

ZELENSKYY: No.

VANCE: Offer some words of appreciation for the United States of America and the president who's trying to save your country.

ZELENSKYY: Please. You think that if you will speak very loudly about the war, you can –

TRUMP: He's not speaking loudly. He's not speaking loudly. Your country is in big trouble.

ZELENSKYY: Can I answer –

TRUMP: No, no. You've done a lot of talking. Your country is in big trouble.

ZELENSKYY: I know. I know.

TRUMP: You're not winning. You're not winning this. You have a damn good chance of coming out OK because of us.

ZELENSKYY: "Mr. President, we are staying in our country, staying strong. From the very beginning of the war, we've been alone. And we are thankful. I said thanks.

VANCE: Just say thank you.

ZELENSKYY: I said a lot of times, thank you, to [the] American people.

Realizing the conversation was going nowhere, Trump concluded what had been yet another sensational press conference with how he felt about dealing with an ungrateful client:

> The problem is I've empowered you (turning toward Zelenskyy) to be a tough guy, and I don't think you'd be a tough guy without the United States. And your people are very brave. But you're either going to make a deal or we're out. And if we're out, you'll fight it out. I don't think it's going to be pretty, but you'll fight it out. But you don't have the cards. But once we sign that deal, you're in a much better position, but you're not acting at all thankful. And that's not a nice thing. I'll be honest. That's not a nice thing.
>
> All right, I think we've seen enough. What do you think? This is going to be great television. I will say that.[20]

The disastrous meeting made headlines across the world.

Lech Wałęsa, the former president of Poland and Nobel Peace Prize laureate, whose country has a direct stake in the outcome of the conflict, was compelled to publish an open letter. He was joined by thirty-eight other former political prisoners of Poland's communist regime, condemning Mr. Trump's views on Ukrainian President Zelenskyy's supposed lack of gratitude toward the United States. As Wałęsa bluntly stated:

> We consider your expectations regarding the showing of gratitude for the material assistance provided by the United States to Ukraine to be offensive. Gratitude should be given to the heroic Ukrainian soldiers who shed blood in defense of the values of the free world.[21]

[20] Adriana Gomez Licon, "What They Said: Trump, Zelenskyy and Vance's Heated Argument in the Oval Office," *Associated Press*, February 28, 2025, https://shorturl.at/7YpD9.

[21] Daniel Tilles, "Wałęsa Condemns Trump Treatment of Zelensky, Likening It to Communist Interrogation," *Notes from Poland*, March 3, 2025, https://shorturl.at/0wFn8.

In Iran's early modern political culture, while the ideal response to the "binding" obligation of gratitude was not uniform across political interactions, it was nevertheless framed as personal and informed by a moral domain that supplied the language and the inner meanings. It also supplied the justification for the severe consequences of reneging on one's obligation of gratitude. Treason against the shah, for example, was thus reformulated as ingratitude and expressed as *kufr*, with connotations of blasphemy, consequences in the afterlife, and the offender branded as *kāfar-i niʿmat*, "the ingrate," who rejected the obligation of gratitude expected in lieu of patronage he received – another ideological way to attempt to inhibit severance of ties and secure the political submission of a client. All these elements are present in the Trump-Zelenskyy quarrel, though their moral substructure is harder to see when not expressed with moral codes.

Such obligation-inducing codes were key in regulating political relations among "Sufi warriors" of the fifteenth century. The obligation of gratitude to strengthen ties of loyalty, for instance, found new iteration in the Sufi master-disciple relationship in which the Sufi sheikh's material and political resources and disciples' desire for political action shaped their perceptions of a new form of legitimate authority. Now Sufis could in earnest ask whether a sheikh could and should be the *rightful* king? I search for answers in Chapters 2 and 3 in the roots of the Safavid Sufi order, when dreams of worldly sovereignty had not entered their loftiest aspirations. Yet, obligation-inducing codes in the political realm are meaningful if understood within the context in which they are evoked such as occurred in political power relations, the type we today term "patronage and clientelism," discussed in Section I.5.

These clientelistic interactions were the result of a significant political shift in the power structure during the ninth/fifteenth and tenth/sixteenth centuries, compared to the ʿAbbasid-Buyid period four centuries earlier, which Roy Mottahedeh explored. This shift was driven by the rise of Sufi orders and other antinomian groups, who consolidated their social power into political movements, ultimately transforming the religiopolitical landscape of the region. Sufi groups exhibit powerful internal dynamism that enabled them to develop organizational capacities for politicization. Roughly between the decline of the Mongol Ilkhanid hegemony in the mid-eighth/fourteenth century and the fall of the Aqquyunlu state at the hands of their cousin Shah Ismail a century and half later was the age of Sufism's experimentation with real political power, with blood and carnage that often accompanies mass uprisings. This was the era when Sufi disciples took up arms to effect political change, such as the Sarbidars, the

Mar'ashis, the Hurufiyya, and the Nurbakhshiyyah, to name just a few. The Safavids were one such group that was undergoing internal changes throughout the ninth/fifteenth century, which included "Shi'itization" of the order (see Chapters 2 and 3).[22]

I.5 ON PATRONAGE AND CLIENTELISM

The theoretical lens of patronage and clientelism can help untangle relationships among political agents and unveil the processes involved in acquisition and maintenance of power. Research has revealed, for instance, that the development of networks of clients and brokers tied by shared ideologies and obligations was instrumental to the formation of early modern states in Europe and across Asia. Kettering, for example, defines the relationship as

> an indirect form of power: a patron influences the behavior of his clients because he can grant or withdraw benefits, thereby rewarding compliance or punishing disobedience. He can manipulate his clients because of their indebtedness for past favors and fear of future reprisals: his control over their behavior gives him power. Patronage is the art of obligation, of manipulation through rewards and punishment.

The *client* reciprocates the patron's political favors, protection, and various forms of economic rewards by offering his loyalty and service, and by extension the acceptance of subordination and obedience. Kettering explains that the role of a client is to be "a reliable, obedient subordinate in what is often a political jungle ... a patron is expected to give material benefits because he can do so, while a client offers in exchange more intangible assets of loyalty and service."[23]

[22] For the history of political movements in this period, see 'Abd al-Rafīʿ Haqīqat Rafīʿ, *Tārīkh-i Junbish-i Sarbidārān va Dīgar Junbish'hā-yi Īrāniyān dar Qarn-i Hashtum-i Hijrī* (Tehran: Intishārāt-i Kūmish, 1374); Abū al-Fazl Nabā'ī, *Awzā'-i Sīyāsī va Ijtimā'ī-i Īrān dar Qarn-i Hashtum-i Hijrī* (Mashhad: Intishārāt-i Dānishgāh-i Firdawsī-i Mashhad, 1375); Zarrīn'kūb, *Justujū dar Tasavvūf-i Īrān*; Shaybī, *Tashayyuʿ va Tasavvuf*; Saʿīd Nafīsī, *Sarchishmah-i Tasavvuf dar Īrān* (Tehran: Kitābfurūshī Furūghī, 1343); Arjomand, *Shadow of God*; Rasūl Ja'fariyān, *Tārīkh-i Tashayyuʿ dar Īrān: Az Āghāz tā Qarn-i Haftum-i Hijrī*, 2 vols. (Tehran: Shirkat-i Chāp va Nashr-i Sāzmān-i Tablīghāt-i Islāmī, 1388); Mansūr Sifat'gul, *Sākhtār-i Nahād va Andīshah-yi Dīnī dar Īrān-i 'Asr-i Safavī: Tārīkh-i Tahavvulāt-i Dīnī-i Īrān dar Sadah'hā-yi Dahum tā Davāzdahum-i Hijrī-i Qamarī* (Tehran: Mu'assasah Khadamāt-i Farhangī-i Rasā, 1381).

[23] Sharon Kettering, *Patrons, Brokers, and Clients* (New York: Oxford University Press, 1986), 3–4; Maria E. Subtelny, *Timurids in Transition: Turko-Persian Politics and*

The Safavids here too enshrined their obligation of service with inspiring terms as *jān-sipārī* (self-sacrifice), *khidmat-kārī* (servitude), and *nīkū-bandagī* (noble-thralldom) as a reflection of their position vis-à-vis their patron. In their attempts to secure patronage ties by offering their loyalty, chiefs used rhetoric of selflessness, self-sacrifice, and submission as seen in their petitions sent to the court throughout the period.[24]

The main form of patronage they sought from the shah, aside from appointment to state offices and protection, was land assignments. The Safavid shahs continued the long-held practice of granting land assignments (*ulkā*, *tiyūl*, and *iqtā*ʾ) to tribal chiefs in exchange for military service. The principal aim of these grants to the chiefs was for the maintenance of troops, cost of their management, and security of their provinces. The size and quality of the land depended on the size of the tribe and the standing of its chief and clansmen. At times of political chaos and war, such as when Tahmasb ascended the throne in 930/1524, distribution of land assignments became a point of grievance and injustice among the chiefs and exacerbated the political instability and infighting.

At the Safavid court, one's client was often another's patron. Clients employed their influence with their patrons who acted as "intermediaries" in a cascading fashion, creating networks of patrons, brokers, and clients. This dynamic, prevalent in court societies of early modern Eurasia, is seen, for example, in the relationship between high-ranking officials who left most of the political imprint on the historical record, often working at the epicenter of power.

In analyzing Safavid-era patronage and clientelism, one encounters a common challenge. Personal ties and the formation of political loyalties

Acculturation in Medieval Iran (Leiden: Brill, 2007); James Scott, "Patron-Client Politics and Political Change in Southeast Asia," *American Political Science Review* 66, no. 1 (1972): 91–113; Frederick Barth, "Political Leadership among Swat Pathans," in *Friends, Followers, and Factions: A Reader in Political Clientelism*, ed. Steffen W. Schmidt, James C. Scott, Carl Landé, and Laura Guasti (Berkeley: University of California Press, 1977), 207–17; Alex Weingrod, "Power and Patronage," in *Patrons and Clients in Mediterranean Societies*, ed. Ernest Gellner and John Waterbury (London: Duckworth, 1977), 41–51; Lawrence Stone, *The Crisis of the Aristocracy, 1559–1641* (Oxford: Clarendon Press, 1965).

24 The Safavids used the long-established military term "amir" in reference to the Qizilbash chiefs. In official court documents, the tiered structure of *khān*, *sultān*, and *beg* are used per individual cases. Given the overlap between the three designations at various times in a commander's career, I have used the general term "chief" to refer to high-ranking Qizilbash amirs. Terms such as "*rīsh-safīvdān-i tavāyif* " (the white-beards of the tribes) and "*buzurgān*" (grandees) are often used in a general collective sense to refer to the tribal elites.

are difficult to observe because such relationships were often based on tacit understandings that obscured declarations of loyalty, which were often self-evident not requiring justification. This difficulty is compounded by the challenge of deciphering the language and occasion of patronage found in the sources, and by the ways used to decrypt the type of political connections that reflects the development or continuation of clientelistic relationships. For the Safavids, the rhetorical language and literary devices often used in official documents, however, do unveil how language is adopted from the literary tradition to the political arena. One finds that the refined rhetoric Safavid court ministers employed in state correspondences reflects the ways that they appropriated poetic language to articulate political power. As sociolinguists have long alerted social historians to the usage of linguistics as codes of power exchange, the language of the Safavids' patronage practices certainly reveals important features of their ideological source of domination and subservience.

Political men engaged with one another in well-trodden paths and knew how to sustain their ties. And when pushed, they knew how to make effective their demands through usage of sacred language. We see this clearly, for example, in the trial of a powerful Qizilbash chief who was accused of treason and "ingratitude" against his patron Shah Tahmasb, explored in Chapter 5.

In our own time, we're no strangers to the cost of flouting the obligation of gratitude to someone who enacts a favor for us regardless of religious interpretation. We use common proverbs such as "don't bite the hand that feeds you," and reflect on the sayings of great literary figures like William Shakespeare, who wrote, "how sharper than a serpent's tooth it is to have a thankless child," or the clever Mark Twain, who explained, "if you pick up a starving dog and make him prosperous, he will not bite you. This is the principal difference between a dog and man." We instantly sense the heavy weight of the obligation to be grateful to the favor-producer.

A reason why the obligation of gratitude resonates deeply with our social decorum and sense of decency relates to the way morality shades the interaction and often grants moral authority to the favor-producer. Such authority is present in even mundane situations. I recall a few times in my childhood when a friend rebuked me by saying, "bishkanah īn dast kih namak nadārah." Persian speakers know this phrase by heart. It means, "may this hand break for it does not have salt," meaning this is a useless limb for it produces no obligation-inducing favor (salt being a symbol of favor or benefit). This would happen precisely at times when the said friend believed that I had offended him by showing ingratitude for some favor he had done for me, and for which he now expected something in return. The offense stirred in him a great deal of indignation caused by a sense of being wronged and produced for me a feeling of shame from having transgressed some norm I should have observed.

Salt has long served as a symbol for the tie of obligation, as common today as it was during the Safavid period, especially during rituals among Sufis, brotherhoods (*futuwwa*s), and guilds. An artisan, for instance, may refer to his trusted apprentice as his "namak-parvardah," that is, he has been raised on his "salt" and is thus under an obligation of gratitude that he must honor. On the other hand, when someone shows ingratitude toward his patron one often hears, "namak khurd va namakdūn shikast" (he ate the salt and broke the saltshaker), that is, he broke the tie of obligation of gratitude that was in effect. In the adult world, ingratitude creates conflict and sometimes causes the severance of friendship or family ties. To avoid the occurrence of a potential conflict, some even try to preempt a possible rejection of putting someone under the obligation of gratitude. In a meeting in which a favor might be exchanged, when the potential favor-producer offers tea, for example, in order to put the prospective recipient at ease, he may say the tea "namak nadārah" (does not have any salt in it) thereby making it clear to the other party to be at ease, with no obligation of gratitude being traded here.

Surrendering one's moral authority is the underlying reason why many avoid accepting favors in the first place. It is not unusual to hear someone under pressure say, "zīr-i dayn-i hīchkas namīram," meaning "I will not go under the obligation of gratitude to anyone," fearing that one day they would say to themselves "rū saram minnat guzāsht." Many know this loathsome phrase. It means, the favor-producer held the obligation that is produced by the favor (*minnat*) over the recipient's head, as though it could drop and crush him with its weight at any time. The client's subservience is clear in the symbolic language used, "zīr-i dayn" (under the obligation), "rū-yi sarash" (placed obligation on his head).

Such symbolism, beyond its everyday societal functions, provides important clues to how power is acquired and maintained, especially in the political realm where stakes can be extremely high. On a fundamental level, obligation of gratitude is often established as follows: (a) the patron acquires the obligation of gratitude because of providing the beneficiary with a favor, (b) the beneficiary is thus under obligation for his acceptance of the favor, (c) the patron would then exploit the obligation as currency to use to *oblige* the client to return the favor. If he does, he has honored his obligation of gratitude. But, if he does not, he is censured as an offender, an "ingrate."

The seemingly universal understanding of the obligation of gratitude appears to play a significant role in creating durable political ties. The formative periods of dynasties, the focus of this book, offer a rare chance to examine this ideological source for the forging of a patronage system in an emergent state. The result of the Safavids' theological articulation of patronage was that the Sufi king acquired the "moral authority of gratitude" over the military chiefs through dispensation of benefits, which he expected them to honor with loyalty and service, and the authority to chastise them if they did not honor their obligation. If the client flouted his obligation (i.e., he denied the value of the favor and its sanctity), the patron had on his side the moral high ground, affirmed by religion to chastise the "ingrate client." In other words, the obligation of gratitude was a currency regulated by the power of morality to inhibit the client's disloyalty.

A strand of inhibitive moral obligations was at work in Safavid political culture of the tenth/sixteenth century, evident in their patron-client interactions. I explain that the obligation was understood in its deontological sense where "obligation as duty" was the normative ethical standpoint in evaluating the morality of an action. This was so because binding moral obligations were believed to be more difficult to break – an attempt to ensure cooperation in an unstable organization. Whether the political agent followed the ethical precepts or not, he was aware of their consequences and recognized their consecrated language with which he could save his neck if occasion required.

These theological deliberations to inhibit disloyalty reflected the wider political consequences for the Safavid state formation. In Chapter 4, for instance, I show how the political outcomes of the court's patronage activities under Shah Tahmasb contributed to the reunification of the Qizilbash tribal confederacy, the backbone of the Safavid military power, during the last Ottoman invasion in Tahmasb's reign, and forced Sultan Suleyman to accept the limits of his eastern imperial ambitions. The Peace of Amasya of 962/1555, which inaugurated a period of peace and stability for the Safavids, I have argued in Chapter 4, was the direct result of such a systemic political transformation.

In order to fully appreciate the Safavids' hard-won political stability, it is necessary to briefly discuss their ideals of kingship, political culture, and the existing "spheres of power" with which the Safavid court negotiated religious authority and political dominance – this is explored in Section I.6.

I.6 ON THE THEORY OF STATE AND THE SPHERES OF POWER

While the Qizilbash tribal chiefs might have adhered to the notion of cooperate rule or sovereignty common to Turco-Mongol tribal organizations, the idea never supplanted the traditional Perso-Islamic principles of kingship that the Safavid political community came to accept and expect in their leadership by the late ninth/fifteenth century. Similar to other early modern states in Eurasia, once the Safavids managed to achieve political stability by the mid-tenth/sixteenth century, they continued the long kingship tradition of hereditary monarchy, close to *Patrimonialstaat* in the Weberian models of authority and *Herrschaft* or "imperative control," in which the ruler, armed with great means of collective violence and the mantle of a divine mandate, could intervene in any social sphere with little or no limitation. Primogeniture was accepted as the legitimate form of the transfer of power at successions, though often contested.

Patrimonial court societies like the Safavids often saw themselves as a type of an extended family. However symbolic the perception, it nonetheless reflected their political realities, for the elite often secured their power and position by creating extensive kinship ties through marriage and intimate patron-client bonds. Routinely, proximity to the ruler and his family determined the level of influence an official attained.

The Safavids were the inheritors of a Persian political culture that had absorbed the literary and the religious, the philosophical and the bureaucratic spheres of the previous centuries. Perso-Islamic courtly tradition by the tenth/sixteenth century underwent a powerful transformation due to the force of ʿAlid Shiʿism. Their kingdom was a Shiʿi one, the only one, and they were keenly aware of this fact, and from their standpoint a political breakthrough to establish the "just state" (*dawlat-i haqq*) denied to ʿAli after Muhammad's passing. The early shahs exercised what can loosely be categorized as a theocracy in a Twelver Shiʿi vessel. Their officials articulated their shahs' principles of legitimation based on the claim of direct descent from the Prophet Muhammad through his daughter Fatimah's marriage to his cousin ʿAli, the holy progenitor of the twelve Imams. Post-establishment, the family became less overt about their descent from their eighth/fourteenth-century ancestor, Sheikh Safi al-Din of Ardabil, the founder of their Sufi order, reflecting the shift in their self-characterization and detachment from their Sufi origins.

Safavid court society functioned under a power-sharing schema among three major overlapping groups reliant on the shah or his surrogates to various degree, which at the structural level reflected the efforts of (a) those who acquired power by force, the so-called men of the sword – the Qizilbash military chiefs and the court elite; (b) those who helped maintain and legitimize it through management of resources and a sacred ideology, "men of the pen," that is, the administrators; and (c) "the men of cloth," the clerics whose functions overlapped with those of group (b), especially during the formative period of the dynasty. Less problematic in terms of negotiating political power were the other Sufi orders in the realm along with urban guilds (*asnāf*) and brotherhoods (*futuwwa*s). Because of their considerable lack of "hard power" to generate and sustain the means of collective violence, the Safavid court during the tenth/sixteenth century either absorbed their leadership into their "political blood" or pacified them through use of force. This is explored separately in Chapter 3.

I.7 ON THE POLITICAL DRIVERS

Preserving ties of loyalty among men of the sword especially during the rise of the dynasty was an art of survival. The disastrous defeat of the Safavids at the hands of the Ottomans in 920/1514 and the subsequent loss of Shah Ismail's divine aura of invincibility, followed by the decade-long civil war after his death, created a fertile ground for deceit and treason, which befell his son and successor, Tahmasb. Not only did the young shah have to confront deadly challenges to his rule at home, but he also had to face a massive Ottoman invasion from the west and devastating Uzbek attacks from the east. Tahmasb's prospects for survival looked bleak by any standards.

Thus, the Safavid court struggled to find ways to prevent severance of ties and to create restraints to combat the widespread treacheries plaguing their politics. Providing material benefit to induce loyalty (i.e., creating patronage ties) among the Qizilbash chief was one effective method and as noted earlier, their patronage's inner moral dimension aimed to render it convincing and increase its odd of resilience. There existed, however, another type of bond, of those who didn't need inducement to "negotiate" their loyalty. This was the Safavid inner core known as the *muqarrabān*, a consecrated political designation related to Sufi thought, meaning those who have gained proximity to the Divine, a sheikh, or in this case the Sufi shah because of their incredible loyalty and faith.

The court's *muqarrabān* were at the epicenter of Safavid power and often served in the *dīvān-i jānqī* (supreme royal council) composed of Shah Tahmasb's most trusted ministers. This category of the officials was institutionalized post Tahmasb era as part of the court society with demarcated duties and remunerations. They often occupied the highest military and bureaucratic offices of the state. There were many who served the shah faithfully, but the focus will be on the main "decision-makers" who, orbiting the shah, were the "political drivers" and shaped policies during the formative period of the dynasty and reflect the convergence of loyalty, patronage, and politics at the heart of the Safavid family. Furthermore, I explore another powerful influence on Tahmasb, namely, his sister Mahin Banu, a commanding political force at court who had the shah's ear and reverence. Close in age to her brother, Mahin Banu was Tahmasb's most intimate friend and confidant. This is explored in Chapter 6.

The importance of these officials' positions is reflected in the fact that they had managed to climb to the lead positions of the three overlapping spheres of power at court during a time of chaos: the military, the administrative, and the religious. These individuals were empowered to shape domestic and foreign policy, managed immense resources, and accumulated wealth and clients. Yet, they lived precarious lives, serving close to absolute power where preservation of ties was a matter of life and death. They were Savinduk Beg Afshar, Tahmasb's head of the royal guards (*qūrchī-bāshī*) and later the realm's chief of the army (*amīr al-umarā*); Shah Quli Khalifah, the keeper of the royal seal and the chief Sufi deputy (*khalīfat al-khulafā*), in charge of validating appointments and various tax exemptions, in addition to his spiritual functions; and Qazi Jahan Qazvini, the chief minister and the head of the bureaucracy (known by various titles such as *vakīl*, *vazīr*, *nāzir-i dīvān-i aʿlā*, *vazīr aʿzam*). These ministers had the longest tenures in their respective offices in Safavid history: Savinduk Beg, twenty-eight years; Shah Quli Khalifah, twenty-six years; and Qazi Jahan, fifteen years.

Tahmasb's political education took place during the maelstrom of the civil war among the leading Qizilbash chiefs. He learned, for instance, the fate of the viziers who served his father, six to be exact, most of whom met violent ends. He learned to recognize the power of the military chiefs and how inconsistent they were in their commitments and loyalty. He experienced firsthand the fragile nature of his kingship, not only in relation to the chiefs but also his own family members who sought to destroy him and take the throne. Unlike his father, he had little chance to prove himself as a charismatic warrior king. He was placed on the throne unexpectedly after Shah Ismail's premature death of cirrhosis and thrown to the wolves.

Tahmasb grew up watching men struggle to retain their loyalty. Understandably, he was wary and distrustful of his chiefs. In such an environment, his inner circle took on a deeper significance not only for his survival and that of his house, but also the Safavid community's collective political aspirations that had begun with his ancestor Sheikh Junayd. He was to carry that mantle of sovereignty for Shiʿis. Against this backdrop, for example, it is easy to see why he would appoint the head of his royal guards, Savinduk Beg, to be the army chief, leaving him in that function for nearly three decades, and not appointing another for several years after Savinduk's death.

The young king, however, had an able chief minister at the most perilous time of his kingship, Qazi Jahan. He was to Tahmasb what William Cecil was to Elizabeth I of England, or Nicolas Perrenot de Granvelle to the Habsburg emperor Charles V. A most extraordinary minister of the early modern courts, Qazi Jahan undertook the immense work of streamlining state revenues in the chaos of the 940s/1530s and restored the bureaucratic practices that facilitated the link between the government and the military, especially during the devasting Ottoman and Uzbek wars. Furthermore, as argued in Chapters 4–6, Tahmasb's inner circle strengthened the crown by their political policies and patronage networks, which proved vital for the restoration of the Qizilbash reunification.

I.8 THE SHIʿI ʿULEMA AND THE CLERICAL ESTABLISHMENT

Shah Tahmasb intensified his father's policies of promoting the new class of Shiʿi ʿulema, native or émigré, in their mission of reshaping Iran's religious landscape. Since there was a dearth of basic Shiʿi educational material in the realm (Iran had been a predominantly Sunni region), he patronized a large cohort of scholars who produced works of theology, law, and devotional literature. This came at a great cost to the Sunni ʿulema and their networks who were persecuted, harassed, and largely prohibited from teaching posts, community leadership, and state-influenced appointments.

The gradual "Shiʿitization" of Iran during the Safavid period set in motion a profound social transformation. Once the Safavids seized power in the opening decade of the tenth/sixteenth century, a new Shiʿi clerical power began to take root and expand into the realm of power politics. Taking the long view, Arjomand's research, for instance, has shown that the tensions that defined the ʿulema's role in the political landscape of the tenth/sixteenth century was linked to the Sunni notables' control of the judiciary, education, and the pious endowments (*awqāf*) prior to the Safavid takeover, forming a kind of a "clerical estate." Arjomand suggests that due to geographical, linguistic, and cultural outlooks, the two groups remained distinct throughout the first half of the tenth/sixteenth century but had their greatest overlap during the reign of Tahmasb's grandson, Shah ʿAbbas I, in the early eleventh/seventeenth century. The conventional view is that after the dust of conquest settled, some Sunni notables took a small leap and professed Shiʿism to enter Safavid service and thereby retained some of their power and influence. The other group of ʿulema, Shiʿi jurists (*fuqahā*), specifically from areas in today's southern Lebanon, Iraq, and Bahrain, arrived to the nascent kingdom patronized by the court, though their impact and number is debated. Yet, other research suggests that the influx of ʿAmuli scholars from Lebanon to Safavid Iran occurred during the second half of the tenth/sixteenth century and speculates the reason for this pattern might be the political stability and the peace with the Ottomans that Tahmasb secured.[25]

During this formative period, the tension between the two groups sometimes played out at court, and given his tenuous hold on power and a faded claim to spiritual authority, Tahmasb was advised to back influential Shiʿi jurists such as ʿAli Karaki (d. 940/1534). The young shah was counseled well, for the potential of a leading mujtahid such as Karaki to strengthen his legitimacy was immense. Karaki was among the luminaries of the legal scholars from the Shiʿi stronghold of Jabal ʿAmel in southern Lebanon and was among the first cohort of Shiʿi ʿulema who joined Shah Ismail's service to the dismay of their peers who were critical of the Safavid brand of Shiʿism.[26]

As Abisaab has suggested, the religious reform Karaki and his camp proposed resonated with the Safavid elite, and their expertise in jurisprudence enabled them to assure the court that they had the authority to standardize the faith in such basics as the "correct" enactments of worship

25 Devin J. Stewart, "Notes on the Migration of ʿAmuli Scholars to Safavid Iran," *Journal of Near Eastern Studies* 55, no. 2 (1996): 81–103; Albert Hourani, "From Jabal ʿAmil to Persia," *Bulletin of the School of Oriental & African Studies* 49 (1986): 133–40; ʿAlī Muruwwah, *al Tashayyuʿ bayn Jabal ʿĀmil wa-Īrān* (London: Riad El-Rayyes Books, 1987); Jaʿfar al-Muhājir, *al-Hijra al-ʿĀmiliyya ilā Īrān fī al-ʿAsr al-Safawī* (Beirut: Dār al-Rawda, 1989); Andrew J. Newman, "The Myth of Clerical Migration to Safawid Iran: Arab Shiite Opposition to ʿAli al-Karaki and Safawid Shiism," *Die Welt des Islams* 33 (1993): 66–112; Abisaab, *Converting Persia*. Andrew Newman disagrees with the entire premise of migrating clerics, though this position remains a distinct minority and is refuted by others.

26 Wilferd Madelung, "Karakī," EI^2 IV (1978), 610; Arjomand, *Shadow of God*, 125–34.

(*ʿibādāt*), contract law (*muʿāmalāt*), and the Shiʿi sacred history and rituals. Karaki produced for the Safavid public simplified legal manuals and commentaries, elucidated Shiʿi doctrine and hadith on the basis of the Jaʿfari legal school, and wrote polemics (*munāzarāt*) against Sufis and Sunni scholars. Abisaab points out that Karaki's treatises, such as *al-Risāla al-Jaʿfariyya* on the fundamentals of ablution and prayer, and the anti-Sufi polemic *Matāʿin al-Mujrimiyya* in which he claimed that several Sufi practices contradicted Shiʿi doctrine, laid the groundwork for Shiʿi orthopraxy and later suppression of Sufis in the eleventh/seventeenth century.[27]

Considering the eminence of Karaki at court, Tahmasb felt justified in patronizing him and granting him hallowed titles such as *nāʾib al-imām* (deputy of the Occulted Imam) and *khātam al-mujtahidīn* (seal of the jurists). Thus empowered, Karaki carried out his policies of religious reform. He created networks of scholars, judges, and officials in major cities to implement his reforms and apply legal rulings based on the Jaʿfari school for cases of crime, family law, and the collection of taxes. He also appointed prayer leaders in towns and villages, broadcasting his interpretations across newly conquered Safavid territories.[28]

By espousing such reforms, the Safavids intruded into the structure of urban society and into people's lives, and introduced new variations on existing public and private forms of piety (e.g., institutionalizing the Shiʿi call to prayer, the public cursing of the first three caliphs, and encouraging theatrical reenactments of Imam Hussein's martyrdom in Karbala). Such public policies, Abisaab argues, helped fulfill a fundamental Safavid goal: to transform the religious and cultural landscape from Sunnism to Imami Shiʿism. Furthermore, doctrinal authenticity helped the Safavids counter the Ottoman accusations of heresy and innovation, as opposition to such religious reforms were violently suppressed.

Karaki and his clients clashed with the local notables such as the *sadr* Mir Jamal al-Din Mohammad Astarabadi and Ghiyath al-Din Mansur Dashtaki Shirazi on several grounds ranging from theological disputes to the correct direction of prayer (*qibla*), to the public cursing of the "rightly guided caliphs" Abu Bakr, ʿUmar, and ʿUthman – a practice that incensed

[27] Abisaab, *Converting Persia*, 156–75.

[28] Eskandar Beg Monshi, *History of Shah ʿAbbas the Great*, vol. 1, trans. Roger M. Savory (Boulder, CO: Westview Press, 1978), 229–31; Arjomand, *Shadow of God*, 133–34; Said A. Arjomand, "Two Decrees of Shah Tahmasb concerning Statecraft and the Authority of Shaykh ʿAli al-Karakī," in *Authority and Political Culture in Shiʿism*, ed. Said A. Arjomand (Albany: State University of New York Press, 1988), 250–62.

the Ottoman court and their ʿulema. The *sadr* was a powerful religious officer of the realm, managed the enormous resources linked to pious endowments, and oversaw the appointing of judges. When Tahmasb had to arbitrate, he nonetheless ruled in support of Karaki, further strengthening his status as the leading cleric.

His decision to consistently back Karaki during this period appears more political than theological. He might have been convinced of Karaki's position on religious grounds, yet the political benefits were clear. By publicly supporting a powerful mujtahid he was able to offset his own lack of religious authority in an era when his father's charismatic rule had ended. His religious policies, therefore, focused on becoming the patron and protector of the Shiʿi ʿulema not only through political support but also by lavish patronage of the Shiʿi shrine cities of Najaf, Karbala, Qum, and Mashhad. Perhaps for this reason, his formal royal epithet *dīn-panāh* (the refuge of faith) was devised to reflect his image.[29]

Given the interwoven nature of the new Shiʿi ʿulema's work within the emerging Safavid political system, Arjomand posits that

> the era begins with the hegemony of a homogeneous mandarin-like clerical estate, with a fairly broad cultural outlook, engaged in a number of judiciary, and quasi-political, quasi-religious functions, and ends with the uneasy coexistence of this estate with a markedly different status group: a group of religious professionals, with a narrowly dogmatic and juristic outlook, forming the nascent Shiʿite hierocracy.[30]

Karaki and his camp did much to facilitate this transformation under Tahmasb's patronage. The network of patrons and clients Karaki created in the formative period continued to impact Safavid politics well into the eleventh/seventeenth century as several of his descendants became high judges and *sadr*s, served as viziers, and even married into the royal family.[31]

[29] Hani Khafipour, "Beyond Charismatic Authority: The Crafting of a Monarch's Image in the Public Sphere," in *The Safavid World*, 111–25.

[30] Said A. Arjomand, "The Clerical Estate and the Emergence of a Shiʿite Hierocracy in Safavid Iran: A Study in Historical Sociology," *Journal of the Economic and Social History of the Orient* 28, no. 2 (1985): 169–219.

[31] Abisaab, "Ulama of Jabal ʿAmil"; Arjomand, *Shadow of God*, 160–88.

1

The Founders

1.1 SAFI AL-DIN

The origin of the Safavid Empire can be traced to a journey of a young man seeking a spiritual teacher.

Abu al-Fath Ishaq, son of Amin al-Din Jibraʾil and commonly known as Safi al-Din (d. 735/1334), was born in 650/1252-3 to a local notable family, in Ardabil, a town situated on an open plain east of Mount Sabalan in northwestern Iran. Ardabil's climate was harsh; its bitter winters were legendary. But it received ample rain and rich soil allowing its farmers to grow an array of agricultural products. The neighboring pastures including the Mughan plain provided fodder for herders and pastoral nomads, who mixed with the sedentary peoples of the region. Ardabil's economy and vitality was also linked to a major commercial and political center of the medieval world, the city of Tabriz, situated on the grand east-west trade route. The diversity of its population was reflected in the languages spoken in the region: Turkish, Persian, Gilaki, Kurdish, Arabic, Armenian, Georgian, and other local vernaculars.[1]

[1] For the life and teachings of Safi al-Din, see Rajabī, *Sharh-i Safā*; Ghulām Rizā Tabātabāʾī Majd, *Dard-i Talab: Zindagānī-i Shaykh Safī al-Dīn Ardabīlī* (Tabriz: Nashr-i Abū, 1376); Tawakkul b. Ismāʿīl (Ibn Bazzāz Ardabīlī), *Safvat al-Safā: Dar Tarjumah-yi Ahvāl va Aqvāl va Karāmāt-i Shaykh Safī al-Dīn Ishāq Ardabīlī*, ed. Ghulām Rizā Tabātabāʾī Majd (Tehran: Intishārāt-i Zaryāb, 1376), 3–16. On his genealogy, see Zeki Velidi Togan, "Sur l'origine des Safavides," in *Mélanges Louis Massignon*, vol. 3 (Damascus: Institut français de Damas, 1957), 345–57; Ahmad Kasravī, *Shaykh Safī va Tabārash* (Tehran: Jār, 2535/1977); Kazuo Morimoto, "The Earliest ʿAlīd Genealogy for the Safavids: New Evidence for the Pre-Dynastic Claim to Sayyid Status," *Iranian Studies* 43, no. 4 (2010): 447–69.

Safi al-Din was born a generation after two violent catastrophes were visited upon the people of Ardabil: a deadly raid in 605/1209 by the Georgians from the north, who sacked the city and slaughtered thousands of its inhabitants, and the Mongol invasion in 617/1220. Though not directly impacted by these devastating events, his generation was taught how to survive in its aftermath. The harsh rule of Ilkhanid and Timurid dynasties in the eighth/fourteenth and ninth/fifteenth centuries forced some Sufi communities to become political in a sustained manner, though many kept their distance from politics and remained focused on the inner journey.

According to his biographer, Safi al-Din exhibited an intense inclination toward a deeper understanding of Islam at an early age. When he reached adulthood, the urge became stronger, and he plunged himself into the "sea of mysticism." Unquenched by the knowledge he acquired from his teachers in Ardabil, he set out to find a spiritual master capable of satisfying his yearning and help him make sense of his acute spiritual emotions.

His search brought him to Shiraz, a town nestled in a valley in the southern Zagros mountains some 1,500 kilometers south of his hometown. He wanted to become a disciple of Sheikh Najib al-Din ʿAli Buzghush Shirazi (d. 678/1279), "the gray falcon of Shiraz." Najib al-Din had been a disciple of the renowned master Shahab al-Din Suhravardi, the author of the influential work *ʿAwārif al-Maʿārif.* This might have strengthened Safi al-Din's determination to seek a master with such a prominent spiritual lineage (*silsilah*). By the time Safi al-Din reached Shiraz, the aging sheikh had passed away. He was told to go to the forests of the north and find the "Ascetic of Gilan," Sheikh Zahid Gilani (d. 700/1301).

At last, he found the old mystic in 675/1276-7 in Lahijan on the southern shore of the Caspian Sea and began a relationship that not only transformed Safi al-Din himself but the future of the entire region. His intense spiritual training changed him into a commanding Sufi teacher and set in motion the processes that created the far-flung communities of the Safavid order. It is extraordinary that the Safavid Empire owed its birth to a disciple finding his spiritual master. The disciple's intense reverence for his sheikh is pointedly illustrated in a miniature painting from the royal illumanited manuscript of Jami's *Haft Awrang* (see Figure 1.1).

Safi al-Din remained in Sheikh Gilani's companionship for some twenty-five years. He seemed to have stood out among the sheikh's disciples as his biographer likes to portray him. He impressed the sheikh

FIGURE 1.1 Murid kissing the murshid's feet. Folio from *The Seven Thrones* (*Haft Awrang*) by the Sufi master Nur al-Din Jami (d. 898/1492). This exquisite manuscript was patronized by Sultan Ibrahim Mirza, Shah Tahmasb's nephew, during his governorship of Mashhad (964–73/1556–65).
Freer Gallery of Art, Smithsonian Institution, Washington, DC: Purchase – Charles Lang Freer Endowment, F1946.12.207

so much that he agreed to his daughter Bibi Fatimah's marriage to Safi al-Din. Union to a well-establish Sufi family was a momentous event and became the foundation for their offspring's claims to spiritual authority and control of the social capital such claims carried. They had three sons together, Muhyi al-Din (d. 724/1324), Sadr al-Din (d. 794/1391-2), and Abu Saʿid (d. uncertain). As the years went on and he inched closer to death, he designated Safi al-Din to lead his order in 700/1301, much to the resentment of his own family. His eldest son, Jamal al-Din ʿAli, was most vocal among Safi al-Din's equals and directly challenged his spiritual authority on multiple occasions. It was rumored that he even tried to assassinate him.[2]

Safi al-Din was no longer a teenager seeking a spiritual guide. He had matured and was now in command of two treasures prized by Sufis, a pure spiritual genealogy (*silsilah*) and the direct experience of the Divine Essence (*mushāhadah*), fruits of years of discipleship on the path to transcendence. He decided that the time had come to return to his native land of Ardabil and to disseminate what he had discovered among his people. The fact that some men in Gilan were trying to kill him certainly hastened that decision.

Safi al-Din's family was of some means and owned land. Upon his return, he was in command of considerable material resources, which freed him from labor and provided the prestige that medieval notables with money enjoyed. Safi al-Din seems to have been a charismatic teacher and before long, he attracted a considerable following.

1.2 THE ARCHITECT OF THE ORDER AND THE BIRTH OF A SACRED HISTORY

After more than four decades of teaching, it was now Safi al-Din's turn to depart the world and to appoint a successor. Upon his death in 735/1334 he designated his son Sadr al-Din Musa (d. 794/1391-2) to lead the order. This was probably not a revelation to Sadr al-Din. No doubt, he had been

[2] Tawakkul b. Ismāʿīl, *Safvat al-Safā*, 788–791, 1088–89; see image 4.3, which depicts Safi al-Din's assassination attempt in a unique illustrated manuscript of *Safvat al-Safā* housed in Agha Khan Museum. For a recent analysis of the manuscript, see Aslıhan Erkmen, "The Visualization of Shaykh Ṣafī al-Din Isḥāq Ardabilī: A Unique Illustrated Copy of the *Ṣafvat al-Ṣafā* at the Aga Khan Museum Collection and Its Illustrations," *Iranian Studies* 50, no. 1 (2017): 45–77; Sholeh A. Quinn, "The Dreams of Shaykh Safi al-Din in Late Safavid Chronicles," in *Dreaming across Boundaries: The Interpretations of Dreams in Islamic Lands*, ed. Louise Marlow (Cambridge, MA: Harvard University Press, 2006), 221–34.

nurtured by his father to progress on the Sufi path and to perhaps one day inherit the order's *sajjādah* (prayer rug; a symbol of the order's leadership). It is no exaggeration to say that Sadr al-Din's managerial talents in maintaining the order's sociopolitical relations were the main reason that its resources and social base expanded. Like Jalal al-Din Rumi's son and successor Baha al-Din Sultan Valad (d. 712/1312), who helped establish the Mawlaviyyah order in Anatolia, Sadr al-Din's fifty-nine-year tenure as sheikh transformed the clusters of Sufi aspirants into an extensive web of masters and disciples enchained to the Safavid spiritual creed.[3]

Sadr al-Din expanded his father's lodge in Ardabil to include a mausoleum, communal kitchen, and various quarters for the daily activities and spiritual practices, an indication of their increasing numbers. In the process, he converted Safi al-Din's gravesite and modest lodge into a major pilgrimage site in the region that hosted wayfarers and devotees from near and afar. What seems to have enabled him and his successor to secure the order's economic resources was a series of tax exemptions and protection guarantees from the Jalayirid rulers of Azerbaijan, namely, Uways I (r. 757–75/1356–74) and Sultan Ahmad (r. 784–813/1382–1410), which safeguarded the family's land revenues and endowments. The Safavids, unlike orders that shunned or kept material possession to a minimum, had many sources of revenue that its leadership sought to preserve and to develop.[4]

[3] Ibrāhīm b. Mīrak Jalāl al-Dīn Amīnī Haravī, *Futūhāt-i Shāhī: Tārīkh-i Safavī az Āghāz tā Sāl-i 920 H. Q.*, ed. Muhammad Rizā Nasīrī (Tehran: Anjuman-i Āsār va Mafākhir-i Farhangī, 1383), 25–32; Qāsim Beg Hayātī Tabrīzī, *A Chronicle of the Early Safavids and the Reign of Shah Ismail*, ed. Kioumars Ghereghlou (New Haven, CT: American Oriental Society, 2018), 81–93, 112; Qāzī Ahmad b. Sharaf al-Dīn Qummī, *Khulāsat al-Tavārīkh*, 2 vols., ed. Ihsān Ishrāqī (Tehran: Intishārāt-i Dānishgāh-i Tehran, 1359), 1:23–34; Amīr Mahmūd Khvāndamīr, *Tārīkh-i Shāh Ismāʿīl va Shāh Tahmāsb-i Safavī: Zayl-i Tārīkh-i Habīb al-Sīyar*, ed. Muhammad ʿAlī Jarrāhī (Tehran: Nashr-i Gustarah, 1370), 21–26.

[4] See, for instance, the detailed audit of Sheikh Safi al-Din's mausoleum undertaken by the court official ʿAbdi Beg Shirazi and commissioned by Shah Tahmasb. ʿAbdī Beg Shīrāzī, *Sarīh al-Mulk: Vaqf-nāmah-i Buqʿah-i Shaykh Safī al-Dīn Ardabīlī*, ed. Mahmūd Hidāyatī (Tehran, 2011); Vladimir Minorsky, "A Mongol Decree of 720/1320 to the Family of Shaykh Zāhid," *Bulletin of the School of Oriental and African Studies* 16, no. 3 (1954): 519–20; Gottfried Herrmann and Gerhard Doerfer, "Ein persisch-mongolischer Erlaß des Ǧalāyeriden Šeyḫ Oveys," *Central Asiatic Journal* 19 (1975): 1–84; Jahāngīr Qāʾim-Maqāmī, *Yak Sad va Panjāh Sanad-i Tārīkhī az Jalāyirīyān tā Pahlavī* (Tehran: Sitād-i Buzurg-i Artishtārān, 1348), 9–15; Jahāngīr Qāʾim-Maqāmī, "Farmān Mansūb bih Sultān Ahmad Jalāyir," *Barrasīʾhā-yi Tārīkhī* 17 (1347): 273–90; Gottfried Herrmann, "Ein Erlass des Ǧalāyeriden Soltān Hoseyn aus dem Jahr 780/1378," in *Göttinger Orientforschungen: Syriaca*, vol. 3, *Erkenntnisse und Meinungen*, ed. Gernot Wießner (Wiesbaden: Harrassowitz, 1973), 135–63.

One of Sadr al-Din's important realizations was understanding the immense value of the order possessing a sacred text of its own. Such a text would preserve in writing the actions and sayings of his father and more importantly, give the burgeoning community a sense of a shared spiritual past. This led to the creation of Safi al-Din's biography, *The Quintessence of Purity* (*Safvat al-Safā*).[5]

Safi al-Din's disciples had many stories to tell about their encounters with their sheikh and did not shy away from passing down even embarrassing memories if it served a pedagogical purpose. Sadr al-Din tasked his disciple Darvish Tavakkuli (known as Ibn Bazzaz) to collect the stories circulating orally among the order's disciples and set them down in writing. The stories furnished the nascent community a way to preserve their collective memory that was distinct from other orders. Darvish Tavakkuli produced what is considered one of the most important hagiographies of the early modern world. He completed this enormous undertaking (approx. 800 folios) in 759/1358, and upon those pages he inked his brethren's spiritual experiences and created the "founding myth" of the order. In essence, what Sadr al-Din and Darvish Tavakkuli gave the Safavid community by creating *Safvat al-Safā* was their own sacred history.

Sadr al-Din's efforts generated the order's worldly orientation in the face of increased sociopolitical instability of the later eighth/fourteenth century. The tenth/sixteenth century chronicler Fazl Allah Khunji, who was hostile to the Safavids, pondered how a Sufi house managed to become a military power, pins the responsibility directly on Safi al-Din, who did not instruct Sadr al-Din to shun material possessions, and it was this "original sin" of wealth accumulation, Khunji contends, that became a custom among his descendants.[6]

Sadr al-Din's actions were well-timed. The decline of Ilkhanid power on the eve of Safi al-Din's death shattered once more the political stability

5 Tawakkul b. Ismāʿīl, *Safvat al-Safā*; variation: Heidi Zirke, trans., *Ein hagiographisches Zeugnis zur persischen Geschichte aus der Mitte des 14. Jahrhunderts: Das achte Kapitel des Ṣafwat aṣ-ṣafā in kritischer Bearbeitung* (Berlin: Klaus Schwarz, 1987); Michel M. Mazzoui, "A 'New' Edition of the *Safvat al-Safā*," in *History and Historiography of Post-Mongol Central Asia and the Middle East: Studies in Honor of John E. Woods*, ed. Judith Pfeiffer and Sholeh A. Quinn (Wiesbaden: Harrassowitz, 2006), 303–10; Serap Şah, "Safvetu's-Safa'da Safiyuddin-i Erdebili'nin Hayatı, Tasavvufi Görüsleri ve Menkibeleri" [The life, Sufic thoughts, and miracles of Safi al-Din Ardabili in *Safvat al-Safā*], 2 vols., PhD diss., Marmara University, 2007; Togan, "Sur l'origine des Safavides."

6 Fazl Allāh b. Rūzbahān Khunjī, *Tārīkh-i ʿĀlam'ārā-yi Amīnī: Sharh-i Hukmrānī-i Salātīn-i Āq Qūyūnlū va Zuhūr-i Safaviyān*, ed. Muhammad Akbar ʿAshīq (Tehran: Mīrās-i Maktūb, 1382), 259.

and forced its population into a closer association with Sufi orders as well as local brotherhoods (*futuwwas*) for food and security. Sadr al-Din's creation of a resourceful order with spiritual authority, a sacred text, and a strong missionizing orientation carried out by its deputies allowed the Safavids to gradually attract a considerable following.

Sadr al-Din's successors, Sheikh Khwadja Ali, the Black Robed (d. 832/1428), and his son Sharaf al-Din Ibrahim (d. 851/1447), who navigated the Timurid dynasty's sociopolitical upheavals, inherited a vast network of devoted deputies, elders, and disciples whom they supported and fostered among them the perception that true spiritual leadership resided in the house of Safi al-Din and his descendants. The ninth/fifteenth century ushered in a new era of Sufi orders' experimentation with developing their sources of social power to wrestle with the political world. The Safavids too were caught amid warring chiefs and the needs of a desperate population.[7]

1.3 THE SAFAVIDS AMONG OTHER ORDERS

The formative period of the order's social cohesion took place roughly between the mid-eighth/fourteenth and mid-ninth/fifteenth centuries, amid the demise of the Ilkhanid dynasty and the rise of the Aqquyunlu state under Uzun Hasan (d. 882/1478). This was a century of great political reconfigurations that witnessed several Sufi and antinomian orders militarizing to lead armed uprisings against their rulers. Chief among them were the Sarbidars of Khurasan under Sheikh Khalifah and his disciple Sheikh Hasan Juri (d. 743/1342); the Marʿashis in the forests of the north under Mir Qavam al-Din (d. 781/1379); Sheikh Fazl Allah

[7] Information on the political life of Khwajah ʿAli and his successor Sharaf al-Din Ibrahim is meager. See, for instance, Ibrāhīm b. Mīrak Jalāl al-Dīn Amīnī Haravī, *Futūhāt-i Shāhī: Tārīkh-i Safavī az Āghāz tā Sāl-i 920 H. Q.*, ed. Muhammad Rizā Nasīrī (Tehran: Anjuman-i Āsā̱r va Mafākhir-i Farhangī, 1383), 25–36; Hayātī Tabrīzī, *Chronicle*, 91–94, 110–13; Qummī, *Khulāsat al-Tavārīkh*, 1:74–76; variation 1: *Die Chronik Ḫulāsat At-tawā rīḫ Des Qāzī Ahmad Qummī: Der Abschnitt Über Schah ʿAbbās I*, Akademie der Wissenschaften und der Literatur – Veröffentlichungen der Orientalischen Kommission Bd. 14. (Wiesbaden: F. Steiner, 1964); variation 2: *Die frühen Safawiden nach Qāzī Ahmad Qummī*, Islamkundliche Untersuchungen Bd. 5. Freiburg i. (Berlin: Schwarz, 1970). The report that Timur released his prisoners of war to Khwajah ʿAli, though suitable and convenient to showcase the sheikh's influence, without further evidence cannot be fully trusted to be true. Similarly, some have suggested that Sheikh Ibrahim was the first of the Safaviyyah sheikhs who took up arms with his followers and participated in a military campaign. However, more evidence is needed before this claim can be corroborated.

Astarabadi (d. 794/1394), the founder of the Hurufiyyah order; Sheikh Badr al-Din in Anatolia (d. c. 818/1416); and Sayyid Muhammad Nurbakhsh (d. 867/1463), the founder of the Nurbakhshiyyah order.[8]

These movements were early iterations with a new vision of political leadership and a new conception of group cohesion for the means of collective political action, both unconventional and impractical. Ultimately, all these groups failed in establishing the infrastructure necessary to control and expand the sources of their social power. Their demise, however, created political communities that understood opposition to the ruling establishment differently, and sought alternatives to leadership not legitimized by Ilkhanid, Timurid, or Ottoman bloodlines, but by the elusive notion of universal sovereignty and justice of which they had experienced very little. These groups formulated their own conception of leadership that had existed in the margins, believing that political power was best practiced in the hands of Sufi sheikhs.

The archetypal spiritual authority that some saw in their sheikhs, often mirroring that of the Shiʿi Imams with their infallibility, wonderworks, and possession of sacred knowledge, found in this century new fertile grounds to flourish. The close association of the perfect mystical guide with the Prophet's household, especially with Imam ʿAli, had taken deep roots in these communities' spiritual cosmos. The Sarbidars, the Hurufis, the Marʿashis, and the powerful Mushaʿshaʿas of Khuzistan all had fundamental Shiʿi connections in their beliefs and principles of legitimation. The Safavid community found its political coordinates in this atmosphere and when Junayd became the sheikh of the militant wing of the order in the mid-ninth/fifteenth century, there existed a political community who already believed in this form of leadership and supported his bid for power.

1.4 SHEIKH JUNAYD AND THE TRANSFORMATION OF THE ORDER

On March 3, 1460 (3 Jumada I 864), the sheikh of the Safavid order lay dead on a bank of the river Kur in Tabarsaran in the southern Caucasus.[9] His full name was Abu al-Nasr Junayd b. Ibrahim b. Khvajah ʿAli, the fifth spiritual leader of the Safaviyyah order, a patrilineal descendant of Safi

[8] For the history of political movements in this period, see n. 22 in the Introduction.

[9] There are some discrepancies in the sources on the exact day of Junayd's death. I. Mélikoff, "Ḏjunayd," *EI*^{2}, http://dx.doi.org/10.1163/1573-3912_islam_SIM_2115.

al-Din, and now the deceased sheikh of yet another unsuccessful movement of the ninth/fifteenth century that failed to gain a foothold in the political realm.[10]

Junayd and his Sufi warriors were slaughtered by the forces of Amir Khalil Allah Shirvanshah (r. 820–67/1418–63), the ruler of Shirvan (in today's Republic of Azerbaijan, some 300 kilometers north of Ardabil), whose territory they had overrun. They had claimed that their only aim was to cross the Shirvanshah's territory to get to Dagestan to undertake "holy war" against the Christian kingdom in the region. Khalil Allah had not been convinced. He had sent his army and routed Junayd's forces, even though the Sufis had the help of Aqquyunlu troops.[11] Junayd's enemies reported that he fell in battle and his head was severed and brought to the Shirvanshah on a tray. Writers in the service of the Safavid house claimed that he died bravely on the field and his men brought his body back to Ardabil to be buried in the grounds of Safi al-Din's mausoleum.[12]

Junayd was the first sheikh of the order to meet a violent end as a result of his political activities. His death and the death of many of his disciples on that day marked a shift in the order's character in two major ways: first, the militant branch of the order that he led crossed the final threshold of commitment, that is, collective self-sacrifice; and second, in contrast to the previous generation, their deaths generated a pain of loss that found a central place in the community's collective memory. The experience of collective suffering and death and its accompanying emotional associations such as valor, martyrdom, and sacrifice possess elements that merit transmission to the next generation. For the first time, the ties of loyalty within the order were hardened by blood sacrifice. When Junayd's grandson, Ismail, a generation later, expressed in his poems how his Qizilbash warriors finally avenged the deaths of their forefathers, it resonated with

[10] For the main sources on Junayd's life and activities, see Amīnī Haravī, *Futūhāt-i Shāhī*, 36–43; Hayātī Tabrīzī, *Chronicle*, 123–42; Aşıkpaşazade, *Tevarih-i Al-i Osman*, ed. ʿAlī Bey (Istanbul: Matbaʿa-i ʿĀmira, 1332), 264–69; Khunjī, *ʿĀlam'ārā-yi Amīnī*, 252–73; Ghiyās̱ al-Dīn b. Humām al-Dīn al-Husaynī Khvāndamīr, *Tārīkh-i Habīb al-Sīyār fī Akhbār-i Afrād-i Bashar*, ed. Jalāl al-Dīn Humāʾī (Tehran: Kitābfurūshī-i Khayyām, 1362), 4:424–26; Qummī, *Khulāsat al-Tavārīkh*, 1:34–36; Khvāndamīr, *Tārīkh-i Shāh Ismāʿīl*, 27–28. For popular tales on Junayd, see the manuscript *Qessa-ye Soltān Jonayd*, Istanbul, Sulaymaniya Library, MS Fatih 4354; Paris, Bibliothèque Nationale de France, MS Supplément Turc 636.

[11] On Uzun Hasan's military aid to Junayd, see Hayātī Tabrīzī, *Chronicle*, 129–30.

[12] Khunjī, *ʿĀlam'ārā-yi Amīnī*, 262–63; Amīnī Haravī, *Futūhāt-i Shāhī*, 43. Qummī, *Khulāsat al-Tavārīkh*, 1:36, states that Junayd was interred elsewhere.

his men who felt a deep connection to that collective past, a connection that placed their struggle, their sacrifice, within their own heroic and sacred history.

Caution must be observed when discussing "Safavid followers" or "devotees" so as not to give the impression that they were a homogenous group. The Safavid community was diverse across the sociopolitical, economic, ethnic, and linguistic spectrums. What I explain here concerns that segment of the Safavid community that was directly bonded to Junayd and Haydar, accepted their spiritual authority, and actively aided them. As the level of their followers' commitment cascaded out, their relationship to the order's leadership also thinned and became elusive in the historical record (see the Introduction).

A myriad of factors compelled Junayd to take up arms, but one event in particular stands out: the fateful day in 860/1456 when he met Hasan the Tall (Uzun Hasan), the chief of chiefs of the White Sheep Turkmen confederacy, the Aqquyunlu. An ambitious ruler, Uzun Hasan would in a few years' time carve out an enormous territory in today's Iraq, Iran, Syria, and eastern Turkey.

Uzun Hasan was a warrior king par excellence, from a long line of great Turkic warrior chiefs with hereditary claim to the lands of Diyarbakir. He was as shrewd as he was energetic in his political dealings, capable of maintaining the loyalty and obedience of lesser chiefs and compelling them to help him build a formidable coalition. He campaigned against his neighbors ceaselessly, and even challenged the Ottoman Sultan Mehmed II, the Conqueror of Constantinople (d. 886/1481).[13]

Banished from his homebase in Ardabil by his uncle Sheikh Jaʿfar, Junayd set out with his followers eastward toward Anatolia and Syria. His uncle had gotten the upper hand in the dispute over the order's leadership and opposed Junayd's growing militancy, though he himself did not stay clear of political power. Sheikh Jaʿfar had the backing of a new powerful ally, Jahanshah Qaraquyunlu (the chief of the Black Sheep confederation, r. 837–71/1434–67), who had given his daughter in marriage to Jaʿfar's son, Sheikh Qasim. Jahanshah, Uzun Hasan's main adversary, ruled a vast territory in northwestern Iran that included Ardabil. He gave Junayd an ultimatum to leave the region. Junayd was in no position to challenge Jahanshah and with his devotees abandoned his

[13] For a detailed study on Uzun Hasan and the Aqquyunlu, see John Woods, *The Aqquyunlu: Clan, Confederation, Empire* (Salt Lake City: University of Utah Press, 1999).

ancestral town. They temporarily settled in the village of Kilis, in today's northern Syria, at a safe distance from his rivals.

Junayd must have appeared to Uzun Hasan as a gift from the heavens. There was a rare opportunity here for Uzun Hasan. Junayd's dispute with his uncle had made him an enemy of Uzun Hasan's main adversary, Jahanshah Qaraquyunlu. Junayd and his followers could be a valuable ally in his efforts to expand his territory at the expense of the Qaraquyunlus. Known to be a patron of Sufis and holy men, Uzun Hasan found Junayd, who carried the saintly pedigree of the Safavid family, a suitable spouse for his sister Khadijah Begum. The fact that Junayd was able to marry into the most powerful military house in the region and solidify his ties with it suggests that he was perceived as a man of great influence.

We have no idea what Khadijah thought of this proposition. Her union to Junayd sometime before 860/1456 formalized their alliance in their communities and created a new powerful branch of the Safaviyyah lineage, one that ultimately produced the founder of the dynasty, Ismail. The marriage offered Junayd a ladder unreachable to most. The marriage also spelled the beginning of his end.[14]

In addition to the political implications of the union, culturally the Safaviyyah-Aqquyunlu princes embraced their mother tongue, Azeri Turkish, which gave them direct access to their devotees on a deep affective level that comes from a shared language. Shah Ismail's poetry, for example, would have meant very little to the Qizilbash community if it were in Persian.[15] Alevi communities today in Turkey still sing his poems in religious gatherings. The house thus became bilingual, intimately linked to its Anatolian supporters on a cultural-emotional plane.[16]

Frequently, sheikhs who did not keep distance from political power actors justified their proximity with the idea that they sought to have some influence over the ruler to prevent him from wanton oppression and

[14] The exact date of their marriage is in dispute. See Mélikoff, "D̲junayd." Roger Savory, however, disputes this date.

[15] Ismail also wrote a handful of poems in Persian in his *Divan* (see Chapter 3). Shāh Ismāʿīl b. Haydar Safavī, *Hatayî Divanı; Şah Ismail Safevı, Edebı Hayatı ve Nefesleri*, ed. Sadeddin Nüzhet Ergun (Istanbul: Maarif Kitaphanesi, 1956); variation 1: *Khatāʾī, Shāh Ismāʿīl Safavī: Kulliyāt-i Dīvān, Nasīhatnāmah, Dahnāmah, Qūshmālār, Fārsjā Shiʿrlar*, ed. Ismāʿīl-zādah (Tehran: al-Hudā, 1380); variation 2: *Hatâyî Dîvâni*, ed. Muhsin Mecit (Istanbul: Türkiye Yazma Eserler Kurumu Başkanlığı, 2017).

[16] The Venetian emissary Michele Membré, who visited the court in 1530s, reports that during a wedding ceremony in which he was present, the Qizilbash Sufis would recite Shah Ismail's poetry. Michele Membré, *Mission to the Lord Sophy of Persia (1539–1542)*, ed. A. H. Morton (Warminster: E. J. W. Gibb Memorial Trust, 1999), 42.

violence and hoped to aid him in spreading justice. This translated in politics as maintaining order by supporting the status quo with occasional minor interventions. Not so for Junayd. He had more ambition than playing the role of a temporary spiritual advisor to some prince and was not afraid to use violence to create political opportunities. This was his major break from his forefathers. He abandoned the title of sheikh for a political-military title of sultan when in exile from the order's spiritual center in Ardabil, and the change seems to have suited him well.

The Syrian chronicler Sabt b. al-ʿAjami (d. 884/1479) reports that when Junayd resided in Antakya and with his followers built a community with wooden houses, "he acted more like a king than a Sufi."[17] Junayd indeed must have appeared to his contemporaries a lot more political than the Sufi sheikhs to whom they were accustomed. Whereas Safavid chroniclers glorify his expulsion, the hostile Aqquyunlu chronicler Khunji likened Junayd's itinerancy in exile to "snakes who do not make homes themselves but seize the dwelling of others."[18] However nefarious Khunji would like to portray Junayd, Junayd had attracted a considerable number of devotees and the backing of influential deputies.[19]

By the time Junayd became politically active, the order's network of deputies had been in existence for almost a century. Their circles of masters and disciples offered Junayd and his inner circle a network of supporters in towns and villages stretching from Azerbaijan to Anatolia and Syria (more below).

The historical record regarding Junayd's life and controversial activities is fragmentary even considering the dynasty's official sources. We know next to nothing about the beliefs of a man who helped militarize the Safavid order. Junayd did not leave any writings behind, making the task of examining his life more difficult, except for a single letter that he sent to Shams al-Din b. Shammaʾ (d. 863/1459) sometime in 861/1457, in which he tried to defend himself against charges of heresy.[20]

[17] Abū Dharr Ahmad b. Ibrāhīm Sibt b. al-ʿAjamī, *Kunūz al-Dhahab fī Tārīkh Halab*, ed. Shawqī Shaʿath and Fālih Bakkūr (Aleppo: Dār al-Qalam al-ʿArabī bi-Halab, 1418), 2:284.

[18] Khunjī, *Tārīkh-i ʿĀlam'ārā-yi Amīnī*, 263–64.

[19] Ibid., 261, 265, 271–74, in which Khunji scorns the support that the order's deputies offered Junayd and later his son Haydar. Mentions of the early *khalīfah*s are numerous in the Safavid sources though many lack detail. Rasūl Jaʿfariyān, *Tārīkh-i Qizilbāshān-i Safavī dar chand Matn-i Tārīkhī* (Qum: Nashr-i Muvarrikh, 1396), 27–28.

[20] Sibt b. al-ʿAjamī, *Kunūz al-Dhahab*, reproduced and examined by Ahmad Khāmahyār, "Maktūbi-i Sultān Junayd-i Safavī bih Ibn Shammāʿ-i Halabī," *Payām-i Baharistān*, D2,

Shams al-Din was a local sheikh in Aleppo, and the only member of the city's ʿulema who appeared sympathetic to Junayd. He even stood up for him when the other judges issued a fatwa calling for his death. Sabt b. al-ʿAjami recorded the letter in his *History of Aleppo* and chronicled in detail Junayd's trial in absentia, which took place on 25 Ramazan 861 (August 16, 1457). The letter provides a small window into his world and his relationship to his followers a few years before his death.

According to al-ʿAjami, two main charges were brought up against Junayd. First, he was accused of being a believer of Messianism (Mahdism), a follower of Muhammad b. Fallah (d. 870/1465), known as the Mushaʿshaʿa (the Radiant One), who claimed to be the awaited Messiah (Imam Mahdi) and with the help of the tribes of Khuzistan controlled most of southern Iraq and Khuzestan. They became much feared after they sacked the Shiʿi center Hilla in Iraq in 857/1453.[21] Second, he was accused of abandoning the community of the faithful, a charge of heresy often levied against nonconformist religious leaders that was punishable by death. In the letter, Junayd dismisses the charges with an air of confidence and honesty. "In respect to accusations of abandoning correct worship, slacking in obligatory acts," he writes, "and promoting prohibitory commands that has reached you, no one is innocent, except for prophets and saints and those that God has kept innocent."[22]

Throughout the letter he cites the Qurʾan and hadith in his defense with a precision that demonstrates his desire to appear as proficient in religious sciences as his accusers. No doubt, Junayd, being in line to lead a Sufi order, had received an excellent education throughout his upbringing. Under the tutelage of his father, Sheikh Ibrahim, he received lessons in reading the Qurʾan, memorizing hadith, exegesis, and mysticism with the order's elders. He certainly would have been intimate with Sufi and occult works, and knew the Shiʿi corpus, hadith, and eschatological literature. He had enough confidence in his learning that he rhetorically challenged his indicters, "I am a man devoted to the Holy Book and the Way of the Prophet (*sunna*); more insightful in the Qurʾan than any other, and more knowledgeable of the Divine Law than any specialist, and whoever doubts

S5, SH20 (1392): 135–39. Ibn al-ʿAjami states that Junayd's trial in absentia took place on Tuesday, 25 Ramazan 861 (August 16, 1457).

21 ʿAlī b. ʿAbd Allāh Mushaʿshaʿī, *al-Rihlah al-Makkiyyah: Tārīkh-i Siyāsī va Ijtimāʿī-i Mushaʿshaʿīyān*, ed. ʿĀrif Nasr (Tehran: Markaz-i Pizhūhishī-i Mīrās̱-i Maktūb, 1396), 4–17. For the founding of the order, see Ahmad Kasravī, *Tārīkh-i Pānsad Sālah-i Khūzistān* (Tehran, 1368), 8–26.

22 Khāmahyār, "Maktūb-i Sultān Junayd."

this, let them come forth."[23] If al-ʿAjami recorded the letter without embellishment, it seems that Junayd cared very little for keeping up the appearance of a pious sheikh who must exhibit humility, the golden virtue of Islamic ethics.

Indeed, one would be hard pressed to view him as a Sufi sheikh anywhere near the rank as his forefathers or contemporaries. He was simply too political. Yet, the idea of a political sheikh on the Prophetic model had been preconfigured long before Junayd's lifetime (see Chapter 2). Furthermore, the composition of his followers had also changed. The people who followed Junayd were not "*ṭarīqah* Sufis" (disciplined in traditional organized orders) of the earlier era, like Pirah ʿIzz al-Din or Pirah Fazl Allah and hundreds of other Sufis who were focused on transcendence alone. Undoubtedly, there were still those type of disciples, wayfaring with the order's elders in Ardabil and elsewhere, but the Sufis who were attracted to Junayd's brand of Sufism and followed him into the battlefield – those in the power orbit of the militant wing of the order – were stirred by a different set of beliefs and motivated into action by a host of new concerns. They defied easy categorization. They identified as Sufi disciples of the Safaviyyah, but they were also militant with enough solidarity to resist government pressure.

When, for example, Junayd refused the summons to appear in the House of Justice (Dār al-ʿAdl) in Aleppo to respond to the charges, al-ʿAjami reports that the governor tried to persuade him a number of times, even sending high-ranking officials, such as Shams al-Din Shafiʿi, the Mufti of Antakya (in modern Turkey), to fetch him. Junayd, instead, arrested the mufti and threatened to take his life. The governor then sent a royal secretary along with troops to secure his surrender. When he refused again, a clash broke out between the two forces in which the court commander was slayed. The secretary reported back that "they [Junayd's followers] battle with whoever tries to capture him."[24]

The chronicler further relates that Junayd's followers had built a mosque and a bathhouse in the village of Kilis (on the border of Syria and Turkey today), where a large group of his followers congregated. He elaborates on their relationship with Junayd. "On his father and ancestor's reputation, people had tremendous faith in him, obeyed him, and never slacked in their service. People would come to him unceasingly

[23] Ibid.
[24] Ibid.

from Anatolia, Iran, and other realms, and would bring him gifts."[25] Al-ʿAjami's description makes two things clear: (1) that Junayd's disciples were militant and political unlike the temperate type of Sufis of whom we read earlier; and (2) that they were deeply loyal to him to a degree that they had taken up arms to defend him against authorities, even though he appears not to have shared their messianic beliefs.

Junayd's group followed a variety of fringe heterodox beliefs and were often accused by the ʿulema of deviancy and corruption of faith. Mahdism, for instance, the belief that the Mahdi's (the Muslim Messiah) emergence was imminent and that the Day of Judgment was approaching, was among the leading convictions that made a deep imprint in this milieu. Sheikhs such as Muhammad b. Fallah and Muhammad Nurbakhsh, for example, had gained a large following based on their claim to be the awaited Mahdi. Junayd, however, despite the accepted view regarding his political life, does not appear to have manipulated his devotees' belief in this regard.[26]

When, for instance, he was defending himself against the charge of being a Mahdist, he likened his situation to that of the Prophet in the pre-Islamic era (*jāhiliyya*). "When someone who in finding the hidden Truth that is not veiled from the people," he complained to Shams al-Din, "is told what was told to the Prophet, [and treated] in the same way as the previous prophets, to what great calamity he is subjected! Especially, someone like me who is among an ignorant tribe (*qawm jahhāl*) amid whom Mahdism (*al-shaʿshaʿa*) has manifested."[27]

The correct interpretation of the Day of Judgment and the Mahdi's appearance among his followers notwithstanding, Junayd's response shows that his milieu had a deep reverence for the mythical and the sacred, both of which they found in the lives of the Shiʿi Imams. Their everyday piety was shaped by their beliefs in Shiʿi holy figures such as Imam ʿAli,

[25] Sibt b. al-ʿAjamī, *Kunūz al-Dhahab*, 2:284. Junayd was already a man of some means and resources that facilitated his political activities, and the offerings that Ibn ʿAjami mentions the Safavi devotees would bring him served a devotional rather than a material purpose. Religious offering was a common practice in establishing spiritual patronage and helped strengthen the bond between the master and the disciples. The Safaviyyah order had a long history of its supporters offering material gifts in exchange of receiving blessings from the order's sheikhs, a tradition that lasted well into tenth/sixteenth century. See, for example, Membré, *Mission to the Lord Sophy*, 41–42.

[26] Arjomand, *Shadow of God*, 74–77.

[27] Khāmahyār, "Maktūb-i Sultān Junayd." Junayd is explicit throughout the letter in clarifying that he speaks of the Twelver Imamis, and not the other Shiʿi sects. There is no consensus among the ʿulema as to the exact details and sequence of events leading up to the Mahdi's emergence.

who had come to symbolize the perfect archetype with divine qualities, his son Imam Hussein, the Prince of Martyrs, and their offspring, the last of the Imams, the Mahdi, the Awaited One, dwelling in occultation and soon to reemerge. As we shall see in Chapter 2, the community harnessed this source of ideological power, and its leadership seized the paramount claim to religiopolitical authority: direct descent from the Prophet through his daughter Fatimah and his cousin and son-in-law Imam ʿAli.

By the time Junayd took his last breath, the Safaviyyah had been an established Sufi order with a hundred-year history that had formed a distinct communal identity with a vision of rightful leadership. Some of his followers were willing to die for him, no doubt, but many others were supporters but not zealous enough to jeopardize their lives.

For those who entered the murshid-murid (master-disciple) relationship under their *khalīfahs*' guardianship (see Chapter 2 on the role of the "deputies"), the order's rituals, practices, and sacrosanct chain of discipleship offered them a sense of belonging to a particular community with a long history. If Junayd's followers had internalized the principles of discipleship, the spiritual surrender (and political loyalty) of even the most apolitical of them would have been provisionally secured.

Junayd was a proto-Sufi king, a minor Sufi sheikh who wielded political as well as spiritual power. With the support of his powerful brother-in-law Uzun Hasan, he provided his core supporters with weapons and military training to fuel their militancy. They were therefore able to organize themselves into a small militia of Sufi warriors of faith (*ghāzīyān-i sūfī*) who benefited from strong ties of spiritual loyalty to one another.[28]

Junayd's death in the battlefield in 864/1460 had a tremendous emotional impact on his devotees but evidently not enough to extinguish their political will. The Safavid order had roots in the community strong enough to survive the consecutive deaths of its leadership. Junayd, the first of three Safavid leaders to be killed off, passed on to his son and successor Haydar two valuable sources of social power, namely, the order's network of deputies who backed Haydar when he came of age, and the activation of the order's Shiʿi political ideology in concurrence with their supporters' religious views.

[28] Hayati Tabrizi reports that with the help of Uzun Hasan, Junayd gathered 5,000 warriors. Hayātī Tabrīzī, *Chronicle*, 130. For information on the Aqquyunlu and Safavid military, see Vladimir Minorsky, "A Civil and Military Review in Fārs in 881/1476," *Bulletin of the School of Oriental and African Studies* 10, no. 1 (1940): 141–78; Floor, *Government Institutions*, 124–280; Sümer, *Safevî Devletinin Kuruluşu*; Haneda, *Le Châh et les Qizilbāš*; Hamīd Asad'pūr and Husayn Iskandarī, *Artish-i Īrān dar Dawrah-i Safavī va Tahavvulāt-i Ān* (Tehran: Nigāristān-i Andīshah, 1398), 103–66.

1.5 SHEIKH HAYDAR

Under the cover of night, a devotee of the Safavid order, Mawlana Sufi Kalaibari, risked his life to retrieve a sacred object, the severed head of his sheikh, Haydar Safavi (d. 893/1488), the son of Junayd Safavi, which was hanging from the city gate of Tabriz.[29]

Mawlana Kalaibari wasn't a high commander, or kin of Haydar. Like many Safavid followers, he was a craftsman. The chronicler Hayati Tabrizi, who focused on the affairs of the early Safavids, relays that Kalaibari was a carpet seller from Tabriz and as his forename "Mawlana" suggests, he was an esteemed Sufi of his community. He must have felt a deep sense of grief for the manner of Haydar's death and had to end the humiliation that the desecration of their sheikh's body had brought upon his community. Kalaibari carried the head down and buried it in a holy site in the city.

The Aqquyunlu chronicler Khunji Isfahani, who resented the Safavid ascendency, portrays in detail the moment of Haydar's capture. When the sheikh was pierced with an arrow, Khunji reports, his commanders tried to get him out of the battlefield. "They circled around him and began to shield him," he writes.

> They resisted, thrashed, and struggled, but the brave men of the Aqquyunlu broke their circle with their swords and spears. The desperate Sufis at last moved to the side and left his injured body to the enemies. ʿAli Agha Qapuchi severed Sheikh Haydar's wickedness from the world and his head from his feeble corpse and took it to the victorious amirs.

Years later, Haydar's son and successor Ismail retrieved it, reunited it with the body, and interred it along with the other fallen Qizilbash men in a separate cemetery in the grounds of Safi al-Din's shrine.[30]

[29] Hayātī Tabrīzī, *Chronicle*, 178–79; Khunjī, *Tārīkh-i ʿĀlam'ārā-yi Amīnī*, 294–95. Later tenth/sixteenth-century Safavid sources omit the detail of the desecration of Haydar's corpse. See, for instance, Ahmad b. Muhammad Ghaffā rī, *Tārīkh-i Jahān'ārā*, ed. Mujtabā Mīnuvī (Tehran: Kitābfurūshī-i Hāfiz, 1343), 262; Khvurshāh b. Qubād Husaynī, *Tārīkh-i Īlchī-i Nizām Shāh: Tārīkh-i Safavīyah az Āghāz tā Sāl-i 972 Hijrī Qamarī*, ed. Muhammad Rizā Nasīrī and Koichi Haneda (Tehran: Anjuman-i Āsār va Mafākhir-i Farhangī, 2000), 3–4; Yahyā b. ʿAbd al-Latīf Qazvīnī, *Lubb al-Tavārīkh*, ed. Mīr Hāshim Muhaddith (Tehran: Anjuman-i Āsār va Mafākhir-i Farhangī, 1386), 270; Qummī, *Khulāsat al-Tavārīkh*, 1:37–40; Būdāq Munshī Qazvīnī, *Javāhir al-Akhbā r: Bakhsh-i Tārīkh-i Īrān az Qarāqūyūnlū tā Sāl-i 984 H. Q.*, ed. Muhsin Bahrām'nizhād (Tehran: Mīrās-i Maktūb, 1378), 109–11; Khvāndamīr, *Tārīkh-i Shāh Ismāʿīl*, 31–33. On the recent discovery of Haydar's tomb, see Temur Aytberov, "The Newly Found Tomb-Stone of Sheikh Haydar the Safavid in Dagestan," *Iran & the Caucasus* 13, no. 2 (2009): 281–84.

[30] Khunjī, *Tārīkh-i ʿĀlam'ārā-yi Amīnī*, 294; Hayātī Tabrīzī, *Chronicle*, 178–79.

The impact of Haydar's generation in the transformation of the Safavid order into a military-political organization was pivotal. Their relative political success and military failure underlines an important step in the maturation of the order's capability: its capacity to manage a sizable political-military organization and retain the loyalty of its core supporters. In the following I show how Haydar helped create a network of powerful allies, who later supported his son Ismail, the first Safavid shah.

It had been nearly thirty years since Haydar's father, Junayd, was killed by the Shirvanshahs. He was an infant at the time. Now, a young man with the support of thousands of militant Sufis and Turkmen riders of tribes such as the Shamlu, Qaramanlu, and Talish, Haydar initiated another round of conflict with the Shirvanshahs. After a series of skirmishes and a siege, they at last clashed with the joint forces of Farrukh Yasar, the son of Khalil Allah who had beheaded Haydar's father, and his cousin Sultan Yaʿqub, who had succeeded his father, Uzun Hasan, as the chief of the White Sheep confederacy. The battle was a complete disaster for Haydar and his men. They were outmatched and outnumbered. For ordinary supporters of the order, like Kalaibari the carpet seller, the defeat must have been dreadful, witnessing the death of their revered leader and his devotees again by the same dynasty in the same cursed region of Tabarsaran.[31]

The Safavid community was, no doubt, devastated by Haydar's death and loss of countless Qizilbash riders. After nearly a decade of successful military raids, they were all but decimated, their sheikh killed, and his sons on the run for their lives, including Ismail, who was five years old at the time. When Sultan Yaʿqub heard that people were rallying in support of Haydar's eldest, Sultan ʿAli, and were gathering in Ardabil, he ordered their capture, including their mother, Halimah Begum (i.e., his own sister), and sent them to the castle of Istakhr in Shiraz. Though Haydar had exceeded his father's political and military undertakings and perhaps even gained an incremental long-term advantage for the order, he too met the same fate at a young age, leaving the survival of his house in jeopardy.[32]

Unlike Junayd, who married into Uzun Hasan's family, Haydar was born into it. He was the son of Khadijah Begum, Uzun Hasan's powerful

[31] Tabasarān, or Tabarsarān, is a district in the eastern Caucasus by the Caspian Sea, south of the city of Derbent, in today's Republic of Dagestan.

[32] Amīnī Haravī, *Futūhāt-i Shāhī*, 59–64; Hayātī Tabrīzī, *Chronicle*, 181–83; Khvāndamīr, *Tārīkh-i Habīb al-Sīyār fī Akhbār-i Afrād-i Bashar*, 4:434–36; Qazvīnī, *Lubb al-Tavārīkh*, 253–54, 269–70; Qummī, *Khulāsat al-Tavārīkh*, 1:37–41.

sister. This fact alone gave him legitimate entry into the military-political domain, an entry that his father did not have. They named him Haydar, Imam ʿAli's popular warrior appellation, and gave him the honorific Shujaʿ al-Din ("the valiant of the faith"), both names harboring connotations of religious militancy. Haydar, as well, would later name his first son with Uzun Hasan's daughter, Sultan ʿAli, in honor of Imam ʿAli.

When Junayd was killed, his mother, Khadijah Begum, and her inner circle raised Haydar (d. 893/1488). No doubt due to Khadijah's sway, Uzun Hasan brought his nephew under his protection and favored him, even though it caused tension with his sons. She was likely instrumental in securing for Haydar his claim to the city of Ardabil when the Qaraquyunlus declined, as well as arranging his marriage to her niece, Uzun Hasan's daughter Halimah Begum (ʿAlam Shah Begum). Shah Ismail, the founder of the dynasty, was born of this union in Ardabil.[33]

Haydar's birth as an Aqquyunlu prince and his marriage to Uzun Hasan's daughter gave him the political legitimacy to find support if he wanted to make a bid for power. His more powerful cousins, Uzun Hasan's sons, knew this well and was the main reason they tried to eliminate him and his sons.

If Junayd had appeared to some as a political leader in the garb of a Sufi sheikh, Haydar was unabashedly political. He was an Aqquyunlu, a "man of the sword," and like his cousins, he fully embraced the political-military life. Safavid sources are silent on Haydar's spiritual practices and give the impression that he was less concerned with Sufi teachings than political affairs. Yet, according to a contemporary outside observer, he raised the saintly charisma associated with his father's side of the family to new heights. The Venetian ambassador Caterino Zeno, who was present at the court of Uzun Hasan on an anti-Ottoman mission, reported that

> Secheaidare [Sheikh Haydar] was a Saint or Master or Prophet, as we should call him, who by preaching a new dogma in the Mahometan creed, that Ali was superior to Omar, obtained many disciples and people who favored his doctrine. So great was his success, that at this time he was considered by all a Saint, and a man almost divine.[34]

[33] Khunjī, *Tārīkh-i ʿĀlam'ārā-yi Amīnī*, 265, 271; Amīnī Haravī, *Futūhāt-i Shāhī*, 43–46; Qummī, *Khulāsat al-Tavārīkh*, 1:36–40.

[34] See the Italian traveler Caterino Zeno's "Travels in Persia," in *A Narrative of Italian Travels in Persia, in the Fifteenth and Sixteenth Centuries*, trans and ed. Charles Grey (London: Hakluyt Society, 1873), 43–46; variation: Josafa Barbaro and Ambrogio Contarini, *Travels to Tana and Persia*, trans. William Thomas (London: Hakluyt Society, 1873).

Zeno's reference to Haydar's preaching a version of sectarianism will be discussed in Chapter 2. Here I will point out two important features in Zeno's report: (1) that Haydar continued his father's embrace of Shiʿism in direct response to their social base's reverence for the Imams, especially Imam ʿAli; and (2) that his followers perceived him as their holy Sufi sheikh, "a man almost divine." These two features – the Safavid followers' devotion to Imam ʿAli and belief in Sufi discipleship – cut to the heart of the order's spiritual vitality that propelled its political ventures at the end of the ninth/fifteenth century. The Safavid leadership's saintly pedigree, and their ability to be a part of and harness the political and religious beliefs of Shiʿi communities, was what attracted their most ardent supporters and what set them apart from most of the contenders for power in Azerbaijan and eastern Anatolia.

Haydar recognized an important feature of group solidarity that had been overlooked by his father, the powerful sense of union that visual symbols produce. Haydar designed the iconic red *tāj* (crown) that his devotees proudly donned and his enemies frequently denigrated.[35] They would thus be known as the Qizilbash, or the Red Heads. The Haydari *tāj* became the centerpiece of the order's initiation rite, and a powerful symbol of belonging to a new Safaviyyah-Qizilbash military class that was not only linked together via their sacred Sufi *silsilah*, but also through the holy lineage of the twelve Imams. It created a visible marker of loyalty to their sheikh and their group identity. It also gave them a great sense of exclusive privilege of being a member of the new political-military elite, one whose roots ran deep in the reservoir of Safaviyyah discipleship and now consecrated by ʿAlid Shiʿism.

[35] Hayātī Tabrīzī, *Chronicle*, 147–48. Haydar, as the legend grew, saw Imam ʿAli in a dream who revealed to him a scarlet turban with twelve folds, representing the twelve Imams. See, for instance, the late eleventh/seventeenth-century anonymous work *Tārīkh-i ʿĀlam'ārā-yi Safavī*, ed. Yad Allāh Shukrī (Tehran: Bunyād-i Farhang-i Īrān, 1350), 30–31, which credits the invention of the *tāj* to Haydar's dream of Imam ʿAli. Iskandar Beg Munshi in his *Tārīkh-i ʿĀlam'ārā-yi ʿAbbāsī* mentions the dream but not Imam ʿAli (Savory's translation, 1:31). Some scholars believe that the twelve folds refer to the Bektashi teachings and not a reference to the twelve Shiʿi Imams. It is likely that it carried both meanings given the convergence of various Sufi/Shiʿi belief and folklore in this milieu (e.g., Hayātī Tabrīzī, *Chronicle*, 147). Many Sufi orders wore particular styles of turbans with various colors. See Floor, *Government Institutions*, 129. Floor does not cite Hayātī Tabrīzī, *Chronicle*, in this book; however, he references Walter Hinz, *Irans Aufstieg Zum Nationalstaat Im Fünfzehnten Jahrhundert* (Berlin: De Gruyter, 1936); Afzar Moin, *The Millennial Sovereign: Sacred Kingship and Sainthood in Islam* (New York: Columbia University Press, 2012), 81.

Their understanding of their order's teachings and history, as discussed above, was nurtured by the order's far-flung network of elders, the *khalīfah*s and the *pīrah*s active among tribes and villagers in eastern Anatolia, Syria, and greater Azerbaijan. These elders helped create the disciples' tie of spiritual loyalty to Haydar as the head of the order and ensured the order's preservation after his death just as they had done when his father was killed in 865/1460.[36] The Safavid elders recognized that their own survival depended on the community's perseverance and continued belief in the order's spiritual primacy. They helped build the order's social base and supported its military-political goals by instilling the principles of discipleship and spiritual loyalty in their activities. This type of constructed loyalty incorporated organized violence for religious and political ends into the codes of discipleship and provided ideological validation for the order's leadership to continue with further militarization.

Haydar had developed a keen interest in the military arts from an early age. As an Aqquyunlu prince, he was expected to learn martial arts as part of his education. The manner of his father's death, no doubt, profoundly shaped his political awareness. Raised in an ideologically diverse environment that included the Turkmen military-political culture from his mother side, and the Sufi militancy of his father's side, he was difficult to label. For some, he was a holy representative of the Imams. For others, like the veteran Turkmen chiefs who put their full force behind him, he appeared more resourceful and qualified as a military commander than his father.

Some of the powerful chiefs in Haydar's circle, whose names have survived the historical record, demonstrate his ability to create an effective coalition. Chiefs such as Hussein Beg of the Shamlu tribe and Qara Pirah of the Qajars commanded his right and left wings, respectively, on the battlefield and were by his side when he fell in the battle in Tabarsaran. Others included the old Khadem Beg, who had served his father and later became the head deputy (*khalīfat al-khulafā*) of Shah Ismail, and Rustam Beg of the Qaramanlus and Dede Beg of the Talish tribe, who were with Haydar's son Sultan ʿAli, when their cousin Rustam Aqquyunlu's guards intercepted them and executed him.[37]

Haydar's military education began when he was in his early twenties. Strong, charismatic, and violent, at first he had the blessings of his

36 See Khunjī, *Tārīkh-i ʿĀlam'ārā-yi Amīnī*, 261, 265, 270–74, where Haydar was warned at the Aqquyunlu court to cut off his communication with his *khalīfah*s of Anatolia.

37 For a detailed study of early Safavid military ventures, see Allouche, *Origins of the Ottoman-Safavid Conflict*, 50–54.

overlord cousin Sultan Yaʿqub, and launched three relatively large-scale military campaigns against the towns and village of southern Dagestan between 883/1478 and 893/1488. "In reality," writes Khunji,

> he was daring and courageous to the limit, and was skillful in the arts of war, sword fighting, shooting, spear throwing, archery ... In no century can anyone point to a sheikh with a cloak of Sufism who could match [him] in breaking [enemy] lines and in swordsmanship, without having traversed the treacherous path of kings and without having to possess the tax revenues of a realm.[38]

An important indicator of Haydar's militarization was his preoccupation with arms manufacturing, which points to the Safavid leadership's orientation toward developing the infrastructure for warfare during these years and beginning to produce arms. His influential uncle Jaʿfar, who was at odds with his father, Junayd, over his political activities with his Aqquyunlu in-laws, had passed away, leaving Haydar at the top of the order's hierarchy and its resources. A modest factory to manufacture basic weapons such as swords, arrows, bows, and spears could have produced a considerable cache of weapons in one year to arm thousands of new disciples and recruits. It was vital for Haydar and his commanders to have control over their basic military and weapon production. Soon enough, he gained access to sufficient resources that in one of his campaigns north, in order to bypass the Shirvanshah's territory and reach Darband (Derbent in today's Republic of Dagestan) via the coast of the Caspian Sea, he had several vessels built to transport his troops.[39]

As Sufi sheikhs, Junayd and later Haydar's motivation to undertake invasions of Shirvan and Dagestan has remained debatable. The likely explanation is that they wanted to carve out an independent territory from Ardabil north to Derbent in Dagestan through Shirvan and Baku on the western coast of the Caspian Sea. Their path to Dagestan ran through the kingdom of the Shirvanshah. Their confidence in challenging an established dynasty such as the Shirvanshahs points to their high level of mobilization, management of resources, and manpower.

Safavid sources generally acknowledge the excessive degree of violence that Haydar allowed in these campaigns, including enslavement and massacre of civilians who resisted his army. Justified as sanctioned holy war by

[38] Khunjī, *Tārīkh-i ʿĀlam'ārā-yi Amīnī*, 267–69.

[39] Hayātī Tabrīzī, *Chronicle*, 151–52. Qasim Beg reports that Sultan ʿAli continued his father's program by putting Amir Fazl Allah Sayyaf, who was Haydar's teacher in sword-making, in charge in Ardabil (ibid., 193–94); Khunjī, *Tārīkh-i ʿĀlam'ārā-yi Amīnī*, 267–68; Amīnī Haravī, *Futūḥāt-i Shāhī*, 50.

the native literati, he gifted many treasures and slaves to the head chief Sultan Ya'qub Aqquyunlu, as was the custom. His actions were more typical of a chieftain during a raid than a Sufi sheikh. Such gestures of subservience did not, however, assuage Sultan Ya'qub's growing concern regarding his cousin's increasing power, and finally the sultan turned on him when Haydar overstepped his bound and attacked Farrukh Yasar Shirvanshah, Sultan Ya'qub's ally.

The impact of Haydar on the Safavid order's transformation into a military organization was twofold. First, he increased the order's military activities and thereby reconfigured their social ties through the experience of war. As such, he helped create within the existing Sufi brotherhood an "intensive power dynamic" not unlike that of military organizations. His decade-long military campaigns (883/1478–893/1488) and arms production laid the foundation for the order's full militarization a decade later under his son Ismail and his veteran chiefs and military allies, several of whom were to become his kin thanks to his father's marriage alliances.

Second, being Uzun Hasan's nephew and son-in-law offered him a great advantage in forging political alliances with powerful chiefs and solidifying some of them with marriage unions. He was able to marry four of his daughters to military chiefs such as Bayram Beg of the Qaramanlu tribe, 'Abd Allah Khan and Hussein Beg of the Shamlus, and Shah 'Ali Beg the Kurdish ruler of Hazo and Sason. These men and the military power they possessed played a pivotal role in the order's militarization, which a decade later helped secure victories for Ismail.[40]

In Haydar was manifested the union between a military house and a Sufi order. His short but intense political-military venture helped expand

[40] Kioumars Ghereghlou, who has carefully charted Haydar's kinship to powerful families, writes, "In addition to his marriages to Uzun Hasan's and Ja'far's daughters, Haydar had concubinage with several Circassian and Georgian women. Ten sons and four daughters are known to have survived Haydar. Soltān-'Ali, Ebrāhim, and Esmā'il had been born from Uzun Hasan's daughter. Sayyed Hasan (d. ca. 931/1525), who under Shah Esmā'il acted as superintendent of the Safavid shrine in Ardabil, had been born in 878/1473-4 from Haydar's marriage to Ja'far's daughter. Fak̲r-Jahān K̲ānom, the eldest of Haydar's daughter, had been married off to Bayrām Beg Qarāmānlu (d. 920/1514), an influential tribal chief from Moğānāt. Her younger sister, Malak K̲ānom, had been given away in marriage to 'Abdallāh Khan Šāmlu, also known as 'Abdi Beg (d. 912/1506-7), a high-ranking military chief from Ardabil and eponymous founder of the 'Abdallu clan of the Šāmlu. Haydar's other two daughters were married off to Hosayn Beg Šāmlu (d. 920/1514), who later acted as Shah Esmā'il's guardian, and Šāh-'Ali Beg (d. after 920/1540), the ruler of Hazo and Sason in Anatolian Kurdistan who claimed descent from the Sasanian kings of Iran." Kioumars Ghereghlou, "Ḥaydar Ṣafavi," *Encyclopædia Iranica*, www.iranicaonline.org/articles/haydar-safavi.

the Safavids' social base and attract several Turkmen tribes into the order's discipleship. These new recruits wore the Haydari crown that he had given them as a symbol of their group identity and loyalty to the sheikh. With the support of an expansive network of deputies, who fostered spiritual loyalty and submission to the order's leadership and its sacred *silsilah*, Haydar and his chiefs transformed the Safavids into a cohesive political-military order.

By the time of his death, Haydar came to embody a type of Sufi leadership that had the doctrinal depth to feed its political ideology and justify its military venture. Under him the order developed the capability to channel a heterogeneous coalition of militant Sufis and Turkmen clans. This variegated community of allies expected him and the Safavid leadership, its *khalīfah*s and *pīrah*s, to fulfill the political as well as spiritual needs that archetypal warrior chiefs and charismatic holy men often provide. The community would find the ultimate fulfillment of such needs in the person of his son, Ismail.

1.6 THE CLIMB AND THE TRIUMPH

Ismail was not meant to inherit the mantle of leadership. He had two older brothers. He was still a suckling child when his father, Sheikh Haydar, was killed in battle against the Shirvanshahs in the summer of 1488 in what is today's southern Dagestan.

When the news of Sheikh Haydar's death reached the Safavid communities, the deputies (*khalīfah*s) and the remaining Qizilbash chiefs met in Ardabil to regroup. There they decided to rally behind Ismail's eldest brother, Sultan ʿAli. This alarmed their cousin Sultan Yaʿqub Aqquyunlu (d. 896/1490), who became convinced that the political ambitions of this order would not be stymied with the death of their leader. He thus ordered the arrest of the entirety of Haydar's family. They were taken south to the castle of Istakhr in Shiraz.[41]

They spent four and a half years in the old fortress at the mercy of Sultan Yaʿqub. As fate would have it, Yaʿqub died under "mysterious circumstances," which most likely meant that he was poisoned. With his death, the Aqquyunlu dynasty fractured irreparably in the ensuing

41 Amīnī Haravī, *Futūhāt-i Shāhī*, 59–66; ʿAlī b. Shams al-Dīn Lāhījī, *Tārīkh-i Khānī*, 101–3; Hayātī Tabrīzī, *Chronicle*, 179–86; Khvāndamīr, *Tārīkh-i Shāh Ismāʿīl*, 34–39; Qazvīnī, *Lubb al-Tavārīkh*, 270–72; Munshī, *Javāhir al-Akhbār*, 109–12; Huaynī, *Tārīkh-i Īlchī-i Nizām Shāh*, 4–15; Qummī, *Khulāsat al-Tavārīkh*, 1:40–49.

infighting. Another of Ismail's cousins, Rustam, who managed to ascent to power, needed auxiliaries to increase his forces against his opponent Baysunghur. He therefore released Ismail and his family from Istakhr and convinced Sultan ʿAli as the eldest Safavid son to join his forces.

When Rustam was assured of Sultan ʿAli's loyalty, he allowed the family to take up residence in Ardabil. That proved to be a mistake as reports of the Safavid supporters' political activities and weapon production continued to arrive. Rustam thus arranged to get rid of Sultan ʿAli along with his brothers all together. He sent a large force led by his trusted commander Aybah Sultan, who caught up with the Safavid retinue outside of Ardabil and put Sultan ʿAli and his devotees to the sword.

Miraculously, some, including Ismail, escaped. Led by the head deputy (*khalīfat al-khulafā*) Khadim Beg of the Talish tribe, together with the royal tutors (*lalah*s) Hussein Beg and Dadah Beg, a small band of survivors managed to flee to the forests of Gilan.[42]

Throughout its long history, rebels and insurgents of Iran have fled to the forests and mountains of the north seeking refuge from the authorities. The Lahijan province, where Ismail hid, was one such region. Nestled in the northern tip of the Alburz mountains over its main western pass into Gilan, Lahijan was hard to reach and easy to defend against assault. As noted earlier, the Zahidi order of Safi al-Din's master and father-in-law, Sheikh Zahid Gilani, had long been dominant in this part of Gilan. Now, the would-be founder of the Safavid dynasty, young Ismail came seeking refuge in the same soil where his ancestor Safi al-Din two centuries earlier sought spiritual refuge.[43]

The mountainous province was governed by Mirza ʿAli, head of the Kar Kiya house, who held power in the region for more than a century and adhered to the Zaydi branch of Shiʿism, which also believed that leadership resided in the House of the Prophet (*ahl al-bayt*) and his progeny from Imam ʿAli and Fatimah. Mirza ʿAli was sympathetic to Ismail. Though his hold on power was tenuous, he had enough military power to withstand Aqquyunlu pressure to hand over the Safavid family. The most Rustam could do coming from Tabriz was to pillage a few villages on

[42] Amīnī Haravī, *Futūhāt-i Shāhī*, 66–73; Hayātī Tabrīzī, *Chronicle*, 194–215; Lāhījī, *Tārīkh-i Khānī*, 102–5; Jean Aubin, "Révolution chiite et conservatisme. Les soufis de Lâhejân, 1500-1514," *Moyen Orient & Océan Indien* 1 (1984): 1–40.

[43] See the introduction by Husayn b. Abdal Zahidi, a later descendant of Sheikh Zahid, who wrote the *Silsilat al-nasab-i Safaviyyah*, reminding the Safavid house of their earlier kinship ties. Husayn b. Abdāl Zāhidī, *Silsilat al-Nasab-i Safaviyyah: Nasab'nāmah-i Pādshāhān bā ʿAzamat-i Safavī* (Berlin: Chāpkhānah-i Īrānshahr, 1343).

the lower slopes.[44] For six years Mirza ʿAli resisted and provided protection for Ismail and his family. It was during these years in the north that Ismail was indoctrinated and instructed in the ways of his father and grandfather.

Ismail's political and religious worldview comes alive in his book of poetry, *Poems of the Sinner*, arguably the finest example of militant Sufi ideology of the era.[45] It is obvious Ismail's knowledge of Persian literature, mystical ideas, and Shiʿi histories (*manāqib*) was not trivial. His poetry often exhibits interwoven strands of history, mythology, and worldly aspirations animating its political message. Ismail was protected by a group of devotees, later known as Sufis of Lahijan and by the moniker "*ahl-i ikhtisās*," the inner circle, some of whom later served in his and his son's government.[46] Sources pertaining to these years are scant but do mention that he came under the influence of one member in particular, a notable of the region by the name of Mawlana Shams al-Din Muhammad Lahiji (d. 921/1515), who instructed him in the Qurʾan, theology, and waited on him when he suffered a prolonged illness. Shams al-Din was an elder of the Nurbakhshiyyah Sufi order and wrote a popular commentary on the mystical treatise *Gulshān-i rāz* by the famed mystic Mahmud Shabistari (d. c. 740s/1340s). Like many Sufi leaders of the time, he also had a long history of involvement with political powers.[47]

"Like a burning sun" Ismail emerged out of the forest to lead his warriors to victory. This was the narrative that later Safavid supporters created to dramatize the rise of their dynasty and glorify its founder. Research has shown, however, that the teenage Ismail had little say in the strategies of the early days and it was his seasoned Qizilbash chiefs and deputies who had supported his father, Haydar, who charted the path of his campaigns.[48]

[44] Lāhījī, *Tārīkh-i Khānī*, 103–4. It was not until the early eleventh/seventeenth century, under Shah ʿAbbas I, that the region became incorporated into the Safavid realm.

[45] Shāh Ismāʿīl b. Haydar Safavī, *Hatayî Divanı*.

[46] Hayātī Tabrīzī, *Chronicle*, 213–14; Floor, *Government Institutions*, 9; Aubin, "Révolution chiite et conservatisme." The first chiefs who gave Ismail their support included Husayn Beg Lalah from the Shamlus, ʿAbd al-ʿAli Beg Dede of the Zup al-Qadrlu, Khadim Beg (*khalīfat al-khulafā*) from Talish, Rustam and Bayram Beg from the Qaramanlu, Elyas Beg Aiqutughlu from Hasanlus, and Qara Piri Beg of the Qajars. Haneda, *Le Châh et les Qizilbāš*, 72–78.

[47] ʿAbd al-Husayn Navāʾī, *Shāh Ismāʿīl Safavī: Asnād va Mukātabāt-i Tārīkhī Hamrāh bā Yadāshtaha-yi Tafsīlī* (Tehran: Bunyād-i Farhang-i Īrān, 1347), 45–49.

[48] For a recent reevaluation of Ismail's military role in the early Safavid campaigns, see Anooshahr, "The Rise of the Safavids"; Togan, "Sur l'origine des Safavides"; Sümer, *Safevî Devletinin Kuruluşu*; Asad'pūr and Iskandarī, *Artish-i Īrān*; Aubin, "Révolution chiite et

These Turcoman tribal confederacies mostly roamed in the land stretching from northwestern Iran to eastern Anatolia and southern to northern Iraq and Syria, and were evidently seven in number: Rumlu, Ustajlu, Qajar, Afshar, Zu al-Qadr, Takkalu, and Varsaq.[49] Their chiefs came together to reunite under their new Sufi shah and prepare for war. They called themselves the Qizilbash, the Red Heads, after Ismail's father, Haydar, invented the tradition of crowning his disciples with crimson headgear as previously noted.[50] They spoke Turkish and were devout ʿAlevis believing in the sanctity and guardianship (*wilāyah*) of Imam ʿAli b. Abi Talib affecting how they perceived Ismail. This is explored separately in Chapter 3. Several other militia contingents, such as the Ardabilis, Gilanis, and several Kurdish clans, from the surrounding areas also joined Ismail's army.[51]

Some believed Ismail to be the long-awaited Mahdi, the occulted twelfth Imam (Muhammad b. al-Hasan al-ʿAskari, b. 255/869). Others believed he was the precursor to the Mahdi and was there to prepare the kingdom for his arrival. Meanwhile the military strategists among them, like the chiefs who had fought the Aqquyunlus and the Shirvanshahis alongside Ismail's father, saw him to be the right child at the right time and in the perfect circumstances to realize their goals and seize power and take Tabriz from the Aqquyunlus. It helped that Ismail was an Aqquyunlu prince himself, a descendant of Uzun Hasan and a grandson of the Christian princess Despina Khatun of the house of Trebizond. He also had a magnificent spiritual ancestry in their eyes; Ismail was the heir to the mantle of their Sufi progenitor Safi al-Din Ardabili, and perhaps more importantly, they believed that he was the direct descendant of their "blessed idol," the first Shiʿi Imam, ʿAli.

The careful strategy devised by his veteran Qizilbash commanders, combined with the religious zeal of his warriors, allowed Ismail to win a string of early victories on the battlefield that gave him much plunder, and confirmed in the eyes of his contemporaries what they had assumed: He was an extraordinary youth whom the Creator favored.[52]

Ismail's triumph was swift and like a dramatic tale of fiction, it started with avenging the death of his father and grandfather, Haydar and Junayd.

conservatisme"; Masashi Haneda, "L'Évolution de la Garde Royale des Safavides," *Moyen Orient & Océan Indien* 1 (1984): 41–64; Minorsky, "A Civil and Military Review."

[49] Haneda, however, has identified the first Qizilbash chiefs who gave Ismail their support with some variation. See n. 46.

[50] Qazvīnī, *Lubb al-Tavārīkh*, 271; Floor, *Government Institutions*, 129.

[51] Floor, *Government Institutions*, 128–32.

[52] Anooshahr, "The Rise of the Safavids."

No doubt, many fighting for Ismail had lost their kin in the previous battle against the Shirvanshahis and revenge might have strengthened their resolve. Ismail's poetry is replete with thoughts of vengeance and retribution against their enemies that at times takes on large mytho-historical significance. Their forces clashed near the city of Baku in 905/1500 in a bloody battle in which Ismail and his Sufi warriors routed the more experienced and professional Shirvanshahis killing their king, Farrokh-yasar.

A year later, Ismail and his Qizilbash chiefs decided the time was ripe to challenge his cousin Alvand Mirza, who commanded the Aqquyunlus forces. Vastly outnumbered but confident from their victory in Shirvan, Ismail's army crushed Alvand's forces at the Battle of Sharur. The path to the capital now lay open.

Ismail stood at the gates of Tabriz, his grandfather's capital, the head of a mighty Qizilbash army, the result of years of sacrifice and preservation of their group cohesion. It had taken the militarized Safavid community nearly fifty years to conquer the ancient city. Ismail then entered the gates like the "awaited Joseph," walked to the grand mosque, and infamously declared Shiʿism the religion of the realm. The event lavishly commemorated as such in Safavid chronicles was nevertheless one of the defining moments in their history and the subject of legendary tales and devotional poetry. It did not only have immense symbolic value in the Shiʿi eschatological doctrine; conquering a capital meant that a legitimate Shiʿi house had at last arrived at the helm of power.

For the next ten years, cities fell one by one to Ismail and his Qizilbash riders: Fars (908/1503); Mazandaran, Gorgan, and Yazd (909/1504); Diyarbakr (911–13/1505–7); and Baghdad (915/1508). In 914/1508 the local rulers of Kurdistan, Lurestan, and Khuzestan recognized his suzerainty. Ismail rewarded his Qizilbash chiefs with governorships of newly gained provinces, which formed the basis and the pattern of the patronage network discussed in Chapters 4 and 5. He thus attracted many allies from the established religious and political communities that began to consider their fortunes tied to that of the Safavid house.

All these victories, however, seemed forgotten when the Qizilbash army was soundly defeated at the Battle of Chaldiran in 920/1514 against the Ottomans led by Sultan Selim the Grim. Ismail was warned at the war council that the Ottomans fight differently – they have mortars, heavy artillery, and legions of gunmen. The Safavid armies were still conventional at the turn of the tenth/sixteenth century and mostly relied on the speed of their calvary, using recurve bows, swords, and spears. At the council before the war, Ismail was advised not to allow the Ottomans time to set up their artillery and to hit them on the move, to which he famously responded, "I'm no caravan thief."

Ismail paid a heavy price for his overconfidence in rejecting the guidance of his senior commanders and suffered the worst and last defeat of his life. As a result, he had a psychological breakdown. Contemporary sources intimate that he only wore black, distanced himself from politics, and never again did he take the field. He took to drinking and died on 19 Rajab 930 (May 23, 1524) near Tabriz at the age of thirty-seven, most likely from liver failure.

Ismail, the charismatic warrior king, was no more and so was the unity of the great Qizilbash confederation that was forged by his presence and what he personified. A faction of Qizilbash chiefs managed to put Ismail's eldest son, the ten-year-old Tahmasb, on the throne, while others prepared for a protracted civil war that was to engulf the nascent kingdom for the next decade, known as the first *fitnah* (revolt). The intertribal war demonstrated to all how fragile the military elites' group cohesion was without a leader of Ismail's caliber. Tahmasb inherited not a throne but the sword hanging above it. To survive, the young shah faced an insurmountable political task, to rebuild the great Qizilbash confederation now scattered and leaderless. For that to happen, he needed to forge his claim to religiopolitical legitimacy on his own terms, distinct from that of his warrior father, whose aura of authority was the result of a host of portentous and sacred beliefs in the eyes of his devotees.[53]

Before examining the challenges Tahmasb faced to assume the throne, a systemic problem at the heart of the dynasty's ascent remained unyielding, even when they were at the helm of power: how to maintain their social cohesion in the face of another disastrous setback and loss of deified leadership even worse than the one before. Safavid historiography has developed enough that we can pause and ask the difficult question of what were the processes that made their brand of cohesion not only possible but particularly resilient. A search for answers forces us to go back further in time to the eighth/fourteenth century, to the very first generation of Safavid Sufi disciples, to see how they perceived their social ties and conceptions of authority in their spiritual leadership – the subject of Chapter 2.

[53] Tahmasb Mirza, the eldest son of Shah Ismail, was born on 26 Dhu al-Hijja 919 (February 22, 1514) in Shahabad village near Isfahan. Khvāndamīr, *Tārīkh-i Habīb al-Sīyār fī Akhbār Afrād Bashar*, 4:468; Khvāndamīr, *Tārīkh-i Shāh Ismāʿīl*, 66; ʿAbdī Beg Shīrāzī, *Takmilat al-Akhbār: Tārīkh-i Safavīyah az Āghāz tā 978 Hijrī Qamarī*, ed. ʿAbd al-Husayn Navāʾī (Tehran: Nashr-i Nay, 1369), 580.

2

The Corpse and the Mortician

2.1 THE DISCIPLE AND HIS SACRED CHAIN

Pirah Fazl Allah, a first-generation Sufi disciple of the Safavid order in the mid-eighth/fourteenth century, recounted the following, an event that nearly snuffed out years of progress he had painstakingly made on the path to transcendence.

I was in Ardabil and Pirah ʿIzz al-Din [my spiritual master] was in Homashahrah. One night, before dawn, I decided to go to the bathhouse. When I went inside the dressing room, the attendee came out and I saw that she was beautiful. I desired her, and since it was at night and the bathhouse empty, I asked her, "Are you also coming to the bath?"

"Perhaps," she responded.

I went inside. She followed me and sat down by the pool. I reached out my hand to touch her and suddenly, I was slapped with such a force that I fell unconscious, blood running out of my mouth, ears, and nose. [In that state] I saw Pirah ʿIzz al-Din wearing an apron like those worn by butchers, sharpening a knife. He seized me and detached all my limbs in such a way that I imagined I was dead.

When people arrived in the morning and saw me on the floor [in a pool] of blood, they became frightened and shouted, "They have murdered someone in the bathhouse." I came to my senses from their cries and at once set out for Homashahrah [to find my guide]. When I arrived there, they informed him that Fazl Allah had come from Ardabil.

"Do not permit him to enter," he told them.

For three days and nights they did not grant me access and I sat across [his abode] and prayed. In the third night, I pleaded inwardly, "If Sheikh Zahid and Sheikh Safi al-Din had gained proximity (*qurb*) to God Almighty, Pirah ʿIzz al-Din will call and forgive me."

At that time, someone came and brought me to Pirah ʿIzz al-Din.

"Is it not enough what you have done already that you now bring Sheikh Zahid and Sheikh Safi at my doorstep as [your] intercessors?!"

Pirah ʿIzz al-Din continued, "If the hand of Sheikh Safi al-Din's *tarīqat* [i.e., teachings] had not struck you at the bathhouse, you would not have failed in depravity and [thereby] would have forfeited your training and spiritual progress."[1]

Medieval Sufis were an extraordinary people, a negligible percentage of the population, living on the fringe, often shunned by the establishment, and disdained by the legalist theologians. Even so, they were often admired for their extreme piety. They had chosen the hardest path of life to find the inner Kaʿba, and they embarked on an inward journey that they believed would free their cognition from the trap of multiplicity and guide them to unimaginable depths of lucidity.[2] They sought the Divine Oneness. In the process, their mental world expanded to accept supernatural phenomena they deemed sacred and developed a methodology and categorization to make sense of their experiences. Sufis would describe wandering for a hundred years in meditation only to awaken and see a mere hour had passed. They would communicate in the dream world with saints and prophets, with visions so intense they felt their death was imminent. They read into ordinary phenomena extraordinary interpretations radically different from normative modes of understanding reality. They lived, it could be said, in a parallel universe within their communities that embodied vastly divergent governing laws.[3]

While Fazl Allah's account may at first appear to be a mere tale of parapsychological phenomena seen in medieval hagiographical literature, a closer look reveals a key component of acquisition of authority with far-reaching political consequences: *silsilah* or the spiritual chain of Sufi

[1] Tawakkul b. Ismāʿīl, *Safvat al-Safā*, 1146.

[2] For studies on medieval Sufi communities relevant to this study, see Ahmet T. Karamustafa, *God's Unruly Friends: Dervish Groups in the Islamic Later Middle Period, 1200–1550* (Salt Lake City: University of Utah Press, 1994); Seyyed Hossein Nasr, *Sufi Essays* (Chicago: Kazi Publications, 1999); Zarrīn'kūb, *Justujū dar Tasavvuf-i Īrān*; Shaybī, *Tashayyuʿ va Tasavvuf*; Nafīsī, *Sarchashmih-i Tasavvuf dar Īrān*; Devin DeWeese, "Spiritual Practice and Corporate Identity in Medieval Sufi Communities of Iran, Central Asia, and India: The Khalvatī/ʿIshqī/Shattārī Continuum," in *Religion and Identity in South Asia and Beyond*, ed. Steven E. Lindquist (London: Anthem Press, 2011), 251–300; Shahzad Bashir, *Sufi Bodies: Religion and Society in Medieval Islam* (New York: Columbia University Press, 2011); Muhsin Kiyānī, *Tārīkh-i Khānqah dar Īrān* (Tehran: Kitābkhānah-i Tahūrī, 1990).

[3] Ahmad b. Muhammad Simnānī, *Chihil Majlis, yā Risālah-i Iqbāliyyah*, ed. Najīb Māyil Haravī (Tehran: Intishārāt-i Adīb, 1366), 133–35.

discipleship. By sharing this rather embarrassing episode about his early training, Fazl Allah (now a "*pīrah*," meaning an esteemed Sufi elder) shows the function of the enchainment in his milieu.[4] He was only saved by virtue of being enchained in a link of discipleship to his teacher Pirah ʿIzz al-Din, who was in turn enchained to his teacher Safi al-Din, and Safi al-Din to Zahid Gilani, and Zahid Gilani to his master Jamal al-Din Tabrizi, and so on, in an unbroken chain of mystics that connected all the way back to the Prophet Muhammad himself, the wellspring of transcendence. Fazl Allah seemed convinced that it was his master-disciple enchainment that gave Pirah ʿIzz al-Din the power of intervention to make his spiritual rescue possible.

The way Fazl Allah arrived at this understanding of his sheikh's *silsilah* reveals the central development in the foundation of the Safavid order: the establishment of Safi al-Din's spiritual authority as the founding sheikh of the order as a distinct branch of his teacher's, the Zahidiyyah. It was this authority that was passed down to his progeny long before the Safavid house's obsession with establishing their legitimacy based on descent from the Prophet through his daughter Fatimah and his cousin ʿAli. And it was this perception of authority that the Safavid disciples recognized as the basis for their discipleship in the nascent order.[5]

The story of how Fazl Allah's teacher Pirah ʿIzz al-Din himself became Safi al-Din's disciple offers another window into how the early Safavid Sufis promulgated and established their order's spiritual legitimacy. As we'll see in Section 2.2, this was done by firmly linking the Safavid chain of discipleship directly back to the source of all mystical knowledge and authority, the Prophet.

[4] According to late Safavid state manuals *pīrah* was the assistant to the *khalīfah*. However, during the eighth/fourteenth century such rankings and hierarchies were fluid.

[5] Having an authentic *silsilah* mattered beyond one's order, to such a degree that certain orders would not accept a disciple in their midst if he failed to produce his *silsilah* and to name the master through whom he was initiated into the path. The Safavid spiritual *silsilah* and descent is recorded in several sources. See, for example, Kiyaʾ Gilani's genealogy of Imam ʿAli's descent, Ahmad b. Muhammad Kiyāʾ Gīlānī, *Sirāj al-Ansāb*, ed. Mahdī Rajāʾī (Qum: Kitābkhānah-i ʿUmūmī-i Āyat Allāh al-ʿUzmā Marʿashī Najafī, 1367), 4–7; Amīnī Haravī, *Futūhāt-i Shāhī*, 1–3; Qazvīnī, *Lubb al-Tavārīkh*, 266–67; Muhammad b. Sultān Muhammad Ardabīlī, *Tazkirat al-Zākirīn; Risālah-i Sūfiyyah-i Safaviyyah; Munājāt* (Kāshān: Hamgām bā Hastī, 1391), 76–79; Zāhidī, *Silsilat al-Nasab*, 10–13. The Safavid genealogy has long been a topic of debate whose key points are discussed in Hani Khafipour, "The Safavid Claim to Sovereignty according to a Court Bureaucrat," in *The Empires of the Near East and India: Source Studies of the Safavid, Ottoman, and Mughal Literate Communities*, ed. Hani Khafipour (New York: Columbia University Press, 2019), 179–92.

Sufi orders are the perfect organization to militarize. They have the intrinsic ideological structures and organizational capability to facilitate acquisition and maintenance of power by force. The Safavid community was a rare example of an order that managed to overcome the main challenges faced by politicalized Sufi orders, that of organization, control, logistics, communication, which translated to the capacity to organize and control people, and the ability to provide material and spiritual benefits long term within an expansive territory. In the following, I sketch the master-disciple dialectic of power embodied in medieval Sufi thought, and its connection to the politicization processes.[6]

2.2 THE MASTER AND THE VISIONS OF THE PROPHET

Pirah ʿIzz al-Din's powers of intercession were made possible by his own discipleship to Safi al-Din. He certainly had not always been a superb mystic capable of penetrating his disciple's dreams. He was not even convinced of Safi al-Din's spiritual authority when he first met him. A long-time Sufi himself, Pirah ʿIzz al-Din had previously made considerable progress on the path and had experienced illuminations, and so he was not initially impressed by Safi al-Din.

In Safi al-Din's biography, Pirah ʿIzz al-Din's son relays how his father eventually became one of the order's first impassioned disciples. Pirah ʿIzz al-Din's story reveals the importance of *silsilah* in the early formation of Safi al-Din's spiritual authority.

> One day, my father was washing a sheepskin in a creek by Ardabil's city gate when he encountered Safi al-Din riding toward him alone.
>
> "How long will you roam aimlessly in this way?" Safi al-Din's heart spoke to Pirah ʿIzz al-Din.
>
> Seeing how Safi al-Din chose to communicate with him, Pirah ʿIzz al-Din's heart responded in kind, "Until I find a murshid."
>
> "Come to us."

[6] Spiritual guides that supervised the adepts were tiered and generally known by titles of *shaykh*, *murshid*, and *pīr*. They each had various duties in the order such as the *shaykh al-taʿlīm*, whose task was to teach Islamic ethics to prepare the murid for the *shaykh al-tarbiya*, the directing master of inner spiritual teaching. The *shaykh al-sufiyya* instructed disciples of the lodge, and the *shaykh al-kull* was the head of the "missionary" sheikhs. There was a great degree of overlap and variation depending on the order's internal dynamics and external sociopolitical circumstances. See the assessment of such classifications in Tanvir Anjum, "Sufism in History and Its Relationship with Power," *Islamic Studies* 45, no. 2 (2006): 221–68.

"What would I gain from you?"

"Illumination (*kashf*), wonderworks (*karāmāt*)," Safi al-Din answered.

"What use do I have for *kashf* and *karāmāt*? Look at the city of Rome," Pirah ʿIzz al-Din's heart said.

Safi al-Din closed his eyes and saw Roman priests in churches discoursing about mystical illuminations.

Pirah ʿIzz al-Din continued, "[You see,] I will not be won by promises of wonderwork."

"We shall give you the supreme illumination," Safi al-Din's heart declared.

"I do not want [your] illumination and will not be enticed with it," Pirah ʿIzz al-Din's heart replied.

At this point, Safi al-Din turned away and rode off.

From that moment, we are told, Pirah ʿIzz al-Din could no longer experience illuminations no matter how intensely he meditated. Helpless, ʿIzz al-Din looked for a master to help him find a solution and was told a sheikh by the name of Shams Ahmad of Hamadan might be the person he is seeking. And so, he headed out with some companions toward Hamadan. The night before his journey, ʿIzz al-Din went to the mosque to pray. He fell into a deep slumber and had an extraordinary dream.

ʿIzz al-Din in a dream state saw himself in a mosque where all the attendees were facing the *qiblah* while he was facing the other way. He became frightened by what he saw, a clear sign of something terrible in his servitude to God. He then heard a voice explaining that he had turned away from a *sāhibdil*, "possessor of hearts." Inquiring who this *sāhibdil* was, ʿIzz al-Din was told to go to the city plaza of Ardabil. He immediately headed toward the plaza and there saw a multitude of radiant people composed of prophets and Sufi saints (*awliyā*). He paid little attention to them and gravitated toward a great throne upon which sat the Prophet of Islam. Next to the Prophet sat a veiled figure.

When I saw the Prophet's countenance, I cried, "O Prophet of God, help, for I have grown stagnant. Show me a murshid [Sufi master]."

The Prophet called me in and said, "I was the first to preach the Path to Truth." Then he named all the other murshids after him, one by one, until Sheikh Zahid [Gilani]. After that, he said, "The person who is seated next to me is the murshid of this age."

"O Prophet of God, who is this person?" I asked.

The Prophet, may God's blessings be upon him, raised his hand and removed the man's veil. I looked up and saw that it was Sheikh Safi al-Din. I felt ashamed that I wanted to go to Shams Ahmad when such a king was in existence. I wondered what to do, when the Commander of the Faithful, [Imam] ʿAli, may God be pleased with him, approached me and said, "Don't be afraid, the Prophet's blessings are upon you. He has forgiven you and placed you into my care."

I then said, "O Prophet of God, intercede for I have offended [Safi al-Din]."

The Prophet, may God's blessings be upon him, took hold of my hand and placed it into the sheikh's hand and said, "Give him repentance (*tawbah*) and mystical instructions (*talqīn*)." The sheikh took my hand, and I began to repent and receive instruction. It was in that state that I screamed and woke up. My companions asked the cause of my scream. I responded that I saw it all in a dream that our guide [Safi al-Din] has been in the house all along and we are [aimlessly] searching around outside.[7]

This account is one of several tales in *Safvat al-Safā* related by Safi al-Din's disciples that aims to affirm their sheikh's *silsilah* and spiritual legitimacy by directly placing him in the presence of the Prophet. Such tales underscore the concern of the early Safavid disciples of proving that they had an authentic Sufi genealogy. In the Islamic mystical tradition, seeing the Prophet Muhammad and speaking with him was not a trivial matter. The vision of the Prophet and his answer to the dilemmas facing the faithful offered absolute certainty. No other vision, save that of the Creator, could match it. Such dreams were therefore meticulously recorded across various genres and passed on within communities for centuries.[8]

In ʿIzz al-Din's dream the Prophet gave him an answer to his predicament of finding a true spiritual master, Safi al-Din, and by naming every teacher in the chain of legitimate masters who passed on their mantle to him. For ʿIzz al-Din and other disciples of the order, this verifiable chain (*isnād*) provided the assurances that Safi al-Din's spiritual teaching was flawless, for absolute perfection in method was the aim and the slightest defect would have far-reaching detrimental effects for the disciple's transcendence.

[7] Tawakkul b. Ismāʿīl, *Safvat al-Safā*, 254–57; Muhammad Nishātī Shīrāzī, *Tarjumah-i Nuskhah-i Khattī-i Tazkirah-i Shaykh Safī al-Dīn Ardabīlī: Mahfūz dar Kitābkhānah-i Sāltīkūf Shichidrīn San Pitirzbūrg Rūsiyyah*, trans. Dāvūd Bahlūlī (Qum: Nashr-i Adyān, 1388), 151–53.

[8] Özgen Felek and Alexander D. Knysh, eds., *Dreams and Visions in Islamic Societies* (Albany: State University of New York Press, 2013); Elizabeth Sirriyeh, *Dreams and Visions in the World of Islam: A History of Muslim Dreaming and Foreknowing* (London: I.B. Tauris, 2018); Nuzhat Ahmadī, *Ruʾyā va Sīyāsat dar ʿAsr-i Safavī* (Tehran: Nashr-i Tārīkh-i Īrān, 1389); Louise Marlow, ed., *Dreaming across Boundaries: The Interpretations of Dreams in Islamic Lands* (Cambridge, MA: Harvard University Press, 2006).

Silsilah is a key principle in both the dreams recounted above. The disciple Fazl Allah believed ʿIzz al-Din was able to rescue him because he was enchained within Safi al-Din's *ṭarīqah*, that is, the order's path, its teachings, its creed. ʿIzz al-Din, meanwhile, was assured, we are told, of Safi al-Din's true spiritual authority by a vision of none other than the Prophet himself.

ʿIzz al-Din, in due time, became a *pīrah* and one of Safi al-Din's closest companions. By retelling their experiences with Safi al-Din, Sufis embedded themselves within this sacred enchainment and legitimized their own training. Pirah ʿIzz al-Din initiated his own son, ʿAbd Allah, into the order, and even tried to persuade his old skeptical father of the truth of Sufi piety.[9]

Eventually, their relationship grew so deep that when Safi al-Din's son Sadr al-Din (who later succeeded him as sheikh of the order) was seeking permission to carry out spiritual conversation with an elder (*suhbat*), Safi al-Din told him to sit with Pirah ʿIzz al-Din. He explained to his son that, "Pirah ʿIzz al-Din has served me the way I served [my own guide] Sheikh Zahid." Note again the hints of authoritative *silsilah* in Safi al-Din's reply.[10]

2.3 SUFIS AND THE LEGACY OF THE PROPHET'S MISSION

Confirmation of a genuine sanctified *silsilah*, however, was not the only principle that established a sheikh's authority. His role as a custodian of his community based on the Prophetic model was just as vital in the post-Mongol era. Safi al-Din was the pole of ʿIzz al-Din's spiritual life. He revered his sheikh as a true guide, an intercessor linked directly to the Prophet. This was not unique to the Safavid sheikh, however. Other Sufi sheikhs in previous eras had paved the way for the type of spiritual authority perceived in Safi al-Din. Masters of mysticism such as Sheikh Ahmad Jam (d. 536/1141) and Sheikh Najm al-Din Razi (d. 654/1256), as well as Razi's sheikh, the renowned mystic Najm al-Din Kubra (d. 618/1221), had advocated for a greater role for Sufi sheikhs in their communities. They had developed their view partly based on their understanding of the Prophet's spiritual as well as sociopolitical mission, and partly as a response to the changing needs of their communities.[11]

9 Tawakkul b. Ismāʿīl, *Safvat al-Safā*, 848–49.
10 Ibid., 259–60.
11 On Sufi sheikhs as the inheritors of the Prophet Muhammad's legacy, see Arthur F. Buehler, *Sufi Heirs of the Prophet: The Indian Naqshbandiyya and the Rise of the*

Sheikh Ahmad Jam, for example, had explained the demanding steps that transformed a sheikh to the height of spiritual perfection, becoming a "deputy (*nā'ib*) of Muhammad the Messenger of God and the *khalīfa* (successor) of God on earth, upon whose holy countenance life flourishes, and from his pure spirit the lifeless hearts ignite to life."[12]

By elevating the sheikhs' roles as custodians of their communities in this fashion, Ahmad Jam pulled the Sufi sheikhs into the controversial arena of *khilāfat* (i.e., the rightful successors to lead Muhammad's community), which was until then the domain of military governors and their supportive ʿulema. A century after Sheikh Ahmad Jam, Najm al-Din Razi (d. 654/1256), who was given the nickname "wet nurse" for his tender care in nurturing his disciples, became entangled in the chaos of the Mongol invasion of Iran and Iraq in the mid-seventh/thirteenth century and advocated for greater involvement of Sufi sheikhs in their communities. He specifically pointed to the social obligations they were under as successors of the Prophet Muhammad's mission. He reminded his disciples with the words of the Prophet himself who said, "The sheikh among his tribe is like the prophet among his community." These sheikhs and many like them confirmed such beliefs in the eyes of their communities with their actions, especially during periods of extreme hardship and insecurity that followed the Mongol conquests.[13]

By the mid-eighth/fourteenth century – Safi al-Din's generation – the notion that a sheikh was the deputy of the Prophet with important social commitments had taken firm root. ʿIzz al-Din Mahmud b. ʿAli Kashani (d. 735/1334), for example, remarked that "after the rank of prophethood, no degree is worthier than the Prophet's deputy in guiding the masses to the truth and following the path of the Messenger of God … the purpose of being a sheikh is this deputyship. The station of sheikhhood is thus the highest of stations."[14] The Safavid biographer Nishati

Mediating Sufi Shaykh (Columbia: University of South Carolina Press, 2008), 1–4. On the Safavid-era religiopolitical landscape, see Rasūl Jaʿfariyān, *Safaviyyah dar ʿArsah-i Dīn, Farhang va Sīyāsat* (Qum: Pizhūhishgāh-i Hawzah va Dānishgāh, 1379); Rasūl Jaʿfariyān, *Kāvush'hā-yi Tāzah dar Bāb-i Rūzgār-i Safavī* (Qum: Nashr-i Adyān, 1384); Jaʿfariyān, *Sīyāsat va Farhang-i Rūzgār-i Safavī.*

12 Abū al-Fath Muhammad b. Mutahhar Ahmad Jām, *Hadīqat al-Haqīqah*, ed. Muhammad ʿAlī Muvahhid (Tehran: Bungāh Tarjumah va Nashr-i Kitāb, 1343), 12–15.

13 ʿAbd Allāh b. Muhammad Najm al-Dīn Rāzī, *Mirsād al-ʿIbād min al-Mabdaʾ ilā al-Maʿād*, ed. Husayn al-Husaynī Niʿmat Allāh (Tehran: Dār Matbaʿah-i Majlis bi-Tabʿ Rashīd, 1312), 126–28.

14 ʿIzz al-Dīn Mahmūd b. ʿAlī Kāshānī, *Kitāb Misbāh al-Hidāya wa-Miftāh al-Kifāya*, ed. Jalāl al-Dīn Humāʾī (Tehran: Intishārāt-i Sukhan, 1394), 226. It is important to note,

Shirazi, meanwhile, took the claim to new heights and wrote, "If the Prophet had not said 'there are no prophets after me,' without a doubt, Safi al-Din would have been God's prophet."[15]

Safi al-Din seemed to be the type of sheikh that was engrossed in the religious and political life of his community (see Figure 2.1). He often used his status to shield them from the Mongol military governors. "He has a large following," wrote a contemporary Ilkhanid historian and official, Mustawfi Qazvini, "and because the Mongols have reverence for him, it prevents them from oppressing the population, and this is a great accomplishment."[16]

The Safaviyyah order was founded long after Safi al-Din returned to Ardabil, in Azerbaijan, where it gradually took root and whence it spread to Anatolia and Syria, no doubt due to his teachings and charisma. One of the reasons for its steady expansion was its strong belief in disciple recruitment and its ability to develop the social infrastructure to sustain it. These activities usually took the form of creating spiritual patronage through the murshid-murid (master-disciple) networks of the order's elders (sing. *pīrah*) and deputies (sing. *khalīfa*), who enlisted new aspirants into the order and undertook to guide and train them.

Safi al-Din had set the example for the commitment to nurturing disciples with an inexorable ardor. Once in a dispute with Sheikh Zahid Gilani's son Jamal al-Din ʿAli, who questioned his authority, Safi al-Din defended his spiritual mission based on the obligation to assist his disciples. "Spiritual leadership," he said

> belongs to he who even if he had only four disciples, one in the east, one in the west, one in the north, and one in the south, would not neglect them . . . and at the time of death when Satan attempts to test their faith, he would have the power to help all four so that they would preserve their faith. If that person is not at that level, the prayer rug [a symbol of the sheikh's authority] and guidance is forbidden to them.[17]

His contemporary Sheikh ʿAla al-Dawlah Simnani (d. 736/1335) relates that a Sufi once complained to him that Safi al-Din missionized constantly,

however, that many Sufi guides and their disciples remained apolitical, the Chishti order being a clear example. See, for instance, Lawrence G. Potter, "Sufis and Sultans in Post-Mongol Iran," *Iranian Studies* 27, no. 1–4 (1994): 86–90.

15 Shīrāzī, *Tarjumah-i Nuskhah-i Khattī-i Tazkirah-i Shaykh Safī al-Dīn*, 24–25.

16 Hamd Allāh Mustawfī Qazvīnī, *Tārīkh-i Guzīdah* (Tehran: Amīr Kabīr, 1364), 675–76.

17 Shīrāzī, *Tarjumah-i Nuskhah-i Khattī-i Tazkirah-i Shaykh Safī al-Dīn*, 606–7; Tawakkul b. Ismāʿīl, *Safvat al-Safā*, 581–82.

FIGURE 2.1 Safi al-Din in ecstasy. The folio illustrates a moment when Safi al-Din, inspired by the profound words of the preacher Tuti, began to engage in *samāʿ*. His energy sparked others to join in the mystical dance. At the center sits a group of veiled women, highlighting the involvement of women in Sufi circles.
Safvat al-Safā, Aga Khan Museum, AKM264 (fol. 282r)

claiming that there is no other murshid than himself, and that the masses ought to come to him to receive guidance. Another Sufi pressed the sheikh regarding Safi al-Din's claims to supernatural powers, time travel, and the occult, to which the great sheikh of Simnan responded that he had experienced them himself and pointed to the Prophet's ascension (*miʿrāj*) from Jerusalem to heaven and back, which occurred in a fraction of second, as an example of the Creator's will regarding wonderworks that Sufi sheikhs routinely experience.[18]

As we saw, when ʿIzz al-Din had a dream vision in which the Prophet designated Safi al-Din as the "murshid of this age," he was struggling to find a sheikh with an authentic *silsilah* to guide him on his transcendental, not political, journey. Yet, the way that disciples like ʿIzz al-Din perceived their sheikh's indisputable spiritual authority to be directly connected to social obligations meant their community embraced an understanding of the sheikh's wider authority upon which political aspirations could be built.

2.4 THE ANATOMY OF SURRENDER

We saw earlier how two early Safavid disciples perceived their visions metempirically (i.e., beyond the realm of sensory experience) and found them instrumental in resolving their spiritual predicaments. Such experiences were rooted in the relationship that flourished between the master and his disciples and was the cornerstone of the order's emerging solidarity. In order to show how that solidarity at the heart of *tarīqah* Sufism was created let's take a microscopic view of what it entailed.

A contemporary of Safi al-Din, the Sufi Mahmud b. ʿAli Kashani (d. 735/1334) wrote a treatise called *The Lantern of Guidance* (*Misbāh al-Hidāyat*). In it, he set out the conditions that a committed disciple like Pirah ʿIzz al-Din must internalize for his training to progress. Inspired by Shahab al-Din ʿUmar Suhravardi's (d. 632/1234) widely known Arabic language treatise *ʿAwārif al-Maʿārif*, he wanted to make Suhravardi's teachings accessible to Persian-speaking Sufis who did not know Arabic. Kashani was the right mind at the right time to amalgamate the collective understanding of the master-disciple dynamic at the onset of a new era, an age when Sufism became political and ideals of leadership shifted. Subsequently, the eighth/fourteenth and ninth/fifteenth

[18] Simnānī, *Chihil Majlis*, 132–34.

centuries witnessed several Sufi orders attempting to seize power by force (see Section 1.3).

What Kashani explained in his treatise was commonly practiced among Sufis of the era. A look at his *silsilah* shows the overlapping nature of discipleship and teachings among various orders. Kashani, for example, was a disciple of Zahir al-Din Buzghush Shirazi (d. 716/1316) and Nur al-Din ʿAbd al-Samad Isfahani (d. 699/1300), both students of Sheikh Najib al-Din ʿAli Buzghush Shirazi (d. 678/1279) (i.e., Zahir al-Din's father). It was this great master that Safi al-Din had sought in Shiraz when he decided to become a serious Sufi. Najib al-Din had been the disciple of Shahab al-Din ʿUmar Suhravardi, who established the Suhravardiyyah order. Sheikh Zahid Gilani, Safi al-Din's spiritual guide, traced his spiritual lineage to Jamal al-Din Tabrizi as well as Abu al-Najib ʿAbd al-Qadir Suhravardi (d. 563/1168), the paternal uncle and teacher of the famed Shahab al-Din ʿUmar Suhravardi. Kashani thus traced his *silsilah* to Shahab al-Din in this fashion.[19]

It was without question that an aspirant should have a sheikh on the Sufi path, though on rare occasions an aspirant might appear without a need for a guide. In his treatise, Mahmud Kashani explains how a Sufi disciple typically begins his training and readies himself to completely surrender his will to his sheikh. This process moves him from inner cognitions to the outer strata of consciousness. The initial relinquishment is often called *taslīm shudan* (to surrender) or *dar band shudan* (to be enchained or to be bound). The surrender was absolute in all its aspects: physical-sensory, mental-emotional, and even in the dream state, the mysterious realm where Sufis believe humankind gains the ability to communicate with other worlds and intellects. The common metaphor of "the disciple as a corpse in the hand of his mortician" was used to describe the disciple's complete surrender to his sheikh if he hopes to perceive ultimate unity.[20]

[19] Kāshānī, *Misbāh al-Hidāyat*, 13–15.

[20] Rāzī, *Mirsād al-ʿIbād*, 146–47. The famous saying belongs to the founder of the Qadiriyyah Sufi order, ʿAbd al-Qadir Gilani (d. 561/1166), and is widely cited in medieval and modern scholarship. Ibid., 136–37, 146–47; Lucy E. Creevey, "Ahmad Bambo 1850–1927," in *Studies in West African Islamic History*, vol. 1, *The Cultivators of Islam*, ed. John Ralph Willis (London: Frank Cass, 1979), 281. For example, influential sheikhs such as Hajji Bektash Vali (d. 669/1271), the eponym of the Bektashiyyah order, Najm al-Din Kubra, the founder of the Kubraviyyah, and his disciple Najm al-Din Razi discuss the necessity of a master. Rāzī, *Mirsād al-ʿIbād*, 126–32; Hacı Bektaş Veli, *Maqālāt-i Ghaybiyyah*, ed. Ihsān Allāh Shukr'khudā (Isfahan: I. Shukr'khudā, 1381), 52–53. For the account of Hajji Bektash's life, see his hagiography *Manakıb-ı Hacı Bektâş-ı Velî*

The symbolic language of surrender and submission was further enshrined in the disciple's rituals of initiation. Among the common initiation rites whose symbolism reflected their intimate relationship was the master fastening the disciple's belt (*shadd*), offering him to drink the salt water from his hand (salt being a symbol of obligation), bestowing his *khirqa* (cloak) on the disciple, donning of the order's turban, and the intimate language that tried to express this extraordinary mystical relationship.

The first step is the disciple's belief in the exclusivity of the sheikh as his main guide. There can be no other. As Kashani puts it, "for if he perceives another as more masterful, the love and intimacy would be fragile and the sheikh's teachings and spiritual states (*ahvāl*) would not penetrate." According to Kashani, the disciple has to be convinced that the *fath al-bāb* (opening of the gate of illumination) is only possible through companionship and service to the sheikh, such that the seeker "would either reach the destination, or surrender his life upon [the sheikh's] abode."[21]

When we look at Pirah ʿIzz al-Din's experience of surrender to Safi al-Din we can see how Kashani's manual translated experientially to the disciple's training. When, for example, Pirah ʿIzz al-Din mentions that he became stagnant and no longer experienced illumination, it was ascribed to his rejection of Safi al-Din's invitation (*daʿwa*) to become a disciple – the point being, without a legitimate sheikh, no illuminations would open for him.

Kashani clarifies the centrality of companionship to the sheikh in this way:

[The disciple] must continuously remain in anticipation of what may pass on the sheikh's lips and believe the sheikh's speech to be an intermediary of God's

"*Vilâyet-nâme,*" ed. Abdülbâki Gölpınarlı (Istanbul: İnkılap Kitabevi, 1958); variation: *Vilāyat-nāmah*, ed. and trans. Esra Dughan and Maryam Sultani (Erbil, 1998). Later sheikhs such as Nur al-Din Isfarāyinī (d. 717/1317) confirmed the earlier views with such statements as, "he who refutes the sheikh and based on ignorance says that one could complete this journey without a teacher and a guide, [hearken that] the masters of the path have said, 'he who has no sheikh, Satan becomes his sheikh'" (Isfarāyinī, *Kāshif al-Asrār*, 147–49). For an example of the Sufi dialectic and experiential metaphysics of this period, see Ahmad b. Muhammad Simnānī and Nūr al-Dīn ʿAbd al-Rahmān b. Muhammad Isfarāyinī, *Murshid va Murīd: Mukātibāt-i ʿAbd al-Rahmān Isfarāyinī bā ʿAlāʾ al-Dawlah-i Simnānī*, ed. Hermann Landolt (Tehran: Qismat-i Īrānshināsī, Instītū-yi Faransavī-i Pizhūhish'hā-yi ʿIlmī dar Īrān, 1351). Husayn Vaʿiz Kashifi Sabzavari, whose works bridged intellectual spirituality with popular piety in the late ninth/fifteenth century such as found in his *Futuvvat'nāmah-i Sultānī*, ed. Muhammad Jaʿfar Mahjūb (Tehran: Bunyād-i Farhang-i Īrān, 1350), 61–64, reiterates previous views on the necessity of a sheikh.

21 Kāshānī, *Misbāh al-Hidāyat*, 218–20.

words … and believe the sheikh's heart to be a tumultuous sea filled with gems of mystical knowledge that Divine Grace bestows and are tossed onto the shores of [his] tongue. Thus, the disciple must continuously be attentive and ready so as not to miss the benefits that come from the sheikh's words.

Once exclusivity is established, the disciple, Kashani writes, must "surrender to the sheikh's piercing power of managing his psychological states (*taslīm-i tasarrufāt-i shaykh*) … He must keep open the path to the sheikh's penetrative teaching in his soul and self, and be obedient and content with whatever he commands, for the essence of his will and love would not ignite except in this manner."[22]

Next, the disciple must abandon the thought of objecting to the sheikh's conduct, no matter how odd it appears. Kashani points to the famous story of Prophet Moses and his spiritual guide, the enigmatic holy figure Khizr, to illustrate his point (Qurʾan 18:65–82). Khizr, though not mentioned by name in the Qurʾan, is a shadowy "servant of God" whose story fascinated medieval Sufis. Along their journey, Khizr carries out three shocking acts that cause Moses, having only a limited capacity to comprehend what he is witnessing, to question Khizr's intentions. He does not realize that the strange acts are meant as deliverances, causing Khizr to eventually take his leave of him.[23]

Now firmly in the hand of the sheikh, the disciple must continue to work on abandoning his self-will (*salb-i ikhtiyār*). He must desert the idea that he has control over his physical body, that he must feed it, dress it, and care for it on his own. The disciple, Kashani writes, "must not on any occasion, religious or worldly, grand or diminutive, act without the will and consent of the sheikh [including] to eat, drink, dress, sleep, nap, to receive and to give benefaction." These prohibitions were part of the comprehensive set of directives that Sufis believed would nurture obedience and help annihilate the "I," that guileless illusion that plagues mankind and separates us from the Creator. Strict directives also extended to the spiritual practices of praying, fasting, *zikr* (remembrance of the link between the Creator and the created), and recitation of the Qurʾan with the aim of perfecting their aspirants' abilities to pierce the veil of false reality. The constraints on outward movement of the body extended to the mystical dance of *samāʿ*. A disciple was expected to refrain from rising to

22 Ibid., 218–33; Rāzī, *Mirsād al-ʿIbād*, 136–77.

23 This story is found in the Qurʾan (18:65–82) and has been subject to several Sufi exegetical writings throughout the centuries.

dance and not to give in to ecstatic utterances (*zaʿaqāt*) in the presence of the sheikh.[24]

Pirah ʿIzz al-Din's training had sharpened his heart's eye so that he was able to comprehend unveilings (*vāqiʿāt*). According to Kashani, however, even at this advanced state Pirah ʿIzz al-Din needed his master's consultation. Kashani explains that "whether in a dream state or conscious, in making sense of unveilings (*kashf-i vāqiʿāt*) [one must] refer to the sheikh's knowledge and not independently and based on self-opinion decide on its correct [interpretation]." The crucial element of the methodology, Kashani writes, is a process of perfection through the sheikh's precision, as even a slight misreading of a vision could lead to defects and result in obstruction.[25]

According to Kashani, the disciple's surrender to the sheikh is further solidified by the telling of personal secrets. This is an inherently difficult request, for secrets are extremely private and some have the potential to bring about an immense amount of guilt and shame. Yet, it is vital for a disciple to reveal his secrets to his sheikh in order to eliminate hidden desires. The idea is to "polish the heart" of all its imperfections.

Kashani knew intimately the significance of divulging secrets to his sheikh, explaining, "If his [i.e., the disciple's] coiled up conscious brings his being under the influence of one of his secrets, it may create a suppressed unfulfilled desire in his inner being and block the path of his sheikh's succor." By unburdening his secrets and thereby exposing an aspect of his true self, the disciple created a void into which the sheikh could channel transcendental yearnings.[26]

Once during his advanced training, for example, Pirah ʿIzz al-Din did not know why the path had become obscure to him. He therefore went to Safi al-Din to seek help.

"ʿIzz al-Din, what have you done that such a veiling has occurred," Safi al-Din asked him.

"I do not know, O sheikh," he responded.

"Do not be troubled, I will tell [you]," Safi al-Din continued. "On such and such day, in such and such alley, you encountered a catamite who captured your thoughts for a moment. This is the reason behind the concealment."

ʿIzz al-Din then remembered what the sheikh revealed and exclaimed, "Upon [my life,] relieve me, O sheikh."

24 Kāshānī, *Misbāh al-Hidāyat*, 194–98, 224.
25 Ibid., 222.
26 Ibid., 225–26.

> Safi al-Din responded, "Do not be disturbed, for there are many such precipices on the path which only a few can escape, but I pulled you out of this abyss. Go and recommence [your] training for tonight what you desire will occur."[27]

Here, Pirah ʿIzz al-Din was saved by virtue of being enchained to Safi al-Din's *tarīqat* (spiritual teaching). This is similar in fashion to how he later saved his student Pirah Fazl Allah, whose story opened this chapter's discussion. The implication, according to Kashani, is that if Pirah ʿIzz al-Din had revealed the encounter voluntarily, the obstruction would have not occurred in the first place.

Sexual desire was among the hardest temptations to tame. Revealing it to the sheikh was one way a disciple could master this powerful primal desire. Cultural norms, however, often made that difficult as it produced the preventative feeling of shame that may imperil one's life. For example, when another Safavid disciple, Pirah Muhammad Darvary, was traveling with Safi al-Din on a ship, Safi al-Din designated him to lead the prayer when they reached the shore. That night, Pirah Muhammad had a nocturnal emission or a wet dream due to prolonged abstinence from sexual activity. He was mortified knowing that he would be impure and therefore unable to lead the prayer if he did not ritually clean himself. He could neither disclose what had happened because he felt ashamed, nor was he able to wash up properly aboard the ship. His choices quickly narrowed; he could either divulge to Safi al-Din what had happened in the dream that caused the impurity or find a way to clean himself. He chose the latter and was about to suspend himself on the side of the ship to submerge his body in the sea, when Safi al-Din, as his biographer often likes to point out, was privy to the whole affair, intervened and prevented what could have led to a fatuous death. This story not only points out how Safi al-Din's acute perceptiveness is constructed but also the idea that discipleship requires all-embracing transparency, and that carnal desires needed to be resolved completely for the disciple to progress.[28]

While the disciple must reveal his secrets to the sheikh, he must not share the sheikh's secrets with others, especially those related to wonderworks (*karāmāt*) and unveilings (*vāqiʿāt*). Kashani states that, "the sheikh may have seen a spiritual or temporal benefit in concealing it that the disciple's intellect could not grasp, and in revealing it a perversion might be born." The privilege of holding the master's secrets was taken with

[27] Tawakkul b. Ismāʿīl, *Safvat al-Safā*, 847–48.
[28] Ibid., 659.

extreme care by the disciple, for a failure may lead to a severance of their bond. The relationship grown in this fashion continuously nurtured their emotional and spiritual intimacy.[29]

The all-embracing submission of disciples, however, was temporary and ultimately led to a greater acquisition of spiritual power and authority as they advanced. Their training involved the extremely difficult task of surrendering their existence to their masters in exchange for what they believed to be true salvation, the experience of ultimate reality. Most failed, few prevailed, and some became elders and deputies of the order. If successful in reaching their destination, elders like Pirah ʿIzz al-Din would acquire the spiritual strength necessary to attract and train their own disciples. Thus, collective submission of an order's disciples led to powerful cooperatives that were sustained by the master-disciple relationship and dispersed in overlapping networks. Over time, during the eighth/fourteenth and ninth/fifteenth centuries, members of the Safavid order became bound by a consecrated group identity that was confirmed by their common spiritual lineage whose authoritative teachings they believed were manifested in the person of their sheikh, Safi al-Din. As in the case of many Sufi communities, the Safavids' ties of spiritual loyalty to their sheikh and his teachings over long distances and across generations were maintained by the deputies, the *khalīfah*s, and the hierarchy of elders who passed on the order's teachings. In Section 2.5, I discuss their role in maintaining the ties of spiritual loyalty between the order's disciples and its leadership.

2.5 THE DEPUTIES

By the mid-tenth/sixteenth century when the order had fully developed into the military powerhouse of the region, its leadership's appeal to spiritual loyalty and submission projected a distorted image of the disciplined Sufism of the eighth/fourteenth century, the apolitical discipleship of Pirah ʿIzz al-Din's milieu.

Even without the direct spiritual leadership characteristic of later Safavid sheikhs/kings, the order's *khalīfah*s and *pīrah*s continued to play a powerful surrogate role, passing on the principles of discipleship with its absolute obedience to the sheikh as a central tenet. The resultant spiritual obedience thus continued to be perceived as self-evident within the

[29] Kāshānī, *Misbāh al-Hidāyat*, 226.

Safavid discipleship, though now in an increasingly political context which in turn attracted armed political men. As explained below, the *khalīfah*s helped create and maintain the order's social ties by crafting overlapping and extensive master-disciple relationships that cascaded within the broader Sufi community that encompassed non-disciple supporters. With their spiritual gravity in the eyes of their communities and guidance, they reproduced for the devotees consecrated relationships that offered them powerful ideological resources to form durable ties when they began to militarize in the later ninth/fifteenth century.[30]

The Safavids were one of many Sufi orders that developed a *khalīfah* system to communicate with their disciples over long distances, to pass on their teachings, vital information, and maintain their ties.[31] This was one of the ways that Sufi orders branched out and created offshoots.[32] *Khalīfah*s were disciples who rose in the order's spiritual hierarchy to become the representatives of the sheikh.[33] They were the elite of the order's Sufis, dedicated to their work and resolute in their devotion to the path. In the early years of the Safavids' development in the mid-eighth/fourteenth century, the order created a proselytizing orientation following Safi al-Din's model and sent out deputies to recruit and train disciples across Anatolia, Azerbaijan, northern Syria, Palestine, and as far east as Khorasan.[34]

Later Safavid sources tend to exaggerate the extent of their early networks, but the order clearly had the spiritual strength and organizational

[30] For studies on *khalīfah*s during the Safavid era, see Muhammad ʿAlī Ranjbar, "Mansab-i Khalīfat al-Khulafā dar Dawrah-i Safavī," *Ganjīnah-yi Asnād: Faslnāmah-yi Tahqīqat-i Tārīkhī* 1–2, no. 33–34 (1378): 4–15; Willem M. Floor, "The Khalifeh al-Kholafa of the Safavid Order," *Zeitschrift der Deutschen Morgenländischen Gesellschaft* 153, no. 1 (2003): 51–86; Roger M. Savory, "The Office of Khalīfat Al-Khulafā under the Safawids," *Journal of the American Oriental Society* 85, no. 4 (1965): 497–502. Regarding the Safavid tradition of assigning *khalīfah*s to every town, see Rasūl Jaʿfariyān, ed., *Tārīkh-i Qizilbāshān-i Safavī dar Chand Matn-i ʿArabi-yi Dawrah-yi Othmānī* (Qum, 1397), 27–28.

[31] Orders such as the Niʿmatullahis, Kabiriyya, Murshidiyya, and followers of Khvajah Ahrar, to name a few, made effective use of *khalīfah* networks. Floor, "The Khalifeh al-Kholafa," 52.

[32] For the Safaviyyah's branch in greater Syria, see Ahmad Khāmahyār, "Mazār-i Du Tan az Mashāyikh-i Safavīyah dar Lubnān va Filistīn," in *Shamʿ-i Jādū-yi Umīd: Vīzha'nāmah-i Marāsim-i Nikūdāsht-i Ustād Duktur Muhammad ʿAlī Muvahhid*, ed. Muhammad Khusruwshāhī (Tabriz: Dānishgāh-i Tabrīz, 1393).

[33] For the first generation of Safaviyyah *khalīfah*s, see Tawakkul b. Ismāʿīl, *Safvat al-Safā*, 1130–67.

[34] Khāmahyār, "Mazār-i Du Tan"; Qasim Beg's description of Qasim Anvar in Hayātī Tabrīzī, *Chronicle*, 109–10; Roger M. Savory, "Some Reflections on the Totalitarian Tendencies in the Safavid State," *Der Islam* 53, no. 2 (1976): 226–41.

infrastructure to attract and retain disciples over long distances largely through the efforts of its deputies. Darvish Tavakkuli (Ibn Bazzaz), who completed Safi al-Din's biography *Safvat al-Safā* twenty-four years after the latter's death, offers a firsthand account of at least seventeen high-ranking deputies like Pirah ʿIzz al-Din, as well as Safi al-Din's little-known Sufi brother Salah al-Din Rashid, and twenty-four junior deputies who were the pulse of the order, attracting and guiding numerous disciples.[35]

Their tasks, in addition to initiating new disciples into the order, included ensuring correct rituals, instructing disciples on the fundamentals of Sufism, and supervising their progress with the help of other elders.[36] On a basic level, a *khalīfah*, for instance, as the sheikh's representative supported the aspirant through the difficult process of repentance (*tawbah*), and prepared him with particular instruction on personal *zikr*, the active remembrance of God's holy names whose repetitions would manifest in his heart and transform his entire being to achieve higher consciousness.[37]

Communal rituals such as *zikr*, a central practice in *tarīqah* Sufism, moreover, reinforced the disciples' sense of brotherhood and companionship. In the case of the Safavids, because they had militarized, such spiritual practices further strengthened their social ties and enhanced their military comradery and cohesion.

This proved an invaluable asset long term, especially when the militant faction of the order faced certain destruction against more powerful opponents.[38]

[35] Tawakkul b. Ismāʿīl, *Safvat al-Safā*, 1114–68, 1169–93. Tawakkul b. Ismāʿīl, or Ibn Bazzāz as he was known, does not rigidly distinguish between the "*pīrahs*" and "*khalīfahs*." It was not until the later tenth/sixteenth century when the order was bureaucratized that we observe a hierarchy of spiritual offices and functions.

[36] An eleventh/seventeenth-century Safavid Sufi, Muhammad Ardabili, in his *Tazkirat al-Zākirīn*, 89–95, describes the order's spiritual hierarchy, that is, in the order of *shāh*, *khalīfah*, *pīrah*, *naqīb*, *khādim*, and so on, to the laborers of the lodge.

[37] One of the best descriptions of the effects of *zikr* is given by the Sufi master Sahl al-Sustari (d. 283/896), who once instructed one of his disciples: "'Strive to say continuously for one day: "Allâh! Allâh! Allâh!" and do the same the next day and the day after, until it becomes a habit.' Then he told him to repeat it at night also, until it became so familiar that the disciple repeated it even during his sleep. Then Sahl said, 'Do not consciously repeat the Name anymore, but let your whole faculties be engrossed in remembering Him!' The disciple did this until he became absorbed in the thought of God. One day, a piece of wood fell on his head and broke it. The drops of blood that dripped to the ground bore the legend, 'Allâh! Allâh! Allâh!'" Annemarie Schimmel, *Mystical Dimensions of Islam*, (Chapel Hill: University of North Carolina Press, 1975), 169. See Section 3.5 for further discussion on *zikr*.

[38] The early Qizilbash army's campaigns under Ismail are detailed in many early Safavid chronicles. See, for example, Amīnī Haravī, *Futūhāt-i Shāhī*, 73–185; Hayātī Tabrīzī, *Chronicle*, 218–59; Qazvīnī, *Lubb al-Tavārīkh*, 266–80.

By the mid-tenth/sixteenth century, the *khalīfah*s operated under the directorship of the chief deputy (*khalīfat al-khulafā*), a Sufi master of the highest order at the center of political power, figures like Khadem Beg of the Talesh tribe, Dedeh Khulafa of the Ustajlus, and Shah Quli Khalifah of the Zul al-Qadrs, who became Shah Tahmasb's keeper of the royal seal (see Chapter 6). The chief deputy worked near the sheikh (i.e., the shah and his inner circle after 906/1501) and served the order in the religious as well the political sphere. He was the intermediary between the order's sheikh and the elders and the disciples in his region. He also helped craft the order's political message that would resonate with the community he served in villages and among tribes in eastern Anatolia. In addition, it is likely he was instrumental in recruiting fighting men. The seeds of the powerful influence these deputies came to hold, however, were planted during the spiritual formation of the order as previously discussed.[39]

Until recently, very little was known regarding the dissemination of the order's teachings and what its leadership communicated with their numerous deputies. This has changed with the reexamination of the Command Papers (the *Buyruk*, also known as *Manāqib al-Awliyā* or *Manāqib-i Shaykh Safī*) preserved by the Qizilbash-Alevi communities in today's Turkey.[40] One such document, part of a *Buyruk*, is a letter, dated to the

[39] For the Safaviyyah order's general teachings, see Ardabīlī, *Tazkirat al-Zākirīn*, 75–109; *Sī Futuvvat'nāmah-i Dīgar: Sī Risālah-i Nāshinākhtah dar Futuvvat va Pīshah'varī va Qalandarī*, ed. Mihrān Afshārī (Tehran: Nashr-i Chishmah, 1391), 41–57; Zāhidī, *Silsilat al-Nasab*, 36–38.

[40] Rıza Yıldırım, "The Safavid Ecumene and the Formation of the Qizilbash-Alevi Community in the Ottoman Empire, c. 1500–c. 1700," *Iranian Studies* 52, no. 3–4 (2019): 449–83. Yıldırım's study establishes the foundational texts of the *Buyruk*, which he has termed "Shah Tahmasb's Vulgate." I am grateful to Yıldırım who graciously afforded me access to his article (before it was published) "The Commandment (*Buyruk*): An Introduction to the Sacred Texts of the Kizilbash-Alevi Community," where he discusses the sources for the Anatolian Qizilbash communities of this period. As he puts it, "Among the 288 manuscripts in private libraries of Alevi *dede*s and elders that I had a chance to consult, the most frequently copied books are the following: the Quran, *Buyruk*, *Faziletname*, *Maktel-i Hüseyin*, *Kumru* [*Kenzü'l-Mesa'ib*], *Hz. 'Ali Cenkleri*, *Vilayetname-i Hacı Bektaş Veli*, *Makalat-ı Hācı Bektaş Veli*, *Hüsniye*, *Ebu Muslimname*, *Battalname*, *Müseyyebname*, *Kitab-ı Cabbarkulu*, *'Ilm-i Cāvidān*, and poetry collections (*divan*) of the prominent Kizilbash-Alevi poets such as Şah Hatayi, Pir Sultan Abdal, Kul Himmet and Virani ... Among these 'Alevi books,' the *Buyruk* has a special place. Kizilbash-Alevis have almost universally accepted it as the most authoritative religious text after the Quran." Rıza Yıldırım, "The Commandment (*Buyruk*): An Introduction to the Sacred Texts of the Kizilbash-Alevi Community," in *Entangled Confessionalizations? Dialogic Perspectives on the Politics of Piety and Community Building in the Ottoman Empire, 15th–18th Centuries*, ed. Tijana Krstić and Derin Terzioğlu (Piscataway, NJ: Gorgias Press, 2022), 289. For the latest research on the Qizilbash communities, see also Karakaya-Stump,

early tenth/sixteenth century, sent by a high-ranking member of the order to an unnamed deputy in Ottoman eastern Anatolia to be read to other disciples. Presumably, it was penned by Shah Ismail's regent and right-hand man (*vakīl-i nafs-i nafīs-i Humāyūn*) Sayyid ʿAbd al-Baqi, who served him in political and religious matters in the early years of his reign. He lost his life in 920/1514 in the infamous Battle of Chaldiran against the Ottomans where the young Shah Ismail and his Qizilbash troops were roundly defeated, having underestimated the new form of artillery warfare.[41]

As has been argued thus far, preservation of ties and finding ways to cultivate cohesion was central to the Safavid order's ascendency. ʿAbd al-Baqi's letter exemplifies the type of communications sent by a chief deputy to distant Safavid elders. His letter offers a glimpse into how the order's leadership maintained its ties with its communities, particularly with its members in eastern Turkey living under fear of persecution by the Ottoman state. In it, ʿAbd al-Baqi affirms their spiritual ties in addressing the recipients as "brothers with pure faith, learning and knowledge, observing the laws, and those who have pledged allegiance to the Ocak [intermediary families] of Shaykh Sayyid Safi al-Din Ishaq Wali, a lover of the noble family of Muhammad-Ali, the chief of dervishes, saints, and king of God-fearing people, a road-guide in the two worlds."[42]

ʿAbd al-Baqi expresses ties of loyalty to the Safavid *tarīqah* when he calls the order's devotees

> brothers who are sincere practitioners of the way, the disciples who reside in the corners of villages and towns, the holy warriors and princes whose hearts' eyes

"Who Really Were the Kizilbash?"; Rıza Yildirim, "The Rise of the Safavids as a Political Dynasty: The Revolution of Shah Esmail, the Founder of the Safavid State," in *The Safavid World*, 56–76.

41 In the early years of the Safavid takeover, some of the officials that served political and military functions were often religious dignitaries. ʿAbd al-Baqi was a member of Ismail's inner circle, the center of political power. Later sources mention that the office of the *khalīfat al-khulafā* (chief deputy) was conferred on Khadem Beg Talesh (Floor, "The Khalifeh al-Kholafa," 55n18), who had fought alongside Ismail's father, Haydar, years earlier. ʿAbd al-Baqi no doubt worked closely with many members of Shah Ismail's high command in communicating with their social base in Anatolia. For a summary of ʿAbd al-Baqi's career, see Floor, *Government Institutions*, 8–10. A late seventeenth-century source, *ʿĀlam'ā rā-yi Shāh Ismāʿīl*, ed. Asghar Muntazir Sāhib (Tehran: Shirkat-i Intishārāt-i ʿIlmī va Farhangī, 1384), mentions a letter from Shah Ismail introducing Nur ʿAli as a *khalīfah* (Floor, "The Khalifeh al-Kholafa," 53). For further information on Nur ʿAli Khalīfah, see *Tārīkh-i Qizilbāshān*, ed. Mīr Hāshim Muhaddith (Tehran: Intishārāt-i Bihnām, 1361), 26.

42 Yıldırım, "The Safavid Ecumene," appendix 1, 478–80.

always look to this sublime lodge [Safi al-Din's lodge in Ardabil], the adherents who long to see the beautiful face of the Shah [Ismail], and who desire a noble and distinct spiritual companionship from a house tracking the Truth.[43]

The overall purpose of the letter makes it clear that ʿAbd al-Baqi wants to elicit their loyalty and affirm their belief in the order's murshid-murid association, that is, the murshid dispenses blessings, the murid benefits and thus is obliged to internalize the gratitude owed to his murshid, a debt that could never be settled. This is further made explicit when ʿAbd al-Baqi attempts to empower the deputies to nurture obedience in their disciples in accordance with the central tenet of discipleship. "They [the disciples] ought to have faith in your [the *khalīfah*'s] actions and pledge allegiance to the lodge of the saints [Safavid house] following the phrase, 'Without the guide, I would not have known my Lord.'"[44]

We saw previously that Sufi sheikhs were unanimous in their views on the centrality of the disciple's enchainment to a guide on the Sufi path. The enduring tie that the master-disciple union produced through the order's spiritual chain, the tie that was at the heart of the order's spiritual legitimacy, thus proved a gift to the order's sense of cohesion when it began to militarize under Sheikh Junayd and his son Haydar.

The presumed submission of the disciple to his guide enabled the order's spiritual leaders to make the final demand in discipleship: self-sacrifice. When ʿAbd al-Baqi, for example, writing in an atmosphere saturated by Ottoman state persecution of Safavid supporters in eastern Anatolia, wanted to explain the necessity of self-sacrifice, he put it this way: "they [the disciples] should be able to give their life for the sake of the common faith, strife [*sic*] against disloyalty, never give up on the path, not to doubt their decision, or have fear in their hearts in their submission to the path."[45] Bodily sacrifice among the order's disciples had previously come in the form of physical diminution due to fasting, isolation, and passivity during discipleship as discussed above. Now, in its militarized form, it entailed the possibility of violent death.

Death under torture or in some distant battlefield was no doubt difficult to accept by many in the order's far-flung and diverse communities. Those who did accept "giving their life," however, and followed Haydar and later his son Ismail into the frontline, to the children of those who were persecuted and killed, their self-sacrifice behind the Safavid banner

[43] Ibid.
[44] Ibid.
[45] Ibid.

became a sacred act, admired by their community. Their deaths "for the sake of the common faith" were honored as martyrdom.[46] These families and clans formed the military branch of the order known as the Qizilbash (Red Heads). Under Haydar, they became an exclusive group whose members wanted recognition for their blood sacrifice and the privilege to which they felt entitled (see Section 1.5). This is one of the reasons why in the formative period of the state, they violently opposed any non-Qizilbash appointments to positions of power in the military.

By the time the order militarized in the second half of the ninth/fifteenth century, the *khalīfah* system had been in existence for over a century and had developed the capacity to offer the Safavids an advantage along the organization-communication axis. Their networks provided an infrastructure of communication across a vast territory, passed on vital information, and shared resources. Better communication allowed them to organize efficiently and form more effective coalitions.

The master-disciple relationship with its appeals to loyalty and obedience that the deputies fostered offered a natural hierarchy that readily lent itself to an intensive power configuration favorable to militarization. This also meant that the order was able to develop the spiritual depth within a variegated community that made strong spiritual connections among themselves to sustain themselves and survive the elimination of their leadership.

These communities of master-disciple circles who committed to the Safavid house politically were influenced by another ideological and deeply emotive current that galvanized their Sufi piety and militarism – that of ʿAlid Shiʿism, or absolute devotion to Imam ʿAli. Haydar's successor, Ismail, and the leaders of the Safavid community harnessed this immense source of social power that reinforced their group solidarity, the subject of Chapter 3.

46 For the Ottoman state's attitudes regarding the Qizilbash and the legal religious reasoning for their persecution, see, for example, Abdurrahman Atcil, "Ottoman Religious Rulings concerning the Safavids," in *Empires of the Near East and India*, 97–107; Fariba Zarinebaf-Shahr, "Qizilbash 'Heresy' and Rebellion in Ottoman Anatolia during the Sixteenth Century," *Anatolia Moderna. Yeni Anadolu* 7 (1997): 1–15.

3

The Shadow of the Perfected Being

3.1 THE ARCHETYPAL DISCIPLE

He lifted the Prophet's decaying body, holding it against his chest, gently washing the limbs of a man who had nurtured him since childhood, as the other male cousins poured water over the robe in which he was wrapped. "Dearer than my father and my mother, how sweet you are alive and dead!" he is reported to have uttered at that moment. Islam's archetypal disciple, ʿAli b. Abi Talib, thus found himself washing the corpse of Islam's archetypal sheikh.[1]

The narration of the Prophet Muhammad's illness and passing became a deep well of inspiration for the reception of Imam ʿAli's extraordinary spiritual authority by the Safavid community. One event in particular, the gathering at the Prophet's deathbed, proved central in tracing the origin and authenticity of their belief in the sanctity and primacy of Imam ʿAli.

It is no exaggeration to say that the Safavid community were obsessed with Imam ʿAli (see Figure 3.1). What was it about this holy man that

[1] According to Ibn Ishaq, six other companions of the Prophet helped ʿAli wash and prepare the Prophet's body for burial (Martin Lings, *Muhammad: His Life Based on the Earliest Sources*, 2nd ed. (Rochester, VT: Inner Traditions, 2006), 687–90); cf. Abū Jaʿfar Muhammad Tabarī, *Tārīkh-i Tabarī, yā, Tārīkh al-Rusul wa-l-Mulūk*, vol. 4, trans. Abū al-Qāsim Pāyandah (Tehran: Intishārāt-i Asātīr, 1362), 1323–39; Ahmad b. Abī Yaʿqūb Yaʿqūbī, *Tārīkh-i Yaʿqūbī*, ed. Ebrahim Ayati (Tehran: Bungāh-i Tarjumah va Nashr-i Kitāb, 2536/1977), 509–512; Shaykh al-Mufīd, *Kitāb al-Irshād*, trans. I. K. A. Howard (Elmhurst, NY: Tahrike Tarsile Qurʾan, 1989), 127–36. For the variations of Shiʿi narrations of this event, see Muhammad b. Yaʿqūb Kulaynī, *Al-Kafi*, 8 vols., trans. Muhammad Sarwar (New York: The Islamic Seminary, 2004), 1:593–97; Husayn Vāʿiz Kāshifī, *Rawzat al-Shuhadā*, ed. Hasan Zulfaqari (Tehran, 1390), 324–25; Khvāndamīr, *Tārīkh-i Habīb al-Sīyār fī Akhbār-i Afrād-i Bashar*, 1:419–21.

FIGURE 3.1 Safavid Sufi elder ʿAli Parniqi dreams of Safi al-Din with the Prophet Muhammad and Imam ʿAli
Safvat al-Safā, Aga Khan Museum, AKM264 (fol. 116v)

engulfed their belief system in the later ninth/fifteenth century with such intensity? By then the Safavid branch of Sheikh Junayd's line claimed direct descent from Imam ʿAli, which corresponded to their supporters' spiritual yearning and ideals of leadership. This interdependence had a profound effect on how the Safavid community demarcated their group identity and cohesion.

The Safavid community, I show in the following, made a particular set of mytho-historical connections to ʿAli that rendered him the bedrock of this community's devotional life, a community that had come to internalize the ideological structures of Sufi orders by the time Shah Ismail began his military quests in the closing years of the ninth/fifteenth century. ʿAli had thus become the personification of their collective political will, the incarnation of the holy, and their aspiration not for a "philosopher king" but for a Sufi king. Their collective reverence for ʿAli reinforced the core of their piety, influenced their sense of group identity, and served as a source of their sociopolitical power.

3.2 THE PROPHETIC LIGHT

The account of the Prophet's death as retold in medieval Shiʿi sources states that when the Prophet sensed his earthly life was ending, he invited his intimate companions, the later caliphs, one by one. The farewells were short and heartfelt. When ʿAli entered, the Prophet held him in conversation for a long while. When ʿAli returned, the companions asked him what the Prophet had told him that took so long. "He taught me about a thousand doors of knowledge and each door opened for me another thousand doors," ʿAli replied.

When the Prophet's death was at hand, it is reported that he whispered his final words to his daughter Fatimah, while

> the right hand of the Commander of the Faithful [ʿAli] was under his jaw and his soul passed into it. He raised it [his hand] to his face and rubbed it with it [the soul, as he was previously instructed by the Prophet]. Then he [ʿAli] put him [the Prophet] in the direction of the *qiblah*, closed his eyes, and laid him out on his waistcloth.[2]

This story is found among the Safavid communities of the late ninth/fifteenth century. A recently reexamined source linked to the communities'

[2] al-Mufīd, *Kitāb al-Irshād*, 132–33. On the transfer of sacred knowledge from Muhammad to ʿAli at Muhammad's death, see Kulaynī, *Al-Kafi*, 1:587–88; Kāshifī, *Rawzat al-Shuhadā*, 268–69; Khvāndamīr, *Tārīkh-i Habīb al-Sīyār fī Akhbār-i Afrād-i Bashar*, 1:415–19.

general beliefs and practices of the time, and considered to be their principal sacred text, the *Buyruk*, begins with this event.[3] The placement of the story makes clear the centrality of ʿAli. According to the *Buyruk*, in Muhammad's final hour when the prophetic light began to fade, in that hour when the age of prophecy was coming to an end, he transmitted to ʿAli the hidden meanings of existence and unveiled for him insights about the Creator only a few ever knew. ʿAli then wrote them down as a testament (*vasiyyat-nāmah*), which was passed down to his sons Hasan and Hussein after his death. The opening of Shah Tahmasb's *Buyruk* dated to the early tenth/sixteenth century states that the text is none other than this testament.[4]

The *Buyruk* states that this testament was transmitted to the subsequent Imams down to the twelfth Imam, al-Mahdi, the Lord of Time, who would one day emerge (*zuhūr*) with Jesus son of Mary on the Day of Resurrection (*yawm al-qīyāmah*). The testament was only to be revealed to the select few in Sufi communities (*ahl-i tarīqah*) who harbor special devotion for the Prophet and his household (*ahl al-bayt*). When al-Mahdi went into occultation in 260/873, the secret teachings were entrusted to the great guides and sheikhs, generation after generation, until Sheikh Safi al-Din became its bearer in the eighth/fourteenth century. Safi al-Din, equipped with this sacred gift, therefore was able to train and guide the Safavid disciples and his offspring with true mystical insight directly linked to the Prophet. The tradition continued down to the second Safavid leader, Shah Tahmasb.

The Prophet's testament as understood by the authors of the *Buyruk* conceives history in sequential spiritual stages, demarcated by the arrival of prophets whom the Creator ordained to guide humanity to the true path. In one passage, it explains that

> in the final epoch of history, Muhammad and ʿAli came and became the last of the prophets and the last of the legatees (*aṣfiyāʾ*). They honored the earth with the felicity of the Prophethood (*nubuwwa*) and the Sainthood (*vilāya*) and issued the

[3] Rıza Yıldırım, ed., *Menâkıb-ı Evliyâ (Buyruk)* (Istanbul: Yapı Kredi Yayınları, 2020), 325–26. The mother text of the extant *Buyruk* is dated to the early tenth/sixteenth century, which Yıldırım has termed "Shah Tahmasb's Vulgate." It is known by various names, *Menâkıb-ı Evliyâ*, *Menāḳib*, or *Menāḳib-i Imām Caʿfer Sādiḳ*, but most commonly referred to as the *Buyruk* meaning "command." According to Yıldırım, "Kizilbash-Alevis have almost universally accepted it as the most authoritative religious text after the Quran … A significant portion of *Buyruk* texts deals [*sic*] with fundamental Kizilbash-Alevi beliefs about such matters as deity, prophethood, sainthood (Ar. *wilāya*, Tr. *vilayet*), humanity, cosmic history, and ways of salvation" ("The Commandment," 296).

[4] For a critical edition of the text based on eleven manuscript copies, see Yıldırım, ed., *Menâkıb-ı Evliyâ*.

Path, the Rituals, the Four Gates, the Forty Ranks, the Seventy-Two Stages, and the Forty Thousand Commands (*Buyruḳ*). [After completing their mission] they retreated into mystery [died in the material world] ... They entrusted to *dede*s and spiritual guides (*mürşid*) the Forty Thousand Commands that were issued in the Four Gates. [True believers] have attached themselves to the Path of Muhammad-ʿAli as per these commands.[5]

The key tenet in Ali's spiritual authority in the testament has to do with the Prophetic Light. In the opening passage of the *Buyruk*, two central hadiths, "I am the city of knowledge and ʿAli is its gate" and "ʿAli and I were created of one Light," make the spiritual implications for Imam ʿAli clear and fortify the spiritual authority of the holy compendium of conduct that the text aims to communicate.[6]

In Sufi metaphysics, the Muhammadan Light (*nur-i Muhammadi*) or the Muhammadan Truth (*haqīqat-i Muhammadiyyah*) in the emanation story refers to the preexistent soul of Muhammad, the Creator's first emanation, and the manifestation of the first reality or principle, analogous to the active intellect in Neoplatonic cosmogony. All the prophets who preceded Muhammad, "the seal of the prophets," therefore held the Muhammadan Light, the spirit of their own prophethood. This notion played a central role in the development of Sufi conceptions of spiritual authority invested in "the perfect human" (*al-insān al-kāmil*) as seen in the writings of early metaphysicians such as Sahl al-Tustari and Hakim al-Tirmidhi. Closer to the early modern era, Sufi sheikhs such as Ibn al-ʿArabi, Mahmud Shabastari, and Mawlana Jalal al-Din Rumi continued to draw connections between their mystical experiences and the divine light or sacred knowledge which ʿAli shared with Muhammad.

The fact that this concept is found among Safavid political men suggests its prevalence in Sufi communities. Hayati of Tabriz, a Safavid devotee who penned one of the early dynastic chronicles and dedicated it to Tahmasb's sister Mahin Banu, explains its importance. In one passage, for example, he narrates the same hadith as the one found in the *Buyruk* to sanctify and strengthen his claim.[7] Influenced by a host of ninth/fifteenth-century occult

[5] Yıldırım, "The Commandment," 300; *Menāḳib*, Istanbul Belediyesi Atatürk Kitaplığı, MS 27, fol. 640b.

[6] Yıldırım, ed., *Menâkıb-ı Evliyâ*, 326. See the various versions of the Muhammadan Light hadith in Abū Jaʿfar Muhammad Tabarī, *al-Mustarshid fī Imāmat Amīr al-Muʾminīn*, ed. Ahmad al-Mahmūdī (Tehran: Muʾassasat al-Thaqāfah al-Islāmiyyah li-Kūshānbūr, 1415), 630–31; al-Mufīd, *Kitāb al-Irshād*, 20–21; Tahmāsb Safavī, *Tazkirah-i Shāh Tahmāsb*, ed. Karīm Fayzī (Qum: Matbūʿāt-i Dīnī, 1383), 119–22.

[7] Hayātī Tabrīzī, *Chronicle*, 30, 33–34; cf. Shīrāzī, *Takmilat al-Akhbār*, 33–35.

and Sufi intellectual currents, such as the teachings of Fazl Allah Astarabadi's Hurufism and Najm al-Din Kubra's Sufi metaphysics, he states that the Safavids' belief in Imam ʿAli's spiritual preeminence came from the conviction that he was the heir to the Prophetic Light.

Shah Ismail makes the connection clear in one of his poems when he places himself in the spectrum of the primordial light of the preeternity:

> No one becomes a Qizilbash, unless his heart is ablaze and his breast bleeding like a ruby … In the epoch of the mystery of the preeternity, he was the Muhammadan Light, and now he has appeared to the world crowned with a red crown. His name is Ismail, he is of the same essence as the Commander of the Faithful [ʿAli].[8]

To be precise, the late ninth/fifteenth-century Safavids were not Shiʿis in the common Twelver tradition that they *became* in the later tenth/sixteenth century. They were ʿAlavis and their connection to Shiʿism was through their devotion to Imam ʿAli and, to a lesser extent, to the other Imams. These connections, I explain in the following, were based on ʿAli's life story as retold and transmitted in the *manāqib* literature, mystical poetry, and folklore, which became part of the Safavid religious culture that fueled their sense of group identity.

3.3 KINSHIP: ʿALI'S PROXIMITY TO MUHAMMAD

On a fundamental level, the Safavid community as reflected in the extant textual sources believed that ʿAli's uniqueness stemmed from his proximity to the Prophet. They accepted the basic facts about his life from earlier sources: that he was born when Muhammad was thirty years of age, approximately ten years before Muhammad received his first prophetic revelation; that ʿAli was the only person who was born in the Kaʿba; and that he was the first male who accepted Muhammad's divine message.[9]

[8] Shāh Ismāʿīl b. Haydar Safavī, *Khaṭāʾī, Shāh Ismāʿīl Safavī: Kulliyāt-i Dīvān, Nasīhatnāmah, Dahnāmah, Qūshmālār, Fārsjā Shiʿrlar*, ed. Rasūl Ismāʿīl-zādah (Tehran: al-Hudā, 1380), 57; see Vladimir Minorsky's translation of the poem, "The Poetry of Shāh Ismāʿīl I," *Bulletin of the School of Oriental and African Studies* 10, no. 4 (1942): 1048a, no. 211.

[9] Abū Jaʿfar Muhammad Tabarī, *The History of al-Ṭabarī*, vol. 6, *Muḥammad at Mecca*, trans. W. Montgomery Watt and M. V. McDonald (Albany: State University of New York Press, 1988), 82–83; al-Mufīd, *Kitāb al-Irshād*, 1; ʿAlī b. ʿĪsā al-Irbilī, *Kashf al-Ghummah fī Maʿrifat al-Aʾimmah*, ed. Ahmad Ishkavari (Qum, 1421), 1:59–61; ʿAlī b. al-Husayn al-Masʿūdī, *Murūj al-Dhahab wa-Maʿādin al-Jawhar*, ed. Charles Pellat (Beirut: al-Jāmiʿa al-Lubnāniyya, 1965–79), 3:93; Kāshifī, *Rawzat al-Shuhadā*, 321–22; Khvāndamīr, *Tārīkh-i Habīb al-Sīyār fī Akhbār-i Afrād-i Bashar*, 2:8–21.

His mother, Fatimah bt. Asad, named him Haydar, meaning "lion." His father, Abu Talib, however, preferred the name ʿAli, a unique name at the time signifying "exaltedness."[10]

When ʿAli reached five years of age, Muhammad took him into his household to help his uncle Abu Talib during a terrible famine that had gripped the region. ʿAli would be part of Muhammad's household until the latter's death. "When I was but a child, he took me under his wing," ʿAli recalls in one of his sermons. "I would follow him as a baby camel follows the footsteps of its mother. Every day he would raise up for me a sign of his noble character, commanding me to follow it."[11]

Perhaps the most powerful statement ʿAli made regarding his proximity to the Prophet is found in one of his sermons:

> He would go each year into seclusion at [the mountain of] Hiraʾ. I saw him and nobody else saw him. At that time, no household was brought together for the religion of Islam, except [the house of] the Messenger of God, Khadijah and myself as the third. I saw the light of the revelation and the message, and I smelt the fragrance of prophecy.[12]

On another occasion, it is reported that ʿAli said: "Not one [Qurʾanic] verse has been revealed of which I know not where it was revealed, what it concerns, and its subject matter."[13]

The sayings of the Prophet reported on the authority of ʿAli constitute a significant part of the *musnad* compilations (collections of the sayings arranged

10 ʿAli's mother was Fatima daughter of Asad and his father, Abu Talib, son of ʿAbd al-Muttalib, a leading member of the Banu Hashim clan. Abu Talib's brother, ʿAbd Allah, was the Prophet's father. Muhammad b. ʿAlī Ibn Shahrāshūb, *Manāqib Āl-i Abī Tālib*, ed. Yūsuf al-Baqāʿī (Qum: Intishārāt Dhawī al-Qurbā, 1421), 2:303–4; Kāshifī, *Rawzat al-Shuhadā*, 323–24.

11 ʿAbd al-Hamīd b. Hibat Allāh Ibn Abī al-Hadīd, *Sharh Nahj al-Balāgha*, ed. Muhammad Abū al-Fadl Ibrāhīm (Beirut: Dār Maktabat al-Hayāt, 1965–67), 13:197; cf. Reza Shah-Kazemi, "Imam Ali," in *The Shiʿi World: Pathways in Tradition and Modernity*, ed. Farhad Daftry, Shainool Jiwa, and Amyn B. Sajoo (London: I.B. Tauris, 2015), 36; Lings, *Muhammad*, 114.

12 Muhammad b. al-Husayn Sharīf al-Radī, *Nahj al-Balāgha*, ed. Muhammad ʿAbduh (Beirut, 1996), 2:182; variation: *Peak of Eloquence, Nahjul Balagha: Sermons, Letters and Sayings of Imam Ali ibn Abu Talib*, trans. Sayed Ali Reza (Elmhurst, NY: Tahrike Tarsile Qur'an, 1996). ʿAli's proximity to the Creator through his immediacy with His Messenger was emphasized by the earliest biographer of the Prophet, Ibn Ishaq, who described him as "the first male to believe in the apostle of God, to pray with him and to believe in his divine message, when he was a boy of ten ... ʿAlī would accompany the Prophet on his spiritual seclusions in the hills of Mecca: 'There they used to pray the ritual prayers, and return at nightfall'" (Lings, *Muhammad*, 114).

13 Sulaym b. Qays al-Hilālī, *Kitāb Sulaym b. Qays al-Hilālī*, ed. Muhammad Bāqir al-Ansārī (Qum: Nashr al-Hādī, 1415), 256; Muhammad b. Masʿūd ʿAyyāshī, *Kitāb al-Tafsīr*, ed. Hāshim Rasūlī Mahallātī (Qum: Chāpkhānah-i ʿIlmiyyah, 1380–81), 1:14.

according to the original narrator). Among the Prophet's companions, ʿAli was one of the most prolific sources of hadith narrations.[14] Moreover, it was widely believed that because of such close proximity to Muhammad, he knew the circumstances of the revelation and understood better than anyone the hidden dimensions of every verse.[15] A number of Sunni as well as Shiʿi traditions claim that ʿAli was the first person to compile the written text of the Qurʾan and was the foremost authority on its exegesis (*tafsīr*). Ibn ʿAbbas, the best-known exegete among the early believers, studied under ʿAli. Such claims regarding the authenticity of ʿAli's spiritual insights compelled many Sufi sheikhs of the post-ʿAbbasid period who sought certitude in their methods to regard ʿAli as their main interpreter of Islamic esotericism.[16]

ʿAli married Fatimah, the Prophet's daughter with Khadijah, whom he knew all his life. This marriage proved pivotal for the history of Shiʿism. With the birth of their two sons, Hasan and Hussein, the holy *ahl al-bayt* (the Prophet's household) was created. The designation and the subsequent interpretation of Qurʾan 33:33, "Truly God only wishes to remove all impurity from you, O *ahl al-bayt*, and to purify you with utter purification," became central to the Shiʿi theological position, namely, members of the *ahl al-bayt* were infallible (*maʿsūm*) and by divine grace incapable of committing sin. They had become perfect beings.

It is this quality that makes descent from ʿAli's line desirable in the political sphere. For those who believed in Shiʿi principles of political authority, it suggested a leader who's holy bloodline makes him less susceptible to corruption and thus keep cruelty and disorder at bay.

3.4 ʿALI THE WARRIOR OF FAITH

A feature of ʿAli's life that deeply resonated with the Safavids was his extraordinary courage and strength on the battlefield. They believed that

[14] For example, according to the prominent Sunni scholar of the thirteenth century Yahya al-Nawawi, the total number of hadiths transmitted by ʿAli was well over 500. Yahyā al-Nawawī, *Tahdhīb al-Asmāʾ wa-l-Lughāt* (Beirut: Dār al-Kutub al-ʿIlmiyya, 1996), 2:345.

[15] ʿAyyāshī, *Tafsīr*, 1:18; Muhammad b. Yaʿqūb Kulaynī, *al-Usūl min al-Kāfī*, ed. ʿAlī Akbar Ghaffārī (Tehran: Dār al-Kutub al-Islāmiyyah, 1362–63), 1:64.

[16] Muhammad b. ʿAbd Allāh al-Hākim al-Nīsābūrī, *al-Mustadrak ʿalā al-Sahīhayn*, ed. Mustafā ʿAbd al-Qādir ʿAtāʾ (Beirut: Dār al-Kutub al-ʿIlmiyya, 1411), 2:360; Muhammad b. Ahmad al-Dhahabī, *Maʿrifat al-Qurrāʾ al-Kibār ʿalā Tabaqāt wa-l-Aʿsār*, ed. Tayyar Altıkulaç (Istanbul: Türkiye Diyanet Vakfı, Islam Araştırmaları Merkezi, 1995), 3:332. See the fuller discussion in Yadollah Gholami, Matthew Melvin-Koushki, and Faramarz Haj Manouchehri, "ʿAlī b. Abī Ṭālib," *Encyclopaedia Islamica*, http://dx.doi.org/10.1163/1875-9831_isla_COM_0252.

no one among Muhammad's companions was as fierce as ʿAli and knew him with such titles as Asad Allah al-Ghalib (the triumphant lion of God), Haydar-i Karrar (unrelenting lion warrior), and Fatih-i Khaybar (the conqueror of the famed fort of Khaibar). They had inherited this perception from hadiths and historical accounts related to the early battles of Muslims under Muhammad's leadership. The Shiʿi sources in particular focused on the ways that ʿAli's performance at all the major early battles was a source of their solidarity and endurance.

The Safavids revered the Prophet Muhammad, no doubt, but ʿAli had attributes that Muhammad had not. Muhammad had many great qualities but warriorship was not among them. ʿAli's warrior persona was cemented during early Islamic clashes, starting with the first battle at Badr, when he was in his early twenties.[17] These battle stories were later circulated through *manāqib* reciters (from literature extolling the virtues of ʿAli and the other Imams), hadith scholars, poets, and storytellers, and were narrated with beauty and passion. The image of ʿAli that emerges from these accounts is one of the ultimate warrior hero, powerful and resolute in the pursuit of justice. One of the features of these battles that captivated the communities, and a popular topic for preachers and storytellers, were the tales of single combat before the battle known as *al-birāz*, a type of duel in which the two armies sent forth their most skilled warrior to fight to the death.[18]

At the Battle of Badr in 2/624, for instance, the monotheistic followers of Muhammad, an inexperienced lot, were vastly outnumbered, while the polytheistic Meccans commanded a sizable army ready to crush Muhammad and his 313 companions.[19] When a duel was called, ʿAli, his uncle Hamza, and his companion ʿUbayda went forth. They overcame their opponents with ease. This was a great start. It gave the Muslims

[17] al-Mufīd, *Kitāb al-Irshād*, 44–45; ʿAlī b. Muhammad Ibn al-Mughāzilī, *Manāqib ʿAlī b. Abī Tālib*, ed. Muhammad Bāqir Bahbūdī (Tehran: al-Maktaba al-Islāmiyyah, 1403), 277.

[18] The eighth/fourteenth and ninth/fifteenth centuries witnessed a flourishing of *manāqib* writings and recitation, so much so that they gave rise to the Sunni practice of *fazāʾil-khvānī* (reciting praises for the first three caliphs). For medieval Shiʿi elite's support for *manāqib* reciters in urban centers as bearers of its culture see, Jaʿfariyān, *Tārīkh-i Tashayyuʿ dar Īrān*, 820–26; Arjomand, *Shadow of God*, 56–57; Husayn Izadi and Mahdi Ziraki, "Manāqib-khvānī dar Dawrah-yi Āl-i Būyah," *Tārīkh-i Islām* 33–34 (1387): 25–56; Bihrūz Vijdānī, *Hazrat-i ʿAlī (ʿa.) dar Naghmah'hā-yi ʿĀmmiyānah-yi Īrān* (Tehran: Sāzmān-i Chāp va Intishārāt, Vizārat-i Farhang va Irshād-i Islāmī, 1380).

[19] The number 313 later became part of the Imami Shiʿi eschatology, such that the Mahdi's army on the Final Day is believed to be composed of 313 soldiers.

momentum and the belief that victory against their powerful enemy was possible. It was reported that during the ensuing battle ʿAli went on to slay a score of the Meccan nobility, like Hanzala b. Abi Sufyan and Nawfal b. Khuwaylid, who had led the fiercest persecutions against the early believers in Mecca.[20]

A year later, at the Battle of Uhud, he slew the great champion Talha b. Talha in a duel, a common practice between each camp's best warriors before the assault.[21] In this battle, however, the Muslims suffered a setback. They were routed and their Prophet was nearly killed. ʿAli led a handful of companions and pushed back the attackers. ʿAli's performance was so fierce that an angel was heard saying *lā fatā illā ʿAlī wa-lā sayf illā zulfīqār*, the famous couplet seen in numerous art forms, engraved on armor, and in literature, meaning, "there is no warrior but ʿAli, and there is no sword but the *zulfīqār*." *Zulfīqār* was the ominous two-pointed sword with a divine origin, which Muhammad had gifted to ʿAli.[22]

At the siege of Khaybar ʿAli surpassed his previous acts of valor. He first killed the legendary warrior Marhab in the duel.[23] He then charged the castle gate and pulled it out of its sockets allowing the believers to overtake the fort. When later his companion asked him: "How were you able to bear the weight of it [the gate]?" ʿAli replied, "It was just like my shield which was on my hands on other occasions." As the story goes, the events of Khaybar convinced Muslims that ʿAli was extraordinary.[24]

Yet, it was at the Battle of the Trench (*khandaq*) in 5/627 when he defeated the great warrior ʿAmr b. ʿAbd Wudd that ʿAli's image as the warrior of faith (*mujāhid*) was cemented, becoming the conception of a warrior that inspired generations of Shiʿis and transforming him into a

[20] al-Mufīd, *Kitāb al-Irshād*, 44–51.
[21] Ibid., 56–57; Tahmāsb Safavī, *Tazkirah-i Shāh Tahmāsb*, 42–43.
[22] al-Mufīd, *Kitāb al-Irshād*, 58–60; Shah Tahmasb recalls this hadith in a somber passage in his memoir when writing about the time when his brother Alqas betrayed him, and led an army supplied by the Ottoman Sultan Suleyman to dethrone him (*Tazkirah-i Shāh Tahmāsb*, 120, 114–15). According to one popular view, the Prophet had gifted the mighty sword to ʿAli after the Battle of Badr to be used as an instrument of justice, to promote good and forbid wickeness. According to another account, the angel Gabriel brought ʿAli the sword (Ibn Shahrāshūb, *Manāqib Āl-i Abī Tālib*, 3:295). ʿAli's warrior aura was further accentuated by his astonishing steed, Duldul. As the legend goes, the governor of Alexandria had offered it to the Prophet as a gift who then gave it to ʿAli (Muhammad Jaʿfar Yāhaqqī, *Farhang-i Asātīr va Ishārāt-i Dāstānī dar Adabīyāt-i Fārsī* (Tehran: Surūsh, 1369), 195).
[23] Ibn al-Mughāzilī, *Manāqib ʿAlī b. Abī Tālib*, 200–201; al-Mufīd, *Kitāb al-Irshād*, 84–86.
[24] Lings, *Muhammad*, 514; al-Mufīd, *Kitāb al-Irshād*, 83–88.

holy legend, an archetypal soldier who was an instrument of the Creator's justice.[25]

ʿAmr was the Quraysh's most feared fighter. According to early sources, not a single man among the Muslim army stood up when ʿAmr taunted them and demanded a duel, except ʿAli, who immediately rose. The Prophet repeatedly told him to stand down fearing that ʿAli was no match for an experienced warrior such as ʿAmr. When time dragged on and no one volunteered to face ʿAmr, Muhammad at last allowed ʿAli to go forth – no doubt one of the most difficult decisions he had to make. And rightly so. ʿAli was young and fearless, a worrisome combination. Hardly anyone expected him to survive hand-to-hand combat with the legendary ʿAmr. In a way, ʿAmr was to ʿAli who Goliath might have been to David. Muhammad held him in his arms and put his own helmet on ʿAli's head and prayed to the Creator for his protection.[26]

ʿAli went forth and offered ʿAmr an invitation to abandon his animosity against the Muslims and leave the battlefield. ʿAmr ridiculed ʿAli's courage and naivete. A fierce contest then ensued in which ʿAli somehow found an opening and caught ʿAmr with a powerful blow that debilitated him. Once the dust dissipated, the two armies watched ʿAli walk over to finish him off when he suddenly hesitated. When later the Prophet inquired about it, ʿAli replied, "He had insulted my mother and spat in my face. I feared that if I struck then, it would have been out of personal anger. So, I left him until I calmed down, and then slew him for the sake of God."[27] The Prophet was reported to have said: "Faith [in Divine Oneness], in its entirety, has appeared before polytheism (*shirk*), in its entirety."[28]

ʿAmr's sister, on the other hand, had an entirely different view of the event. It is said that she recited the following poem after she heard ʿAli was the victor:

> Two lions attacked one another in a narrow field of battle, each of them was a noble and brave equal.

[25] al-Mufīd, *Kitāb al-Irshād*, 65–72.

[26] Ibid.

[27] Abū Hāmid Muhammad al-Ghazālī, *Kīmīyā-yi Saʿādat*, ed. Husayn Khadīvjam (Tehran: Markaz-i Intishārāt-i ʿIlmī va Farhangī, 1371), 1:517; Jalāl al-Dīn Rūmī, *The Mathnawī of Jalāl al-Dīn Rūmī*, trans. Reynold A. Nicholson (repr., Cambridge: Trustees of the E. J. W. Gibb Memorial, 2001), 1:202–8.

[28] Muhammad Ray'shahrī, Muhammad Kāzim Tabātabāʾī, and Mahmūd Tabātabāʾī, eds., *Mawsūʿat al-Imām ʿAlī b. Abī Tālib fī al-Kitāb wa-l-Sunnah wa-l-Tārīkh* (Qum: Muʾassasat Dār al-Hadīth, 1421), 1:218–19.

Both of them wanted to tear the souls away from each other in the middle of the battlefield, either by stealth or by fighting.
Then ʿAli, go, for you have never gained a victory like this. That is a true statement in which there is no unfairness.
ʿAli, vengeance will be mine. Would that I could come upon him, then my blood-vengeance would be complete.[29]

ʿAli embodied the chivalric ideals as a warrior to an extent that even hostile tribes whose heroes had been killed by ʿAli would write poetry expressing their pride in the fact that ʿAli had slayed their warriors.

Tales of ʿAli's feats were in wide circulation prior to the rise of the Safavids as they were used by Sufi sheikhs and theologians alike to teach their disciples higher ideals and virtues. When the Safavids seized power, they reinvigorated ʿAli's legend and helped amplify their communities' devotion to him. The Venetian emissary Michele Membré, who reached Iran in 1539 when storytellers could hold public audience without harassment, reported:

The Sophians [Safavid Sufis] paint figures, such as the figure of 'Ali, riding on a horse, with a sword; and when they see the said figure of 'Ali, they take hold of their ear and bow their head, which is a kind of reverence.

In their squares there are many Persian mountebanks sitting on carpets on the ground; and they have certain long cards with figures; and the said mountebanks hold a little stick and point to one figure after another, and preach and tell stories over each figure. So everybody gives them some money. There are also others with books in their hands, reading of the battles of 'Ali and the combats of the Princes of old, and of Shah Ismail; and all give money to hear.[30]

The tragedy that befell ʿAli's eldest son, Hussein, further heightened ʿAli's lore for his followers.[31] Hussein rose up against Yazid, the powerful governor of Syria and son of Muʿawiya, who was ʿAli's sworn enemy. His small band of companions and family on their way to Kufah (in today's southern Iraq) were intercepted and brutally killed by Yazid's forces. Membré describes that year's ʿAshura commemoration:

for that martyrdom they perform the passion for ten days, and for it they all wear black, black turban-cloths and black clothes … From evening to one hour of the

29 al-Mufīd, *Kitāb al-Irshād*, 72.

30 Membré, *Mission to the Lord Sophy of Persia*, 52.

31 Khvāndamīr, *Tārīkh-i Habīb al-Sīyā r fī Akhbā r-i Afrād-i Bashar*, 2:670–91; Rıza Yıldırım, "Beylikler Dünyasında Kerbela Kültürü ve Ehl-i Beyt Sevgisi: 1362 Yılında Kastamonu'da Yazılan Bir Maktel'in Düşündürdükleri," in *Kuzey Anadolu'da Beylikler Dönemi Sempozyumu: Bildiriler*, ed. Halil Çetin (Çankırı: Çankırı Karatekin Üniversitesi Yayınları, 2012), 344–72.

night the companies go round through the city and through the mosques chanting in Persian the passion of the said Imam Hussein ... in the evening all the ladies betake themselves to their mosques and a preacher preaches the passion of the said son of ʿAli and the ladies weep bitterly.[32]

Such stories had become an integral dimension of the Safavid communities' spirituality. It echoes for them a divinity that was reachable through ʿAli and his holy progeny. Thus, their communal reverence for them continually reaffirmed their faith and strengthened their sense of group identity.[33]

3.5 ʿALI THE ARCHETYPAL MASTER

"Since thou art the gate of the city of knowledge," prayed the great mystic of the thirteenth century Mawlana Jalal al-Din Rumi, "since thou art the beams of the sun of Clemency, Be open O gate, to him that seeks the gate, so that by means of thee the husks may reach the core. Be open unto everlasting, O gate of Mercy."[34]

Mawlana points in his supplication to "the city of knowledge" hadith, the famous occasion when Muhammad said to his companions, "I am the city of knowledge and ʿAli is its gate." This hadith was as familiar to Sufis as dry bread, and affirmed for the disciple that the path upon which he trekked led him to the gatekeeper of the sacred consciousness.

Such hadiths eternalized ʿAli as an archetypal mystic in possession of sacred knowledge among the luminaries of the Persianate world, like Sheikh Hujwiri of Ghaznah (d. 464/1071), the Sheikh of Simnan (d. 736/1336), the Ghazali brothers of Khurasan, Sheikh Attar of Naishapur, Najm al-Din Kubra of Khvarazm, and many others. They seemed to believe that ʿAli held the key to the mysteries of existence beyond the gate, for he understood the esoteric meaning of the Prophetic Message. For this reason they knew him as the *mazhar al-ʿajāʾib*, "manifestation of mysteries."[35]

32 Membré, *Mission to the Lord Sophy of Persia*, 43.

33 Jean Calmard, "Popular Literature under the Safavids," in *Society and Culture in the Early Modern Middle East: Studies on Iran in the Safavid Period*, ed. Andrew J. Newman (Leiden: Brill, 2003), 315–39; Derviş Muhammed Yemînî, *Fazîlet'nâme*, ed. Yusuf Tepeli (Ankara: Atatürk Kültür, Dil ve Tarih Yüksek Kurumu Türk Dil Kurumu, 2002).

34 Rūmī, *Mathnawī*, 203–4; Leonard Lewisohn, "ʿAli ibn Abi Talib's Ethics of Mercy in the Mirror of the Persian Sufi Tradition," in *The Sacred Foundations of Justice in Islam: The Teachings of ʿAli ibn Abi Talib*, ed. M. Ali Lakhani (Bloomington, IN: World Wisdom, 2006), 109–45.

35 Abū al-Hasan Hujwīrī, *Kashf al-Mahjūb*, ed. Valentin Zhukovski (Leningrad, 1344), 84; Simnānī, *Chihil Majlis*; Isfarāyinī, *Murshid va Murid*; James J. Elias, *The Throne Carrier of God: The Life and Thought of ʿAlāʾ ad-Dawla as-Simnānī* (Albany: State University of

Nearly all Sufi orders, including the Safavids, trace their spiritual chain (*silsilah*) to the Prophet Muhammad through ʿAli, whom they believed the Prophet had directly taught the principles of mysticism. The founders of Islamic mysticism, al-Hasan al-Basri, al-Shibli, al-Junayd, Bayazid Bastami, and Maʿruf al-Karkhi, trace their spiritual teachings to ʿAli.[36] The Safavid order's founder, Sheikh Safi al-Din, was linked to Imam ʿAli through al-Hasan al-Basri (who was ʿAli's companion), Junayd of Baghdad, and Maʿruf al-Karkhi, the companion of the eighth Imam, Reza.[37]

Regarded as the epitome of sanctity (*walāyah*) and the "friend of God" (*walī Allāh*) ʿAli was considered among the Sufis as the *qutb al-awliyā* (pole of sainthood), the "perfect human being" (*al-insān al-kāmil*). ʿAli's *walāyah* (spiritual authority) was considered to be the inner dimension of prophethood. The idea conveyed to Sufi communities such as the Safavids that after the death of the Prophet, whose revelations established the Creator's law (*sharīʿah*) as the outer meaning of the faith, the inner meaning remained accessible to believers through ʿAli. After ʿAli's departure from the world, his descendants, the twelve infallible Imams, kept the inner truth of revelation alive and in turn passed it on to their disciples.[38]

The impact of ʿAli on Sufism is clear in the many Sufi rituals that are traced back to him. It was through ʿAli's grace (*barakah*), for instance, that disciples were initiated into the esoteric meaning of the Revelation. The disciple's path began with the process of repentance (*tawbah*), which was undertaken through Imam ʿAli's intercession.[39]

New York Press, 1995); al-Ghazālī, *Kīmīyā-yi Saʿādat*, 1:517; Farīd al-Dīn ʿAttār, *Dīvān-i Sheikh Farīd al-Dīn ʿAttār*, ed. Mahmud Darvish (Tehran: Javid, 1402); Kubrā, *Fawāʾih al-Jamāl*, 87–89; B. Todd Lawson, "The Dawning Places of the Lights of Certainty in the Divine Secrets Connected with the Commander of the Faithful by Rajab Bursi (d. 1411)," in *The Heritage of Sufism*, vol. 2, *The Legacy of Medieval Persian Sufism (1150–1500)*, ed. Leonard Lewisohn (Oxford: Oneworld, 1999), 261–76.

36 Though ʿAli was the central figure for the foundation of Sufism, his kin and companion Abu Bakr, the first of the four rightly guided caliphs whom the Naqshibandiyyah holds as their initiator, is also considered a great spiritual authority in Islamic mysticism. ʿAli's companions and disciples such as Kumayl b. Ziyad, al-Hasan al-Basri, and Salman al-Farsi were widely believed to have preserved and passed on to their disciples what they learned from ʿAli. See, for instance, Haydar b. ʿAlī ʿĀmulī, *Jāmiʿ al-Asrār wa-Manbaʿ al-Anwār* (Beirut: Dār al-Muhajja al-Baydāʾ, 2007), 224–25.

37 Amīnī Haravī, *Futūhāt-i Shāhī*, 22–23; Ardabīlī, *Tazkirat al-Zākarīn*, 78–79.

38 Yıldırım, ed., *Menâkıb-ı Evliyâ*, 325–26.

39 Kāshānī, *Misbāh al-Hidāyat*, 366; ʿAbd al-Razzāq Kāshānī Samarqandī, "Tuhfat al-Ikhwān," in *Rasāʾil-i Javānmardān: Mushtamil bar Haft Futuvvat'nāmah*, ed. Murtazā Sarrāf (Tehran: Qismat-i Īrānshināsī-i Anstitū-yi Pizhuhish'hā-yi ʿIlmī dar Īrān, 1352), 51. The concept of *tavassul*, loosely translated as intercession, is evoked in many spheres of piety, from Sufi practices to common prayer for healing and prosperity. There are

A key Sufi practice that was believed to have originated with ʿAli was *zikr*, the methodic remembrance and whispering of the Creator's names and attributes. The Prophet had taught ʿAli the techniques of *zikr* and the divine mysteries that the practice could unveil. In later centuries, Sufis articulated its ultimate purpose as the catalyst for the gradual dissolution of the self into the Divine Reality.[40] ʿAli then taught the methods to his disciples, who in turn became teachers themselves and passed on its metaphysical meanings to the few initiates in an unbroken chain of masters and disciples.

In one of his sermons, for example, ʿAli encapsulates the well-known metaphor that *zikr* is like "polishing the heart" referenced by many later Sufis: "Truly God has made al-dhikr a polish for the hearts, by which they [disciples] hear after being deaf and see after being blind." He further explains, "remember Him with perfect remembrance, a remembrance in which your heart and tongue are in harmony, and what you conceal conforms with what you reveal. But you will not remember Him according to the true reality of the remembrance until you forget your own soul in your remembrance." *Zikr* is only one of many Sufi practices that are linked to Imam ʿAli.[41]

Later Sufi communities nurtured a deep connection to Imam ʿAli. Expressed through poetry, medieval and early modern mystics during the eighth/fourteenth and ninth/fifteenth centuries crafted the emotional language of reverence for one who represented the manifestation of the perfected human being the likes of whom had never before appeared. Infallible, epitome of justice, and the fountainhead of mystical knowledge, ʿAli was reincarnated, this time for the Persianate world. Collectively they reveal the flow of ʿAlid devotion among the

differences in terms of permissibility of *tavassul* between various Sunni and Shiʿi schools, complicated by the overlap of *tavassul* and *shifāʿah*, the latter often defined as when a supplicant seeks an intercessor's help specifically for forgiveness of sin.

40 Abu Hamid al-Ghazali describes in detail the result of *zikr* on the Sufi's mind as recorded by ʿAbd al-Rahmān Jāmī, *Lawāʾih: A Treatise on Ṣūfism*, trans. E. H. Whinfield and Mīrzā Muḥammad Ḳazvīnī (London: Royal Asiatic Society, 1906), 70–71; see also David Dakake, "The Practice of *Dhikr* in the Early Islamic Community," in *Knowledge Is Light: Essays in Islamic Studies Presented to Seyyed Hossein Nasr by His Students in Honor of His Sixty-Sixth Birthday*, ed. Zailan Moris (Chicago: ABC International Group, 1999), 169–95. For the Safavid practice of *zikr* after the dynastic establishment, see Ardabīlī, *Tazkirat al-Zākarīn*, 29–74, 83–84.

41 Reza Shah-Kazemi, *Justice and Remembrance: Introducing the Spirituality of Imam Ali* (London: I.B. Taurus, 2011), 160–72.

literati and Sufis in the century prior to the militarization of the Safavid order.[42]

This body of literature reflects these communities' need for intimacy with their imperceptible Creator by managing the complexity of their religious experience through a perceptible connection. ʿAli offered that connection. What the poets and storytellers did by dramatizing the life of ʿAli was to weave a cultural tapestry of the mythical and the sacred, with filigree of the spiritual desire and the shade of the eternal struggle of an archetype who stood for universal absolute goods against iniquity. They infused the story of his life with an infinite pulse that arose from the Sufi conception of the ultimate union of a created being with his Creator.

Encounters with ʿAli in dream-states were not uncommon among Sufis. Sheikh Najm al-Din Kubra (d. 618/1221), the founder of the Kubraviyyah order, for instance, recalls that once in a mystical reverie he found himself in the presence of the Prophet and Imam ʿAli. He greets and shakes ʿAli's hand. He then asks ʿAli if it is true what the Prophet had once said, that whoever shakes ʿAli's hand goes to paradise. ʿAli reassured the sheikh that it is indeed true, confirming the sheikh's spiritual standing.[43] As may be recalled in Chapter 2, the first-generation Safavid disciple ʿIzz al-Din, too, saw Imam ʿAli in a pivotal dream during his discipleship in which Imam ʿAli in the presence of the Prophet Muhammad helped him realize Sheikh

[42] See, for example, the ʿAlid verses of Fakhr al-Dīn Mahmūd Ibn Yamīn, *Dīvān-i Ashʿār-i Ibn Yamīn Farnawmadī*, ed. Husayn ʿAlī Bāstānī'rād (Tehran: Sanāʾī, 1359); Muhammad b. Husām al-Dīn, *Dīvan-i Mawlanā Muhammad b. Husām*, ed. Ahmad Birjandi (Mashhad, 1366); Rabīʿ, *ʿAlī-Nāmah*, ed. Shafiʿi Kadkani (Tehran, 2009); ʿAbd al-Rahmān Jāmī, *Dīvān-i Kāmil-i Jāmī*, ed. Hashim Razi (Tehran: Chāpkhānah-i Pīrūz, 1341); Bābā Faghānī Shīrāzī, *Dīvān-i Ashʿār-i Bābā Faghānī Shīrāzī*, ed. Ahmad Suhaylī Khvānsārī (Tehran: Iqbāl, 1362); Mahmūd b. ʿAlī Khvājū-yi Kirmānī, *Dīvān-i Kāmil-i Khvajū-yi Kirmānī*, ed. Hasan Anvari (Tehran: Behzād, 1374); Awhadī Marāghāhʾī, *Dīvān-i Kāmil-i Awhadī Marāghāhʾī*, ed. Amīr Ahmad Ashrafī (Tehran: Intishhārāt-i Pīshraw, 1362); Shāh Niʿmat Allāh Valī, *Kullīyāt Dīvān-i Shāh Niʿmat Allāh Valī Kirmānī*, ed. Muhammad ʿAbbāsī (Tehran: Kitābfurūshī-i Fakhr-i Rāzī, 1362). Poets who mainly wrote in Turkish, such as Nesimi and Pir Sultan Abdal, echoed similar veneration of ʿAli. See, for instance, Hüseyin Ayan, *Nesîmî Hayatı, Edebî Kişiliği, Eserleri ve Türkçe Divanının Tenkidli Metni* (Ankara: Türk Tarih Kurumu Basım Evi, 2002); Kathleen R. F. Burrill, *The Quatrains of Nesimî, Fourteenth-Century Turkic Hurufi, with Annotated Translations of the Turkic and Persian Quatrains from the Hekimoğlu Ali Paşa MS* (The Hague: Mouton, 1972); Ramiz Faseh, *Seyyid İmadäddin Näsiminin Seçilmiş Bäzi Şeirlärinin Şärhi* (Bakı: Şärq-Qärb, 2007); Abdülbâki Gölpınarlı, *Pir Sultan Abdal: Hayatı, Sanatı, Eserleri* (Istanbul: Varlık Yayınevi, 1963); Cahit Öztelli, *Pir Sultan Abdal: Bütün Şirleri* (Istanbul: Milliyet Yayinlari, 1971); Sabahattin Eyüboğlu, *Pir Sultan Abdal* (Istanbul: Cem Yayınevi, 1977).

[43] Kubra, *Fawaʾih al-Jamāl*, 88.

Safi al-Din's spiritual authority. A similar phenomenon occurs with Shah Tahmasb who vividly describes his visions of ʿAli in his memoire.

Sacred brotherhoods (*futuwwas*, *ahīs*, *akhīs*) and urban guilds that predated the Safavids by centuries and overlapped with Sufi communities scattered in towns and villages across the region left behind their own narratives about ʿAli, their spiritual primogenitor, their epitome of chivalry and holiness.[44]

3.6 THE BROTHERHOODS AND GUILDS

A prominent preacher in the late ninth/fifteenth century struggled to explain the sacred nature of the brotherhoods (*futuwwas*): "What more can one say about the holiness of an order that has Prophet Ibrahim as its originator, Imam ʿAli as its axis, and Imam Mahdi [the twelfth Shiʿi Imam in occultation] as its seal." For him, the brotherhoods were centuries old and their origins mysterious but linked to the sacred. ʿAli had become the paragon of justice who consecrated their circle and legitimized their moral teachings and ethical codes.[45]

In the medieval and early modern era, *futuwwas* or brotherhoods (Ar. sing. *fatā*, pl. *fityān*; also, *ahī*, *akhī*) played a prominent role not only in the spiritual life of their communities but in their political life as well, sometimes reaching the center of power, such as happened with the ʿAbbasid caliph al-Nasir li-Din Allah (r. 575–622/1180–1225). He became a powerful patron of the brotherhoods and an outspoken devotee of ʿAli. His successor, the caliph al-Mustansir (r. 623–40/1226–42), was initiated and became a *fatā*. They both declared ʿAli their spiritual master and the archetype of chivalry, and they both attempted to use the brotherhoods for political ends.

The dominant personality trait of ʿAli was his passion for social justice. Brotherhoods who often found themselves defending their communities and assisting the needy in the absence of effective government sought inspiration in the stories of ʿAli's compassion for the poor and the marginalized. ʿAli was specifically recognized to be the guardian of the vulnerable, the orphans, widows, and prisoners of war. Stories of his gentleness in Shiʿi sources and his own sermons are too numerous to recount. It is

44 ʿĀmulī, *Rasāʾil-i Javānmardān*, 226.

45 Kāshifī, *Futūvat'nāmah-i Sultānī*, 6. On Imam ʿAli's role in the origins of *futuwwat*, see ʿĀmulī, "Risālah-i Futuvvatīyah," in *Rasāʾil-i Javānmardān*, 63–65; cf. Kāshifī, *Futūvat'nāmah-i Sultānī*, 17–20.

clear, however, that ʿAli was a host to a pantheon of virtues that together projected the manifestation of the perfected being in the hearts of his devotees.[46]

A *javānmard* (Pers. sing. of *fatā*) entered a brotherhood when he had first purified himself enough to be able to follow strict ethical codes of spiritual chivalry (*javānmardi*).[47] ʿAli would be his guide who inspired in him courage, strength, and faith. ʿAli's influence was felt at once in the initiation rites into brotherhood, rites common to many Sufi orders that were traced back to ʿAli's relationship with his own teacher, the Prophet Muhammad. The drink of salted water from the sheikh's hand, for instance, the fastening of the *shadd* (cummerbund) around the disciple's waist, and the bestowal of the patched cloak (*khirqah*) to the disciple by his sheikh were believed to have first begun when Muhammad gave ʿAli his mantle. The spiritual relationship between the Prophet and ʿAli became the model for all subsequent Sufi discipleships. As the eighth/fourteenth-century Sufi *fatā* ʿAbd al-Razzaq Kashani put it, "*futuvvat* is part of *tasavvuf* the way *vilāyat* (guardianship of ʿAli) is part of *nubuvvat* (prophethood of Muhammad)."[48]

Many Sufi orders and *futuwwa*s shared similar pedagogical structures and spiritual ethos. They transmitted, for example, their teachings via a murshid-murid schema, gained spiritual legitimacy through chains of knowledge-transmission (*silsilah*) back to ʿAli, and adhered to firm codes of ethics, ranging from everyday social decorum to almsgiving to armed revolts. Their mode of conduct in their communities was supposed to be guided by abiding to such virtues as humility, courage, generosity, and loyalty.

The long-established association of urban guilds (*asnāf*, unions of merchants and artisans) and sacred brotherhoods further intertwined during the ninth/fifteenth and tenth/sixteenth centuries as new generations in the Persianate world sought to understand the inner meaning of their vocations and origins of their associations. The vast majority of guilds continued to recognize ʿAli as their initiator.[49]

46 Shah-Kazemi, *Justice and Remembrance*, 160–65. Some believed that "and give food – despite their desire for it – to the poor, the orphan, and the captive" (Qurʾan 76:8) is a reference to ʿAli. See Kāshānī Samarqandī, "Tuhfat al-Ikhwān," 10.

47 Ibn Yūsuf, "Zubdat al-Tarīq ilā Allāh," in *Rasāʾil-i Javānmardān*, 220–22.

48 Kāshānī Samarqandī, "Tuhfat al-Ikhwān," 12–15.

49 *Futuvvat'nāmah'hā va Rasāʾil-i Khāksāriyyah: Sī Risālah*, ed. Mihrān Afshārī (Tehran: Pizhūhishgāh-i ʿUlūm-i Insānī va Mutāliʿāt-i Farhangī, 1382); *Chahārdah Risālah dar Bāb-i Futuvvat va Asnāf*, ed. Mihrān Afshārī and Mahdī Madāyinī (Tehran: Nashr-i Chishmah, 1388); *Sī Futuvvat'nāmah-i Digar*.

It would be imprecise to discuss the relationship between the urban *futuwwa*s, *asnāf*, and Sufi orders with the Safavid court as disconnected autonomous groups. Though there were major distinctions in their traditions and internal narratives, there was a great deal of overlap in their relationships. One may be a member of an artisan guild, for instance, participate in his local brotherhood, and have had formal Sufi training. Furthermore, such individuals were part of their own nucleus families whose members might had various levels of commitment to the three groups – caution therefore must be observed against generalized demarcations. The *futuwwa* and *asnāf* treatises of the period, for example, disclose the overlay of the three spheres in terms of ideology, spiritual tradition, and power dynamics in their organizations that made up a member's social matrix.

Much of the detail concerning Iran's medieval and early modern guilds, however, comes from the eleventh/seventeenth century demonstrating that they viewed their history as ancient. Their internal narrative takes the origins of their profession even back to the first prophets. Like many guilds in Eurasian societies, they shared common traits such as their hierarchical organizational structure and communal consensus in terms of the guild's legitimacy and operations.[50] Let's consider, for a moment, a typical Safavid guild's hierarchy of command. The guild of tanners, for instance, was led by a trusted elder (*kadkhudā*) elected by at least two-thirds of the guild's craft masters and confirmed by the town's mayor (*kalāntar*), who garbed him in a robe of honor in the appointment ceremony.

A *kadkhudā* gained his power within the group through having the authority to adjudicate among its members to resolve internal conflicts; through his role in the assessment and collection of the guild's taxes; and the arrangement of corvée (unpaid labor due to the overlord). Given these particulars, it is easy to see a *kadkhudā*'s political clout in the community and the guild's importance for the court.[51] The brotherhoods and the guilds, however, were not perceived as hostile, not because of their

[50] Sjoberg draws the following commonalities among preindustrial guilds: (i) guilds have the cartel on a particular trade; (ii) they have rules for the selection of membership; (iii) instruction of the apprentice only occurs within the guilds; (iv) there is a mechanism of quality control; (v) guilds display collective bargaining power vis-à-vis the ruler; (vi) guilds exercise communal welfare for members in need; (vii) guilds enjoy strong feeling of group cohesion and (viii) play an integral role in religious rituals. Gideon Sjoberg, *The Preindustrial City: Past and Present* (Glencoe, IL: The Free Press, 1960), 5, 190–94.

[51] Vladimir Minorsky, trans., *Tadhkirat al-Mulūk: A Manual of Ṣafavid Administration (circa 1137/1725): Persian Text in Facsimile (B.M. Or. 9496)* (Cambridge: Trustees of the E. J. W. Gibb Memorial, 1943), 48, 81–83.

veneration of Imam ʿAli that paralleled the Safavids, but because they lacked any real means of collective violence and military power to pose a threat. Aside from paying tax revenues to the treasury, they were a valuable resource for organizing religious festivals and public rituals such as commemoration of the martyrdom of ʿAli's son Imam Hussein in Karbala and the feast of Eid al-Fitr marking the end of the month of Ramazan.[52]

The Safavid court's reaction to major Sufi orders who possessed organizational capabilities and social influence varied during the first half of the tenth/sixteenth century when the Safavids were still amassing the sources of their ideological power. It is difficult to simplify the reactions of the Sufi orders to Shah Ismail and his brand of Sufism. In Herat, for instance, ʿAbd Allah Hatifi (d. 927/1521), a nephew of the famed Sufi poet Jami and the head of the Naqshbandi order with ties to the city's former patron king Sultan Husayn Bayqara (d. 912/1506), accepted Shah Ismail's authority, while many Naqshbandis abhorred the move and left in protest for India. Another prominent Naqshbandi, Sheikh ʿAbd al-Vahhab of Hamadan, entered Ismail's entourage to the dismay of many of his followers. This trend continued into Ismail's successor Tahmasb's reign. As noted earlier, Tahmasb supported the Shiʿi ʿulema's religious reforms, which came with the added bonus of suspicion and hostility toward Sufis. Yet, when he moved his capital from Tabriz further east to Qazvin in the 950–60s/1550s and away from Ottoman reach, he maintained the court's relations with the Naqshbandis who remained in the new capital and flourished while many followed their elders and abandoned the city.[53]

Likewise, Nurbakhshi sheikhs found an agreeable tenor with Shah Ismail and reticently accepted the authority and patronage of the young Sufi king. As previously discussed, the revered sheikh and confidant of Ismail, Shams al-Din Muhammad Lahiji (d. 814/1515), for instance, established a Nurbakhshi lodge (*khānaqāh*) in the city of Shiraz to train disciples, while his son Ahmad

[52] Yıldırım, "Shīʾitisation of the Futuwwa Tradition"; Mehdi Keyvani, *Artisans and Guild Life in the Later Safavid Period: Contributions to the Social-Economic History of Persia* (Berlin: Klaus Schwarz, 1982).

[53] Jean Calmard, "Naqshbandis and Safavids: A Contribution to the Religious History of Iran and Her Neighbors," in *Safavid Iran and Her Neighbors*, ed. Michel Mazzaoui (Salt Lake City: University of Utah Press, 2003), 9–10, 22–23, 25–26; Andrew J. Newman, "Sufism and the Safavids in Iran: A Further Challenge to 'Decline,'" in *Routledge Handbook on Sufism*, ed. Lloyd Ridgeon (London: Routledge, 2020), 370–86; Andrew J. Newman, "Sufism and Anti-Sufism in Safavid Iran: The Authorship of the *Hadiqat al-Shiʿa* Revisited," *Iran* 37 (1999): 95–108.

took on direct political duties for the Safavid court. He once served as Shah Ismail's envoy to the Uzbek leader Muhammad Shaybani Khan during his eastern campaigns to secure Khurasan. Others like Sayyid Muhammad Nurbakhsh, on the other hand, spurned getting involved with the court and refused royal patronage. Refusing to go "under" the protection of a powerful patron can be risky. Sayyid Muhammad Nurbakhsh's loyalty came under suspicion and might have led to his execution in 944/1537.[54]

Prominent members of the Niʿmatallahi order too joined the Safavids early in the dynasty's rise. Sayyid ʿAbd al-Baqi of Yazd, a descendant of the famed founder of the order Shah Niʿmatallah, became Ismail's close advisor and trusted enough to be appointed *sadr*, the highest religious official in the realm. Shah Tahmasb too maintained a close relationship with the Niʿmatallahis when he succeeded his father. He appointed Sayyid ʿAbd al-Baqi's son Nur al-Din as governor of Yazd, who in 942/1535 managed to climb to the center of power and marry one of Tahmasb's sisters. Some twenty years later, Tahmasb married his son, the heir apparent Ismail II (r. 984–85/1576–77), to his niece, the daughter of this union. The close affinity between the two houses continued well into the eleventh/seventeenth century. By the mid-tenth/sixteenth century, the Safavids had managed to politically absorb and incapacitate these powerful Sufi orders.[55]

Imam ʿAli was the gravitational pole around which Sufi piety, *futuwwa* morality, and Shiʿi theological speculation revolved. The overlap among these groups added an affective complexity in ʿAli's reception among militarized Sufi orders who had a diverse community of supporters with deep veneration of ʿAli. For a devout Safavid militant, ʿAli epitomized the hero of the age; he gave him strength when he was weak in loyalty and courage when was tested on the battlefield.[56]

ʿAli's impact on the mysticism of the Persianate world was such that by the last quarter of the ninth/fifteenth century the military wing of the Safavid order under the guidance of Sheikh Haydar came to champion ʿAlid Sufism (*tasavvuf-i ʿAlavī*) that was both political and militant. The

[54] Shahzad Bashir, *Messianic Hopes and Mystical Visions: The Nūrbakhshīya between Medieval and Modern Islam* (Columbia: University of South Carolina Press, 2003), 175–95; Hamid Algar, "Nūrbakhshīya," *EI*[2].

[55] Terry Graham, "The Niʿmatu'llāhī Order under Safavid Suppression and in Indian Exile," in *The Heritage of Sufism*, vol. 3, *Late Classical Persianate Sufism (1501–1750)*, ed. Leonard Lewisohn and David Morgan (Oxford: Oneworld, 1999), 165–200; Newman, "Sufism and the Safavids in Iran"; Calmard, "Naqshbandis and Safavids," 26.

[56] Yıldırım, "Shīʾitisation of the Futuwwa Tradition."

Safavid leadership did not have to convince their disciples what ʿAli meant for their community; the road had already been paved for the reemergence of ʿAlavism deepened by two centuries of Sufi thought. When Shah Ismail began to put into words his devotion to ʿAli in his *Divan* at the turn of the tenth/sixteenth century, he had a rich literary heritage to draw upon. His poetry reflected the tenor of the time and expressed the affective ways with which ʿAli inhabited the community's spiritual world.

3.7 ʿALID DEVOTION AT THE HEART OF SAFAVID LEADERSHIP

Shah Ismail's poetry and the memoir of his son and successor Tahmasb offer vivid images of what ʿAlid piety entailed in their lives as heads of the Safavid order during the foundational phase of the dynasty (see Chapter 4). Shah Ismail, for instance, demonstrates for his Sufi warriors the nature of Imam ʿAli in this poem excerpted from his *Divan*:

> Know for certain: 'Ali is the Sea of Truth, he is the eternal life of honour. The day the ghazis with red pennons and banners, don their red taj, will be the day of warning. Mo'awiya's horde on seeing one ghazi will grow worse than that sheep in the wolf's clutches. The *akhi*s (brothers) who recognize the *pir* [sheikh] are the true pearls … In the path of the Shah [i.e., ʿAli], Khata'i (Ismail) sacrifices his soul, to say nothing of the kingdom, silver, and gold.[57]

Many of the elements of ʿAlid veneration that we have seen so far that constituted the heritage of the Safavid communities are present in this poem; the *Buyruk*'s discourse on the authenticity of ʿAli's mystical knowledge, Sufi devotional poetry, and the gallantry of ʿAli are reflected in the *manāqib* literature. Ismail thus places himself and his devotees in a metaphysical realm that affirms their loyalty to their immortal ʿAli, their "Sea of Truth."

Many of Ismail's poems are snapshots of his intense devotion to ʿAli, which his son also shared. In Tahmasb's memoire, for instance, he recounts several dreams in which he has visions of Imam ʿAli. In his own words, "it is the belief of this lowly servant Tahmasb al-Safavi al-Musavi al-Husseini that whoever sees the Commander of the Faithful in a dream, that which he commands will be so, and in this there is no doubt."[58]

[57] Minorsky, "The Poetry of Shāh Ismāʿīl I," 1042.
[58] Ṭahmāsb Ṣafavī, *Tazkirah-i Shāh Tahmāsb*, 70–71.

One dream in particular is revealing. It occurred in Herat during Tahmasb's campaign against the Uzbeks in 939/1532. He recalls:

> I saw the Commander of the Faithful in Zaynal Khan's house in Qazvin; he was seated, a young man of approximately twenty-five years of age with black hair. I kissed the ground of servitude and sat down on my knees in front of him and asked:
>
> "Ya Hazrat, may I be a sacrifice for you, I am going that direction, will I clash with the Uzbeks or not?"
>
> The Commander of the Faithful responded, "O Tahmasb, which of your important affairs were determined by war that this will be the second?"

Not satisfied with ʿAli's response, Tahmasb persists:

> I asked again, "May I be a sacrificed for you, tell me what will happen on the other side of the river?"
>
> ʿAli responded, "There is nothing on the other side; whatever it is, it will be on this side of the river."[59]

ʿAli's presence in the intimate space of the dream suggests that Tahmasb was convinced of the powers of intercession, a pillar of ʿAlid piety, that ʿAli can indeed intervene and save a hopeless situation. The dream world offered the supplicant king a realm in which he could speak to the holiest of men and seek answer.

ʿAli then summons Tahmasb closer and requests three favors in return: for Tahmasb to complete the *nahr-i ʿalqami* (a canal of the Euphrates that was used to bring water to Karbala), to build a dome for ʿAli's tomb in Najaf, and to appoint Fathi Beg to be the overseer of Imam Reza's mausoleum in Mashhad. Tahmasb summoned his commanders the next day and shared his encounter with Imam ʿAli.

The exchange of favors at the heart of the dream shows how ʿAli's spiritual patronage was affirmed and kept alive by the Safavid ruler's spiritual clientelism in the political realm. The episode further reveals how Tahmasb understood that ʿAli's patronage carried an obligation of obedience and service in the physical realm.

[59] Tahmasb recalls the exact date as "14 Dhul Hijjah" when he had fallen ill. He uses *wāqiʿah*, a technical term in Sufism, to assure his readers that he experienced a "pure vision" and not a dream that may have been influenced by the *nafs* (lower self). Tahmāsb Safavī, *Tazkirah-i Shāh Tahmāsb*, 70–72. Medieval Sufis categorized *wāqiʿāt* into three groups: (a) pure unveiling: psychic events that are true and require no interpretations; (b) imaginative unveiling: those events that are symbolic and thus require interpretation because of the interference of the *nafs* upon the *rūh*, the soul; and (c) pure imagination: those that are patently false, the product entirely of the *nafs*.

Tahmasb often attributed his victories to his faith in ʿAli, such as when he captured his rebellious brother Alqas.[60] Prince Alqas's betrayal of his brother Tahmasb and joining his archfoe Sultan Suleyman in 954/1547 was a devastating blow to the Safavid house and the kingdom as it inaugurated another destructive invasion of Iran (discussed fully in Chapter 5). In his recollection of those years, Tahmasb writes:

> In that moment [of Alqas's capture], I prostrated in gratitude to God. I had consigned Alqasb to my master the Commander of the Faithful, the Imam of the Virtuous, the Victorious Lion of God, Haydar, ʿAli b. Abi Talib. He captured him in this fashion and placed him [in my care]. When he came in front of me, I said, "Do you see how my master [ʿAli] was more powerful than your patron [i.e., Sultan Suleyman]; and returned you to me once again?" I said nothing more.[61]

Shah Ismail and his son Tahmasb's views on Imam ʿAli, as leaders of the Safavid order in the formative period, shed light on how such an ideological power in the face of continuous betrayals, defeats, and loss of leadership contributed to the preservation of their community's sense of cohesion.

As may be recalled, we ended Chapter 1 on a pause (when the child king Tahmasb ascended a rickety throne) to explore in Chapter 2 how the early Safavid Sufis formed spiritual ties of loyalty to the nascent order's leadership, followed in Chapter 3 by the development of the Safavid brand of Shiʿism in the later ninth/fifteenth century. We now return to the early tenth/sixteenth century to the time of chaos, when Shah Ismail had exhaled his last breath and bequeathed to his son a realm in crisis.

For the next decade, the community's cohesion, the cornerstone of their social power, would be severely tested under Tahmasb, who inherited from Ismail not the crimson crown but an empty treasury, a dysfunctional bureaucracy, and a raging civil war. To make matters worse, the boy king did not have the divine charisma his father had enjoyed in the eyes of his devotees, which helped forged part of his legitimacy. Unable to lean on such charismatic authority, Tahmasb and his inner circle tried to strengthen his legitimacy by constructing an image of the young shah not as a charismatic warrior king but as a patron king and protector of the Shiʿi community. In political terms, this translated into patronage of the Shiʿi ʿulema, negotiating the challenging task of including the previous

60 Throughout his memoire Tahmasb expresses his absolute devotion to ʿAli and credits him for his survival. *Tazkirah-i Shāh Tahmāsb*, 114, 136, 119–22.

61 Ibid., 136–37.

Sunni clerical estate into his administration, and enacting a public campaign to garner wide support for the new shah and his version of Islam among Iran's predominantly Sunni population.[62]

Tahmasb's focus on the patronage of the emerging Shiʿi clerical estate to bolster his legitimacy was matched by an explicit strategy of regenerating the ties of loyalty with the Qizilbash chiefs that had withered. With Ismail's death, a half-century of charismatic authority that defined the Safavid leadership with its devotees after its militarization had come to an end. The bloody civil war that broke out upon Tahmasb's ascension in 930/1524 was a testimony to the unifying force that had brought them to the apex of power a generation ago; their strong cohesion that had given them an edge against their powerful enemies had completely shattered. In these circumstances, how Tahmasb and his ministers attempted to forge new ways to preserve their ties of loyalty and work to rebuild the Qizilbash confederacy against the backdrop of civil war and foreign invasion is the subject of Chapters 4 and 5.

[62] Khafipour, "Beyond Charismatic Authority"; Abisaab, *Converting Persia*.

4

Loyalty and Patronage

4.1 ON THE PRECIPICE

In the autumn of 941/1534, Tahmasb's forces, exhausted from campaigning against the Uzbeks in the eastern frontiers, reached the winter pastures near Qazvin and soon marched westward to face the massive Ottoman invasion led personally by Sultan Suleiman the Magnificent. This was the mighty army that intended to end the Safavids once and for all. Plagued by inadequate supplies and fighting men, and wary of treachery in his high command, Tahmasb and his ragtag army was marching toward a death zone.[1]

The last time the Safavids had met the Ottomans was on the field of Chaldiran twenty years earlier, where they were led by the warrior king Ismail himself. The Safavid armies might have been better fed but were as ill-quipped then as they were now. With their heavy reliance on traditional light cavalry, they were no match for the Ottoman army's new field artillery. The Qizilbash chiefs were slow to adopt to the changing methods of warfare and paid a heavy price. The kin of many chiefs and soldiers serving Tahmasb had perished on that day at Chaldiran.

Tahmasb was now in his twenties, having survived the civil war by playing one chief against another and surrounding himself with loyal men. Still, his military high command was susceptible to enticements to defect. The Ottomans paid well for turncoats and collaborators by offers

[1] Tahmāsb Safavī, *Tazkirah-i Shāh Tahmāsb*, 82–83. Munshī Qazvīnī, *Javāhir al-Akhbār*, 173–74, reports 5,000 riders remained with Tahmasb, "most of them disloyal and dejected."

of titles and land. Knowing their odds of survival against arguably the most powerful army of the early modern world, the Qizilbash chiefs began deserting Tahmasb one by one. Even trusted men such as Hussein Sultan of the Takallu tribe, the son of the late Burun Sultan (governor of the holy city of Mashhad) who had fought alongside Shah Ismail, and Muhammad Sultan of the Zu al-Qadrs, the governor of Tarum and Khalkhal, fled to join the Ottoman camp. News had reached Tahmasb that his cousin Hussein Khan, chief of the Shamlu tribe, the backbone of his military contingents, who had helped him defeat the Uzbeks at the battle of Jam a few years earlier, would be next to desert. Such was the dismal state of their loyalty and cohesion.[2]

Tahmasb recalls this period in his memoirs:

> At that time 7,000 men were with me, and only 3,000 were useful. We had marched speedily from Herat, our horses were frail, and among us there was a group such as Hussein Khan, Ghazi Khan, and Malik Beg Khuyi and their men who were friends in speech but enemies at heart, constantly waiting for calamities to befall [us]. At this time, I became exceedingly desperate. Taking refuge with God, I surrendered the fate of religion and state to Him.[3]

Hussein Khan's defection was the most threatening. Aside from being the chief of the powerful Shamlu tribe of Khurasan, whose fighters Tahmasb desperately needed, Hussein Khan was also the *amīr al-umarā*, the chief military officer of the realm. If that was not sufficient power to challenge Tahmasb, Hussein Khan benefited from the prestige of having Safavid blood: He was Tahmasb's cousin, his mother being Shah Ismail's sister. He was also the guardian of Tahmasb's son, the heir apparent Muhammad Khudabandah, as well as father-in-law to Tahmasb's brother Sam Mirza. The combination of his kinship ties and military power in an important frontier province made him an extremely dangerous rival should he decide to challenge Tahmasb and try to seize power. Rumors were spread that he was behind the failed attempt to poison Tahmasb and to place his brother Sam on the throne.[4]

The source of the intelligence concerning Hussein Khan's defection was credible and made it clear that the Safavid military chief had taken an oath with Ghazi Khan of the Takallu, Malik Beg Khuyi (the governor of Khuy),

[2] Munshī Qazvīnī, *Javāhir al-Akhbār*, 173.

[3] Tahmāsb Safavī, *Tazkirah-yi Shāh Tahmāsb*, 83–87; Munshī Qazvīnī, *Javāhir al-Akhbār*, 170–74.

[4] Hasan Rūmlū, *Ahsan al-Tavārīkh*, 3 vols., ed. ʻAbd al-Husayn Navāʼī (Tehran: Bungāh-i Tarjumah va Nashr-i Kitāb, 1371–75), 1222–23.

and Muhammad Sultan Zu al-Qadr (who had just fled the camp) to defect to the Ottomans with their men the next time they went on reconnaissance.[5] Vais Beg and Jaʿfar Beg, cousins of the powerful governor of Baghdad, Muhammad Khan Sharaf al-Din Takallu (whose trial of treason we will examine in Chapter 5), had also earlier joined the defectors with their men and fled the camp. Tahmasb was watching his debilitated army, the once mighty Qizilbash confederacy that his father, Shah Ismail, and his devotees had built, fall apart before his very eyes.[6]

This dangerous situation highlights the insufficiency of such principles as a sacred ʿAlid genealogy, and the Sufi master-disciple dynamic to induce loyalty and obedience once the "Sufi warriors" wanted power and competed for resources. And they looked to the shah for intercession, protection, and patronage. But what happens when the shah faces a crisis that removes his ability to ensure patronage (*niʿmat*) to his chiefs, as was happening to Tahmasb? No doubt, the chiefs deliberated whether the young shah could still be the purveyor of divine *niʿmat* when, instead of *niʿmat*, discord and death were passing through his hands. The political calculations of such powerful chiefs as Hussein Khan and Ghazi Khan as reflected in their actions discussed above suggest that they did not expect Tahmasb and the Qizilbash confederacy to survive. Indeed, it was a good bet given the massive Ottoman army poised to take the Safavid capital once more.

In an atmosphere of war and disorder when men's loyalties were severely strained, the task of uniting the Qizilbash confederation seemed insurmountable. It is in this period that we see in their communications a host of prohibitive ideological devices being evoked to inhibit disloyalty among the chiefs, such as consecration of ties of political loyalty (*ikhlās*), invocation of the obligation of gratitude (*shukr-i niʿmat*) toward their patron king, and again the assertion of the Safavid shah's right to rule as the legitimate descendant of Imam ʿAli.

The following pages shed light on how Tahmasb's appeal to the spiritual dimensions of loyalty to strengthen his ties to his military chiefs was accompanied by material patronage and royal largesse. The policy was devised within a wider context of an emerging network of patronage and

5 Munshī Qazvīnī, *Javāhir al-Akhbār*, 173–74. Rūmlū, *Ahsan al-Tavārīkh*, 331–32, adds that Hussein Khan had previously tried to poison Tahmasb and place Prince Sam on the throne (variation: *Ahsan al-Tavārīkh*, ed. Navāʾī, 1222–13); Qummī, *Khulāsat al-Tavārīkh*, 1:236; Khvāndamīr, *Tārīkh-i Shāh Ismāʿīl*, 162–63; *Tārīkh-i Qizilbāshān*, 9.

6 Munshī Qazvīnī, *Javāhir al-Akhbār*, 174; Tahmāsb Safavī, *Tazkirah-yi Shāh Tahmāsb*, 87.

clientelism that facilitated negotiating power upon well-trodden paths of associational ties that political agents recognized. By the end of the chapter, I demonstrate that the impact of Tahmasb's patronage activities, specifically the appointment of provincial governors to major political and commercial centers, helped consolidate their power across Iran and stabilize their political system.

4.2 LOYALTY RECONCEIVED

For the Safavids, establishing general ties of patronage, where the infrastructure of power was clientelistic, was not difficult. Preserving them, on the other hand, was a challenge, especially during intervals when key power agents openly abandoned their obligations such as during times of power-transfer, inter/intra-tribal conflict, and existential threats to the Safavid family. These three threats – succession to the throne, civil war (*fitnah*), and foreign invasion – converged during the first half of Shah Tahmasb's reign, roughly beginning with his accession in 930/1524 to the Peace of Amasya with the Ottoman Empire in 962/1555. It was in such a critical period that the Safavid political men were compelled to redefine and reimagine the nature of their political ties.[7]

As discussed in the Introduction, the Safavids commonly expressed the idea of political loyalty as *yak-jahatī* (sincerity), *dawlat-khvāhī* (faith in the order's "turn of fortune" or even the idea of a "state"), and more importantly *ikhlās* (devotional loyalty), a spiritual concept that had the effect of encoding political loyalty with spiritual and moral value. In its ideal form, they used the term *ikhlās* as reference to a type of loyalty of those who supported their patron king without thought of personal gain or loss.

Ikhlās's sacred origin (see Section 4.3) gave it immense potential for political use in a militarized Sufi order. Medieval and early modern thinkers viewed *ikhlās* in a variety of ways as reflected in its wide usage in works of ethics, exegesis, politics, and mysticism. So central was the concept that it was woven into the fabric of sociopolitical and religious life in many different ways: as an abstraction of a virtue, as a principle of sincere political intention, as an expression of pure spiritual devotion, as

[7] The main chiefs in this conflict were Div Sultan of the Rumlu tribe, who was Tahmasb's royal tutor (*lalah*), Köpek Sultan of the Ustajlus (the governor of Tabriz), Chuha Sultan and Ghazi Khan of the Takkalus with Isfahan as the tribe's stronghold, and Hussein Khan of the Shamlus of Khurasan, Tahmasb's cousin and a royal tutor.

an ideal type of unconditional and lifelong social tie, and/or as one of the mystical stations on the Sufi path. It is difficult to produce an English equivalent that would encapsulate its multiple meanings throughout many centuries, but in the context of the early modern political theology, "devotional loyalty" may come close.[8]

There are many reports and anecdotal stories in the sources recounting the *ikhlās* of early Safavid followers, the bravery that it inspired, and the violence that it unleashed. Such stories included the "devoted groom," who was with his bride on their wedding night when he received Ismail's call to arms; or the Qizilbash riders that went into battle without armor believing they would be unharmed in the presence of their Sufi leader; or Ismail's royal guards and devotees (*qūrchīyān-i bā-ikhlās*) who devoured the corpse of Shaybani Khan, the Uzbek leader, in a cannibalistic frenzy at the command of Ismail.[9]

Such tales were nostalgically circulated throughout Tahmasb's reign to convey the extraordinary *ikhlās* of the first generation. Granted, these stories were embellished and made into legend over time, as seen in the series of later Safavid-era "heroic chronicles" of the reigns of Shah Ismail and Shah Tahmasb. Yet by highlighting important social values they hold clues as to how the social cohesion of militarized Sufi orders such as the Safavids was fostered.[10]

As we saw in Chapter 3, betrayal of the Sufi king, whom some of the Qizilbash chiefs viewed as their *valī-yi ni'mat* (divine patron), was defined as *kufr*, a capital sacrilege, and the one guilty of such a transgression was castigated as a *kāfar-i ni'mat* (one who has become an unbeliever because of ingratitude to his patron). These concepts, including *ikhlās*, were firmly rooted in Qur'anic ideas and interpretations that impacted the era's political theology.

[8] See note 15 in the Introduction on the definitions of *ikhlās* and for other important philological information.

[9] Munshī Qazvīnī, *Javāhir al-Akhbār*, 114–15, recorded the story of a Zu al-Qadr warrior retold by the Keeper of the Royal Seal Shah Quli Khalifah Muhrdar, who was of the same tribe. To show his "*ikhlās*" the young groom abandoned his wedding at once, gathered his weapons, and set out to join Ismail. Shah Quli adds that the warrior was elevated to a great rank. Barbaro and Contarini, *Travels to Tana and Persia*, 49:114–15; Khvāndamīr, *Tārīkh-i Shāh Ismā'īl*, 70–72; Shahzad Bashir, "Shah Isma'il and the Qizilbash: Cannibalism in the Religious History of Early Safavid Iran," *History of Religions* 45, no. 3 (2006): 234–56; Qummī, *Khulāsat al-Tavārīkh*, 1:83; Shīrāzī, *Takmilat al-Akhbār*, 43.

[10] *Tārīkh-i 'Ālam'ārā-yi Safavī*; *'Ālam'ārāy-i Shāh Ismā'īl*; *'Ālam'ārā-yi Shāh Tahmāsb: Zindagī-i Dāstānī Duvvumīn Pādishāh-i Dawrah-i Safavī*, ed. Īraj Afshār (Tehran: Dunyā-i Kitāb, 1370).

4.3 LOYALTY AND THE CREATOR

The concept of *ikhlās* in the Qur'an often arises in reference to those who embody it, *al-mukhlasīn*, suggesting it was recognized as an abstraction of absolute faithfulness to their one true Creator.[11] In fact, *ikhlās* is so elemental to the fabric of humankind's spiritual and moral world, it is referenced at the moment of human creation. In a conversation with God about His intention to create humanity, Satan admits he has no power over God's servants that have *ikhlās*, the *mukhlasīn*:

Behold, thy Lord said to the angels: "I am about to create man from clay: When I have fashioned him [in due proportion] and breathed into him of My spirit, fall ye down in obeisance unto him."

So the angels prostrated themselves, all of them together: Not so Iblis [Satan]: He was haughty, and became one of those who reject Faith.

[GOD:] O Iblis! What prevents thee from prostrating thyself to one whom I have created with my hands? Art thou haughty? Or art thou one of the high [and mighty] ones?

[IBLIS:] I am better than he: Thou createdst me from fire, and him Thou createdst from clay.

[GOD:] Then get thee out from here: For thou art rejected, accursed. And My curse shall be on thee till the Day of Judgment.

[IBLIS:] O my Lord! Give me then respite till the Day the [dead] are raised.

[GOD:] Respite, then, is granted thee, till the Day of the Time Appointed.

[IBLIS:] Then, by Thy power, I will put them all in the wrong, except Thy servants amongst them, sincere and purified (*al-mukhlasīn*).

(Qur'an 38:71–83)[12]

[11] For example, in Qur'an 15:40, 37:128, 38:83, 39:2, 12:24 (on the prophet Joseph), 19:51 (on the prophet Moses), 37:40 (in some exegetical writings, this section is tied to a broader commitment to absolute monotheism (*tawhīd*) and exemplified in the Surat al-Ikhlas). For instance, in a hadith narrated by Abu Sa'id al-Khudri, "A man heard another man reciting: Surat ul-ikhlās (The Unity) 'Say: He is Allah, the One,' and he was repeating it. The next morning, he came to Allah's Apostle and mentioned the whole story to him as if he regarded the recitation of that Sura as insufficient. On that, Allah's Apostle said, 'By Him in Whose Hand my soul is! That [Qur'an 112] equals one-third of the Qur'an.'" Muhammad b. Ismā'īl b. Bukhārī, *Sahīh al-Bukhārī: The Translation of the Meanings of Sahīh al-Bukhārī: Arabic–English*, trans. Muhammad Muhsin Khan (Riyadh: Dār al-Salām, 1997), book 83, hadith 6643, 8:338.

[12] The conversation between God and Iblis occurs in a similar manner in Surat al-Hijr. Iblis's banishment has been a rich subject of exegetical literature. One of the most prominent commentaries of the medieval era that drew upon the previous interpretations and influenced later mystical exegesis was *Kashf al-Asrār* by Rashīd al-Dīn Maybudī (reprinted and translated several times). He draws on this dramatic story to convey that God expects

Satan recognizes that the *mukhlasīn* are a distinct group within the larger community of believers. In the Qur'an, then, *ikhlās* emerges as a quality that safeguards those who possess it against disobedience to the Creator. Herein lies its political import: It presents *ikhlās* as an important quality that secures the possessor against the breaking of a bond, be it spiritual or political.

The Qur'an reveals that a distinct group, such as the prophets, exemplify this bond to the Creator. The prophets Muhammad, Joseph, and Moses, for example, are paradigms of faithfulness and submission in the holy text for their embodiment of *ikhlās*.[13]

Qur'anic commentaries on prophetic *ikhlās*, especially Sufi ones, were widespread in the centuries before the rise of the Safavids. The Safavids were particularly receptive to such interpretations and in fact benefited from several Sufi interpretations of *ikhlās* in formulating their political theology.

One such Sufi exegete was Sheikh Abu al-Qasim al-Qushayri (d. 465/1072), an influential Sufi who clarified much of the lexica of Sufism employed by later mystics. He states that "according to an authentic tradition, 'The Prophet – may God bless and greet him – said on the authority of Gabriel, who spoke on the authority of God Most High – praise be to Him – who said: "*Ikhlās* is the greatest mystery that I have deposited in the hearts of those servants of Mine whom I love."'" Al-Qushayri after recording a long line of transmission, reports a hadith that explicitly highlights the political significance of *ikhlās* in its bridging the spiritual and political realms: "The Messenger of God – may God bless and greet him – said: 'There are three things that prevent the heart of the believer from disloyalty: *ikhlās* in his actions to God, counseling those in power, and always holding on to the community of Muslims.'" *Ikhlās* is thus seen in a concentric arrangement of loyalties: *ikhlās* to the Creator at the center prevents one from severing their spiritual tie to God; then *ikhlās* to the just exercise of power keeps one connected to justice; and lastly *ikhlās* to the maintenance of ties in the community of the faithful holds the community together.[14]

The preservation of the sacred bond to the Creator at the center of it all, however, hinges on humankind's submission and devotion to Him,

loyalty (*ikhlās*) from His servants and points to the dismal predicament that has befallen humanity since the disobedience of Iblis as well as Adam. Maybudī, *Kashf al-Asrār*, 5:301–3.

13 For example, Qur'an 12:24, 19:51.

14 Qushayrī, *Risālah-i Qushayriyyah*, 322–27. For other relevant Sufi treatises, see, for instance, Kubrā, *Fawā'ih al-Jamāl*; Isfarāyinī, *Kāshif al-Asrār*; al-'Abbādī, *al-Tasfiyah*.

and the subsequent reward for faithfulness or punishment for ingratitude (*kufr*). This point is clarified in another passage of the Qurʾan, when the Creator speaks to Muhammad:

> Say: [unto them, O Muhammad,] "Verily, I am commanded to serve God with sincere devotion; And, I am commanded to be the first of those who bow to God in Islam." Say: "I would, if I disobeyed my Lord, indeed have fear of the Penalty of a Mighty Day." Say: "It is God I serve, with my sincere [and exclusive] devotion." (Qurʾan 39:11–14)

In the transcendental dialectic, therefore, *ikhlās* and submission are intimately linked as revealed by the devotion of the Prophet – the archetypal creation, the apotheosis of humanity – to his Creator.

Deeply influenced by the Prophet's life and their esoteric interpretations of the Qurʾan, Sufis recognized *ikhlās* as one of the *maqāmāt* (spiritual stations) and a sine qua non on the path of transcendence. Along with other stations such as repentance (*tawba*), patience (*sabr*), and trust in God (*tawakkul*), *ikhlās* marked a progression of behavioral, emotional, and psychological breakthroughs that the disciple (*murīd*) attains on the path to spiritual ascension. Sufi thought had fundamentally shaped the Safavids' political culture and their understanding of loyalty. Such concepts in Sufism proved useful for creating categories to help regulate political interactions. Terms such as *muqarrabān* in reference to the members of their inner circle (from the Sufi concept *qurba*), *sālik* (a Sufi disciple, a reference to a Qizilbash warrior), and *sūfī-garī* (adherence to Sufi codes of behavior) provided the spiritual hermeneutic needed to consecrate their political language with a deep connection to their Sufi heritage – a source of their social power.

4.4 DEVOTIONAL LOYALTY IN THE POLITICAL REALM

However much the Safavid political men wanted to honor the obligation of gratitude owed to their Sufi king for his *niʿmat* as a divine intermediary, transactional loyalty was easily shaken by the winds of fortune. Appealing to sacred concepts such as *ikhlās* and *shukr al-niʿmat* were reflections of their attempts to inhibit severance of their ties during difficult times.

While the chiefs' obedience and loyalty to join the confederacy limited their political power, the bargain offered them wealth, prestige, and the protection of a powerful patron. Their loyalty also produced a greater level of collective ideological strength that created long-term consistent political and military cooperation. During the 940s/1530s and 950s/1540s, in the early years of Shah Tahmasb's reign, when the Safavid confederacy had fractured, enough of the chiefs were convinced of the shah's authority to remain in the confederacy. Many had not forgotten the unity they had enjoyed during Shah Ismail's conquests. They had routed the larger and more experienced armies of the Aqquyunlus, the Shirvanshahis, and the Uzbeks. They saw those years as the old days of glory, conviction, and faith. Finding ways to prevent disloyalty was key in retrieving that unity.

In a political order with spiritual roots, moral liabilities were compelling and proved advantageous in deterring disloyalty. A clear sign of this is when we find that the regulating force to inhibit severance of consecrated ties is none other than the members of the order themselves who hold one another accountable. Most Qizilbash chiefs were not compelled to remain loyal because their loyalty was preconfigured for them as sacred to serve their political relations as needed; it was the transcendental value that they assigned to those ties that made their contravention morally liable.

When, for instance, in 936/1530 in the chaos of the civil war, Zulfiqar Beg of the powerful Mawsullu tribe with a prominent lineage (he was the son of Nukhud Sultan son of Gulabi Beg, loyal chiefs of Ismail) became convinced that he could carve out Baghdad while Tahmasb struggled to survive amidst his warring chiefs, his brothers, ʿAli Beg and Ahmad Beg, wanted to remain loyal to the shah. Reaching an impasse, they conspired to murder their brother. One night when Zulfiqar Beg was in his sleeping chamber, they seized the opportunity to slip into his bed chamber and cut him down. They severed his head and brought it to Tahmasb to show their *ikhlās*.[15]

Murdering one's brother must have been incredibly difficult even considering the extreme level of violence to which these men were accustomed. Their show of loyalty was characterized as *ikhlās* and made a strong enough impression on Tahmasb that he retained Ahmad Beg for service close to him at court and appointed ʿAli Beg to the governorship of Savah and Jurbadiqan. He then, as was expected of him, proceeded to

[15] Munshī Qazvīnī, *Javāhir al-Akhbār*, 158–59; Tahmāsb Safavī, *Tazkirah-i Shāh Tahmāsb*, 59; Rūmlū, *Ahsan al-Tavārīkh*, 3:1223; Qummī, *Khulāsat al-Tavārīkh*, 188–89. As bloody rivalries among brothers and cousins were common in court societies, it is, however, unclear whether Zulfiqar Beg was their half or full brother.

make an example of the rebels. Whomever the brothers endorsed he pardoned but put the rest to the sword.[16]

Switching loyalties, however, was not a move that political men took lightly. Devotional loyalty was such an important concept, and its betrayal such a crime, that chiefs usually found it difficult to trust tiebreakers, men who betrayed their patrons. Even so, they were ready to exploit any opportunity that switching loyalties produced. Tahmasb was particularly skilled at this. When his brother Prince Alqas in 953/1546 rebelled against him, for example, one of Alqas's retainers, Aruj Aqa of the Rumlu tribe, fled to inform Tahmasb of Alqas's plan. The chiefs present at court did not find Aruj's intentions of loyalty to the shah to be genuine and urged that he be apprehended and sent back to the prince for retribution. Tahmasb, however, disagreed: "How could I be so unjust as to disgrace a group who has come to express their *ikhlās*. If it becomes known [that I turned them away], no one else would come forth [i.e., defect]." Tahmasb promoted the informant, instead. He was right. His decision to protect Aruj Aqa and make him his client paid off, for soon thereafter Sultan Mahmud Mirza and Karam Mirza with their riders broke with Alqas and joined the royal camp.[17]

4.5 PATRONAGE AND THE ARTIFICE OF POWER

Lasting patronage without assurances of loyalty was untenable. Shah Tahmasb and his inner circle certainly were aware of how tenuous their hold on the chiefs' loyalty was – the very basis of patronage. This is discernable in their usage of the language of loyalty to create the illusion of power and patronage for Tahmasb in an attempt to inhibit disloyalty among the chiefs. In 941/1533-34, for instance, with the order near collapsing as Tahmasb struggled to hold together the Qizilbash confederacy, he sent a dispatch to Zainal Beg, one of his chiefs in an eastern frontier province. As mentioned above, the Safavids were amidst a two-front invasion by a large Ottoman army from the west and the Uzbeks from the east. These invasions severely strained the Qizilbash chiefs' ties to their shah, causing several of them to defect and aid the Safavids' archenemies in eliminating the Safavid order from the political scene. The letter is exceedingly insecure and lacks authority compared to his letters in the

[16] Munshī Qazvīnī, *Javāhir al-Akhbār*, 156–59; Qummī, *Khulāsat al-Tavārīkh*, 190.
[17] Munshī Qazvīnī, *Javāhir al-Akhbār*, 198–99.

second half of his reign. Its repeated appeal for loyalty displays uncertainty and divulges the dismal state of his ties to the chiefs.

> May the great amir Zainal Beg, who has been privileged with receiving infinite royal munificence, know that the demonstration of his devotional loyalty (*ikhlās*), faithfulness to the state, and sincerity has once again been manifested upon the radiant heart of the shining sun [Shah Tahmasb], which has caused a surge of royal generosity in his regard.
>
> He [Zainal Beg] must, with all his capacity, be of aid and bound by oath in exalting the land; strive in expressing truthfulness; and day by day make apparent to friends and foes the obligations of self-sacrifice, so that the level of his trustworthiness may reach its pinnacle … be hopeful [of our beneficence] and send forth day-to-day reports concerning [your] district. Inscribed in 6/20/941 [December 27, 1534].[18]

Tahmasb's ministers who were behind composing the letter attempt to create an illusion of power and patronage demonstrating that their Sufi king is a capable patron who can provide "infinite royal munificence" to faithful clients who honor their "obligations of self-sacrifice."

The Safavid ministers, who knew how to employ the language of power, tried to create a larger shadow out of Tahmasb's diminished power. They often present him in the royal missives as someone who could provide his Qizilbash chiefs with protection, material well-being, sociopolitical advancement, and all the prestige and pride that accompanied royal favor in exchange for their submission, loyalty, and service.

Sometimes, however, the ruler's assertion of dominance and demand of loyalty reveals more of his deficiency in power than capability. Appeals to valor and masculinity often accompany such demonstrations of power at times of weakness. Even the ministers of Shah Ismail, the charismatic founder of the dynasty, found recourse to this approach helpful when they faced the calamity of their time. After the disastrous rout at Chaldiran when Shah Ismail was trying to assemble his commanders against a possible new offensive by the Ottoman Sultan Selim in 923/1517, he sent a missive to Shahab al-Din ʿUmar Beg of the Zu al-Qadr tribe summoning him and his family to join his camp. He writes:

> Shahab al-Din has been subject of [our] boundless royal patronage; know that prior to this time, [officials] had related [your] devotional loyalty (*ikhlās*) to this

[18] TSMA, E. 8324, in Lajos Fekete and György Hazai, eds., *Einführung in die Persische Paläographie: 101 Persische Dokumente*, trans. Manfred Lorenz (Budapest: Akadémiai Kiadó, 1977), 375–77.

[Safavid] house of blessing and guidance. Thus, our kingly attention and royal patronage in your regard is at its height; be assured and with hope come to the august court with your brothers and nephews ... without apprehension and distress, for having revenge as aim [against the Ottomans] for the honor of [your] house is considered noble and chivalrous. Without any doubt regarding aforementioned [assurances], you will be privileged with royal rewards.

With purity of intention and true creed seize the opportunity and come forth without delay for all of our august effort and benefaction is dedicated to exalting you with infinite royal generosity in such a manner that will be the envy of the world, so that the splendor of your rank will become apparent to all.[19]

Ismail was a shattered man at the time of sending this letter. He had lost many of his inner circle three years earlier on the plane of Chaldiran where the Qizilbash army was finally defeated under his command. As discussed earlier, the defeat destroyed his aura of invincibility and was a turning point in the Qizilbash confederacy's sense of solidarity. Ismail would not take to the battlefield again and drank himself into an early grave at the age of thirty-seven.[20]

Neither Ismail nor his son Tahmasb's inner circle, who helped craft these letters, were so naive as to expect that appealing to devotional loyalty in exchange for continued patronage would be enough to keep the chiefs from reneging on their commitments. Sometimes, they sent agents to make sure their ties of loyalty held. When in 947/1540, for example, Tahmasb was suspicious of the governor Kamal al-Din Yaʿqub Beg's loyalty, he dispatched the courtier Fasih al-Din Muhammad to investigate. Upon receiving the envoy's reportage, Tahmasb sent a letter to the chief reassuring him that

Amir Fasih al-Din Muhammad arrived at the court of the world-refuge portraying [your] *ikhlās*, truthfulness, devoted service, and faithfulness to the state (*nīkū-bandagī va dawlat-khvāhī*) upon the mirror of the sun's heart [i.e., Tahmasb], which resulted in the increasing of compassion and kindness in [your] regard. Upon this very path may [you] tred and in the majestic path of service and self-sacrifice (*khidmat-kārī va jān-sipārī*) remain unwavering.

Tahmasb then reassures him of further patronage: "by no means allow any distress and trepidation to come upon [your] thoughts; be completely self-

[19] TSMA, E. 9670, in ibid., 335–38; see a similar appeal to loyalty at times of crises in Shah Ismail's letter to Ghiyath al-Din Hamzah Beg dated 920/1514 in Muhammad Rizā Nāsirī, "Chand Sanad-i Tarīkhī," *Barrasī'hā-yi Tārīkhī* 9, no. 5 (1353/1974-5): 113–36.

[20] The Battle of Ghujduvan in 918/1512 was the Safavids' first defeat, but Shah Ismail was not present. He later returned at the head of his army and routed the Uzbeks, further enhancing his warrior charisma in the eyes of his fighters.

assured and hopeful of boundless royal generosity. And [you] may send forth petitions to the grand majestic court."[21]

Like Kamal al-Din, the majority of Qizilbash leaders were not treacherous men under ordinary circumstances. They obeyed the Safavid court's directives for the most part as military governors in terms of facilitating the production, consumption, and exchange of goods, providing basic security in their districts, and supplying fighting men at times of war. They were not, however, such champions of political virtue as to allow moral codes to constrain their ambition for power when opportunities presented themselves, and especially in times of war they proved exceedingly fickle. Their patron-client relationships, however, brought with them clear expectations in order to counter such unpredictability and to induce cooperation. One prominent feature was the dyad of generous patronage for acts of loyalty and dishonorable death for acts of treachery.

4.6 THE DYAD OF REWARD AND PUNISHMENT

The Safavid political elite knew the channels to the exercise of power and they ran through somewhat predictable outlets. Reward for loyalty, for instance, and severe punishment for disloyalty was the time-honored pattern for patrons to project power, persuade, and induce their client's cooperation. Hence, when they undertook an act of devotional loyalty, they expected to be rewarded.

ʿAli Beg and Ahmad Beg's decision to murder their brother when he tried to betray Tahmasb and seize Baghdad was framed as an act of *ikhlās*, and we saw how well Tahmasb patronized them. Indeed, conspicuous rewards for acts of devotional loyalty offered an opportunity for Tahmasb to project power and win clients on whose loyalty he could count long term. For instance, the account of his cousin Hussein Khan, who attempted to betray him by defecting to the Ottomans, that we left unsettled at the beginning of the chapter is an excellent instance of how Tahmasb created exceptionally loyal clients.

Even though Tahmasb and his council must have known that challenging Hussein Khan directly was dangerous, for if they harmed him, they ran the risk of facing a legitimate rebellion by the Shamlu tribesmen, they planned to make an example of him. Hussein Khan was all too aware of

[21] TSMA, E. 8924, in Fekete and Hazai, eds., *Einführung in die Persische Paläographie*, 395–96.

his own rising power in relation to the much-weakened Tahmasb to perceive the danger, and when they finally summoned him to the royal tent, he arrived completely unaware that his treachery had been uncovered.

In the tent waited one of Tahmasb's inner circle, the head of the royal guards (*qūrchī-bāshī*) Savinduk Beg Afshar, as well as Tahmasb's brother Alqas. After a brief exchange, Savinduk Beg suddenly thrust his dagger into Hussein Khan's side. Prince Alqas then cut him down with his sword.[22] Afterwards, they cut off his head and tossed it outside into the camp, inflicting a disgraceful death upon the powerful chief for his attempted treachery. Qanbar Ughli, a royal guard, then picked up the severed head and placed it on a spear to parade it about the camp.[23]

Hussein Khan's aides-de-camp Hasan Aqa and Shaʿban Aqa were the informants who had told the shah that their chief intended to defect, effectively sealing his fate. They had no reason to expect that Tahmasb and his house would survive the war with the Ottomans and that Tahmasb could guarantee their patronage. Such rewards, of course, would have entered into their calculations. Their steadfastness not to betray their shah during his moment of weakness, thus, exemplified *ikhlās* from the shah's perspective even though they had betrayed their own patron.[24]

For their *ikhlās* in helping to bring down a powerful rival, Tahmasb elevated Hasan Aqa from a guard (*qūrchī*) to the coveted post of guardianship (*lalagī*) and councilor (*vakīl*) of his brother Prince Bahram, who was now placed in charge of the Shamlus. He also appointed Shaʿban Aqa as military mayor of Isfahan (*dārūghah*), a prosperous town whose resources Tahmasb needed and incorporated into crown domain at that time. Remarkably, the Shamlus did not revolt, indicating that the lesser Shamlu chieftains were given sufficient incentives to remain loyal when Tahmasb reassigned them to Prince Bahram.[25]

22 Munshī Qazvīnī, *Javāhir al-Akhbār*, 174; Qummī, *Khulāsat al-Tavārīkh*, 1:236; Rūmlū, *Ahsan al-Tavārīkh*, 2:331–32.

23 Rūmlū, *Ahsan al-Tavārīkh*, 3:1222–23; Qummī, *Khulāsat al-Tavārīkh*, 1: 236; Munshī Qazvīnī, *Javāhir al-Akhbār*, 174.

24 Munshī Qazvīnī, *Javāhir al-Akhbār*, 172–74. The group designated as *āqāyān* generally corresponds to the middle stratum of Safavid court society and served various duties. Hasan Aqa, for example, was a guard (*qūrchī*) and the bearer of his patron's arrows and bow (*qūrchī-yi tīr va kamān*).

25 Munshi Qazvini later refers to Hasan Aqa only as *vakīl*, suggesting that his position as *lalah* might have only been temporary since Bahram Mirza's previous *lalah*, Ghazi Khan Takallu, had defected to the Ottomans at the time of Hasan Aqa's appointment (*Javāhir al-Akhbār*, 186). Shaʿban Aqa appears to have not held the post for long as others such as

Tahmasb had made a daring gamble and won. His political victory secured something valuable for his survival – the assertion of his power and authority as the chief of all chiefs capable of executing the most powerful among them. The illusion of power and patronage that Hussein Khan's elimination produced, and the reward that the informants gained, helped set the course for Tahmasb to become the pivot of a religiopolitical patronage system that was taking shape.

4.7 THE QIZILBASH REUNIFICATION

Now that we have seen the nature of devotional loyalty in the political environment and the patron-client relationship that intersected the spiritual-political plane, let us examine what the political effects of this patronage were on the early Safavids' attempt to stabilize their political realm and strengthen their hold on power. While it is impossible to prove a direct causation between loyalty and dynastic success, it is clear that by appealing to the twin bonds of *ikhlās* and obligation of *niʿmat*, Tahmasb and his high command were able put together a committed political regime in a patronage system that appeared to its participants sufficiently genuine and equitable.

Undoubtedly, the Safavid political system experienced a high degree of stability in the aftermath of the Peace of Amasya with the Ottoman Empire in 962/1555. Fending off the most powerful army of the early modern world was not easy and forced the Qizilbash chiefs to develop strategies to form stronger ties to survive. Their patronage system facilitated that process and offered them predictable models of interaction regulated by moral codes such as *ikhlās* and *niʿmat*. Furthermore, the court's decision to transfer the capital from Tabriz, which was too close to the Ottoman border, to Qazvin further east, and away from the entrenched power interests of the old Tabrizi network of notables, brought about a sense of a new beginning.

Initially, the appointment of Qizilbash chiefs to govern important provinces and economic hubs when Tahmasb ascended the throne, with a few exceptions, had a high rate of turnover due to insubordination to Tahmasb and elimination by rival chiefs during the civil war. By the mid-930s/1530s, however, when Tahmasb and his inner circle emerged dominant

Khavajah Niʿmatullah Malamari, who was appointed vizier of Isfahan when the city became a crownland (*khāssah*) in 940/1534, managed it from 942/1535 to 955/1548.

from the chaos, they made a series of new appointments, and in the following two decades subdued and absorbed several local dynasties like the Mushaʿshaʿa in Khuzistan in the southwest, and Kar Kiyas of Gilan in the northern forests.[26]

What was extraordinary about these appointments is that even though they were made at a time when Tahmasb lacked political authority and

[26] There are several revealing royal communications with Qizilbash chiefs that illustrate how Shah Tahmasb tried to secure a frontier chief's loyalty and submission by patronage and projection of power. One letter in particular is a decree of appointment sent to Shams al-Din Khan at a time when Tahmasb was facing an Uzbek invasion of Khurasan in 940/1533 and urgently needed support. The decree appoints Shams al-Din to his father's position of chief (*khān*) due to the latter's death. This letter reveals the general statement of power and patronage that the early Safavid state-builders formulated in their negotiations with the military chiefs. As such it contains the following three components that are often found in such letters: the assertion of the shah's dominance as a resourceful king capable of offering patronage and protection in time of disunity (section 1); patronage (i.e., an appointment in this case) and the imposition of obligation of loyalty (section 2); and demand of service often followed by a pledge of future patronage in exchange for continued loyal service and obedience (section 3).

> [1] Decreed the August Prince that the Splendor of the Dignitaries Hajji Sharaf al-Din Aqa had been privileged with the receiving of infinite royal bounty. Know that all the majestic strengths [of the shah] is [*sic*] employed so that the loyal servants of this lofty [Safavid] house could be in the cradle of safety and security. And when the absolved [and] departed Sharaf Khan, who had been a continual recipient of kingly affection and whose patronage (*tarbiyat*) was observed daily by all as we privileged him with infinite royal benefaction.
>
> [2] At this time that he has honored God's Invitation to return, we grant the deceased's official post, treasury, and lands to his son, the refuge of state and governance, and the virtuous of the nobles Shams al-Din Khan as we enlisted [you] into the order of chiefs (*silk-i khanan*), and God-willing, glory be to Him, we shall patronize [you] in such a fashion the increase of which could not be imagined.
>
> [3] [You] must be hopeful of our support and do [your] utmost to protect the province so with the aid of God Almighty, the affairs of Khurasan will be ordered upon the aspirations of [our] loyalists and partisans. Be assured that we shall set course in that direction; [in the meantime] undertake the commands of the royal companions, and until the arrival of the Princely troops, send forth news of the region. Await [our] kingly favors and mercy [and] do not be wanting. Inscribed in Rabi' al-thani, 940/ October, 1533. (Topkapi Sarayi Müzesi Arşivi, E. 5698, in Fekete and Hazai, eds., *Einführung in die Persische Paläographie*, 371–73)

I have not been able to verify to which district of Khurasan exactly Shams al-Din was appointed, for governorship of Herat seems unlikely even though the city's governance was chaotic and changed hands four times in the span of seven years until the appointment of Muhammad Sharaf al-Din Takallu in 943/1537, who held it for nearly twenty years. See Mīrzā Naqī Nasīrī, *Titles and Emoluments in Safavid Iran: A Third Manual of Safavid Administration*, ed. and trans. Willem Floor (Washington, DC: Mage Publishers, 2008), 200–204. For the sake of clarity, the convention of using the third-person singular pronoun is translated as second-person singular.

FIGURE 4.1 Appointments to major provincial centers

military power, they lasted unusually long, an average of twenty years. Bayandur Khan, chief of the Talish, for instance, held his post as the governor of Astara in the north for over forty years (946–89/1539–81).[27] Shah Quli Sultan of the Afshar tribe governed Kirman for twenty-six years. In no other period in the history of the Safavids was there such constancy in provincial governance and state offices (the tenures in Tahmasb's inner circle also mirror this phenomenon as discussed in Chapter 5). These are shown in the figures below. The closest we come to such lengthy governorships is during the reign of Tahmasb's grandson ʿAbbas I, who is credited with inaugurating the Safavid "golden age" due to unprecedented political stability and economic prosperity.[28]

Figure 4.1 shows the distribution of governorships of major cities and commercial hubs among chiefs of the paramount tribes of the Qizilbash confederacy (Ustajlu, Zu al-Qadr, Afshar, Takallu, Talish).[29] Heads of the

[27] Ibid., 149–50. Astara would remain preserved for the Talish until 1014/1605 when the city became a crownland, and according to Iskandar Beg until 1039/1630 Bayandur Khan's descendants held this post.

[28] Ibid., 214–15.

[29] Notes on the appointments: Khuzistan, also referred to as ʿArabistan, was centered at the towns of Huvayzah and Dizful under Sayyid Bakran Shujaʿ al-Din b. Sayyid Fallah (930–48/1524–42) and later Mawla Sajjad b. Sayyid Badran (948–95/1542–87) (ibid.,

FIGURE 4.2 Appointment of crownland and provincial governors

other major tribes, Qajar, Rumlu, Shamlu, Turkman, and Mawsullu (not shown here), also held important military-state positions close to the center of power and throughout their newly acquired territories. This resulted in the creation of a balance of power among the main Qizilbash tribes, which the civil war had destroyed. The chiefs' long-held loyalty and service ensured steady tax revenues and supplies of trained, reliable troops during times of conflict.

Similarly, Figure 4.2 shows that Tahmasb's court secured the submission of major frontier provinces that were governed by established local houses such as the Mushaʿshaʿa in Khuzistan in the south, the Ardalans of Kurdistan to the west, and in the northern mountains, the Kar Kiyas of eastern Gilan. The Kar Kiyas held fast in an uneasy allegiance with the

142–46); Sista, also referred to as Sijistan, was a large province far from Safavid control. Tahmasb appointed Ahmad Sultan Shamlu (943–57/1536–50) to govern four out of twelve of its districts of Garmsir, Khvash, Khushkrud, and Nih-va-Bandan (ibid., 275–78); Kurdistan: Surkhab Beg (946–75/1540–58), who accepted the Safavid lordship, controlled the regions of Sanandaj, Hashli, Sulaymaniyah, and Marivan (ibid., 225–28).

Safavid house due to their close history. They had sheltered the young Ismail when his cousins, the Aqquyunlus, sought to eliminate him. The Kar Kiyas were mostly absorbed and pacified by the early eleventh/seventeenth century under ʿAbbas I, who pursued greater centralization of the state and wanted to bring the northern territories under his control. Figure 4.2 also shows the conversion of Isfahan, Yazd, and Qum to "crownlands" governed and taxed directly by the court.[30]

Having the long-term loyalty of powerful provincial governors guaranteed steady sources of revenue, political cooperation, and reliable troops. It produced, moreover, a renewed sense of solidarity among the Qizilbash confederates at times of war. This was most evident in the three years leading up to the monumental Peace Treaty of Amasya in 962/1555.[31] A Qizilbash commander who was also a court historian and member of the royal guards (*qūrchī*), Hasan the grandson of the prominent Rumlu chief Amir Sultan (governor of Qazvin, later the second Safavid capital), provides careful details of the military affairs of this period, especially during the Ottoman invasion that led to the peace accord. His report reveals a new level of cooperation among the tribes not experienced since the days of Ismail. As may be recalled, conflict with the powerful Ottoman Empire was one major trigger that tested the Qizilbash chiefs' loyalty.[32]

Hasan Rumlu meticulously records his fellow Qizilbash chieftains, who showed up to the royal camp, and their assignments to repel the new Ottoman invasion. We learn that in 959/1552 the tribes that joined the

[30] Taxes were such an important issue that Tahmasb exempted the population of the burden and had the decree inscribed in stone and placed in the Friday mosque (see Khafipour, "Beyond Charismatic Authority"). Yazd became a crownland from 946/1539 onward and was governed by viziers. Muhammad Sharif Tehrani was the first at this appointment and held it for sixteen years (Nasīrī, *Titles and Emoluments*, 300–302); see also Muhammad Mufīd Mustawfī Bāfqī, *Jāmiʿ-i Mufīdī*, 3 vols., ed. Īraj Afshār (Tehran: Asātīr, 1385), 3:167–77, in which Bafqi reports another date for Tehrani's tenure.

[31] Mikheil Svanidze, "The Amasya Peace Treaty between the Ottoman Empire and Iran (June 1, 1555) and Georgia," *Bulletin of the Georgian National Academy of Sciences* 3, no. 1 (2009): 191–97. The treaty was honored while Tahmasb was alive but discarded soon after his death at the onset of another Ottoman invasion. Monshi, *History of Shah ʿAbbas the Great*, 129–31; Allouche, *Origins of the Ottoman-Safavid Conflict*.

[32] It is clear how tenuous Tahmasb's command was in preserving the confederacy's cohesion in the fact that three years earlier, in a military review that took place in 936/1530, major tribes gathered to show their support (such as the Qajars, who could field as many as 6,000 riders; the Ustajlus 16,000; Turkmans 1,000 (underreported); Afshars 6,000; Zu al-Qadr 8,000; in addition to other smaller clans and Mazandarani and Georgian contingents). See, for instance, Qummī, *Khulāsat al-Tavārīkh*, 1:198–206; Floor, *Government Institutions*, 134–36.

defense were formerly hostile toward each other during the civil war:[33] Shahvirdi Sultan Ziyad Ughli and Shah Quli Beg of the Qajar tribe; Badr Khan, Shah Quli Sultan, and Amir Ghaib of the Ustajlu tribe; Muhammad Beg of the Turkmans; Adham Beg and Qanqara Sultan of the Rumlus; Khalifah Ansar of the Qarajah-Daghlu; Alagh Khan (or Beg) of the Saʿdlus; and Zulfiqar Beg of Pazuk. When the main Ottoman army from Istanbul approached and camped at Nakhchivan in 961/1553-54, members of the Safavid family such as Sultan Ibrahim Mirza, Sultan Hussein Mirza, and Maʿsum Beg Safavi, along with military court officials Shah Quli Khalifah Zu al-Qadr (Keeper of the Royal Seal) and their troops composed of the elites selected from various the Qizilbash tribes, joined the camp.[34]

A later report states that when Tahmasb reviewed his forces to prepare to defend against the invasion, 40,000 riders were at his command, a substantial force compared to twenty years prior when he could retain the loyalty of only 7,000 men to face the Ottomans.[35]

The Safavids' guerilla warfare wreaked havoc on the exhausted Ottoman troops' morale and the wide campaign of scorching the earth and poisoning the wells further deprived the massive Ottoman army of food and fodder. The elite Qizilbash contingent under the command of Tahmasb's eldest son and heir apparent Ismail Mirza was then able to route a large contingent of Ottomans under vizier Iskandar Pasha's command and force them to retreat. It was during this campaign that Sultan Suleyman and his high command reached the realization that the invasion of Iran was too costly and unsustainable. The subsequent Peace of Amasya

[33] The Rumlus were led into the conflict by Div Sultan, who was Tahmasb's designated royal tutor (*lalah*); the Ustajlu tribe was led by Köpek Sultan, the governor of Tabriz; Chuha Sultan and Ghazi Khan led the Takkalus with Isfahan as the tribe's stronghold; and Hussein Khan, whose downfall was discussed in Section 4.6, led the Shamlus of Khurasan.

[34] Rūmlū, *Ahsan al-Tavārīkh*, 1354–60, 1371–75; *Tārīkh-i Qizilbāshān*, 56–57. I have not been able to further verify tribal designations of other commanders, such as Quli Beg Ichak Ughli, Ibrahim Khalifah Alpavut, and Allah Hamzah Beg, who participated in the campaign.

[35] Monshi, *History of Shah ʿAbbas the Great*, 129; Floor, *Government Institutions*, 134–36; Tahmāsb Safavī, *Tazkirah-i Shāh Tahmāsb*, 82–83, on the march back to Tabriz in 939/1532-3. For more information on Qizilbash tribes during the reign of Tahmasb, see Faruk Sümer, *Naqsh-i Turkān-i Ānātulī dar Tashkīl va Tawsiʿah-i Dawlat-i Safavī (Safevi Devletinin Kurulusu ve Gelismesinde Anadolu Turklerinin Rolu)*, trans. Ihsān Ishrāqī and Muhammad Taqī Imāmī (Tehran: Nashr-i Gustarah, 1371), 105–31. For other insights into the Safavid military, see, for example, Haneda, *Le Châh et les Qizilbāš*; Hūshang Jalālī, *Tārīkh-i Nizāmī-i Īrān az Dawrah-i Safavī tā Pāyān-i Difāʿ-i Muqaddas* (Tehran: Īrān-i Sabz, 1389); Khānbābā Bayānī, *Tārīkh-i Nizāmī-i Īrān: Dawrah-i Safaviyyah* (Tehran: Tulūʿ-i Qalam, 1379).

between the two states was the rational outcome and an indication of a shift in the power dynamics of the region. The peace treaty brought an end to nearly half a century of hostility and held fast for the remainder of Tahmasb's life.

Sultan Suleyman's final campaign against the Safavids had failed to dethrone Tahmasb and force a change in geopolitics of the region. The reunification of the Qizilbash confederation and the stability in the provincial governance – the result of the relative success of the patronage system that Tahmasb sustained – were the primary reasons for the Ottoman defeat and the resulting Peace of Amasya.

By the mid-tenth/sixteenth century, the young king had survived the bloody civil war, managed to stabilize the political system, and forced the Ottoman Empire to change, for the time being, its aggressive foreign policy vis-à-vis Iran. These political achievements were not brought about without immense ideological spadework by the Safavid power agents and the producers of the dynasty's political theology. Yet, there existed among them men whose ambitions often turned to treachery. Developing strong ties of patronage and clientelism among the chiefs, though effective at times, did not seem sufficient to secure obedience and service – Tahmasb needed to craft a new image of a Sufi king distinct from his predecessors to inhibit disloyalty on the material as well as the ideological plane if he hoped to remain in power, the subject of Chapter 5.

5

The Divine Patron

5.1 THE TRIAL

He sat in silence, proud and self-assured, but there was no hiding his heavy heart from his enemies. The court was crammed with chiefs, grandees, and high-ranking courtiers who had gathered there to witness the downfall of the most powerful Qizilbash chief in the realm, Muhammad Khan Sharaf al-Din of the Takallu tribe, the governor of Herat and the royal guardian of the heir-apparent Sultan Muhammad. He had arrived in haste and without notice with 300 of his men at the court held at the summer pastures near the city of Qazvin. An old veteran had tipped him off that a plot had been hatched against him. It was 953/1546, the year that Prince Alqas rebelled against his brother Shah Tahmasb, a revolt that prompted yet another Ottoman invasion previously alluded to. Budaq Munshi, the khan's secretary during his governorship of Baghdad, meticulously recorded what happened next to his patron.[1]

According to Budaq Munshi, Muhammad Khan stood accused of treason. His adversaries, mostly the chiefs of the rival Ustajlu tribe, had filled the shah's ear with tales that the khan had grown too powerful in the frontier province of Khurasan and had plans to rebel. To further damage his reputation and tighten the noose around him, they claimed that the khan's loyalty to the shah was disingenuous. They argued that when he

[1] Munshī Qazvīnī, *Javāhir al-Akhbār*, 196–98; Mīrzā Bayg Junābādī, *Rawzat al-Safaviyyah*, ed. Ghulām Rizā Tabātabā'ī Majd (Tehran: Bunyād-i Mawqūfāt-i Duktur Mahmūd Afshār, 1378), 503; Khvāndamīr, *Tārīkh-i Shāh Ismā'īl*, 221–23.

was the governor of Baghdad, he had planned to defect to the Ottomans when they invaded the Safavid western territories in 941/1534.[2]

During the gathering, the cabalists denounced Muhammad Khan repeatedly. They were in possession of incriminating communications against him. They testified that when the khan abandoned Baghdad and was marching toward the royal encampment to join the shah, he had not heard that his brother-in-law Ghazi Khan Takallu had switched his allegiance to the Ottoman Sultan Suleyman. When the news finally reached him in Shushtar that Ghazi Khan had in fact defected, he had a change of heart and intended to return to Baghdad to join the Ottomans. They had men of the Aqajari clan present to provide the corroborating evidence of the khan's betrayal.[3]

The conspirators seemed to have known Tahmasb's weakness. They were aware of his hatred of Ghazi Khan (the khan's in-law), whom he once called "a deceitful, satanic, devious little man."[4] Tahmasb had good reason to hate him. Ghazi Khan had been the royal tutor (*lalah*) of Tahmasb's younger brother, Prince Bahram – a position of utmost trust, which at that time also carried the power and prestige of the governorship of Herat. At a desperate moment, when the Safavid troops had marched nonstop from Khurasan toward Azerbaijan to counter the main Ottoman army in 940-1/1534, weakened by lack of provisions and suffering from low morale, and when only 7,000 men remained on Tahmasb's side, Ghazi Khan and his cavalry had abandoned him to join the Ottomans. The Ottomans had also well-rewarded another defector, a fellow Takallu chief by the name of Ulamah, the former governor-general of Azerbaijan. The Ottoman sultan made Ulamah the governor of Erzurum to buy his loyalty. Tahmasb considered Ulamah an even more loathsome character, calling him an ingrate (*namak bih-harām*) for his treachery, one of the culture's worse insults (see Section 5.3). These high-level defections, along with the infamous Takallu tribe's rebellion during the civil war a few years earlier, had made the shah extremely distrustful of the tribe and its ambitious chiefs.[5]

Now, Muhammad Khan, the most powerful of the Takallu chiefs, was on the brink of a disgraceful end to a long and illustrious career in the service of the Safavid house. He remained silent during the accusations.

[2] Khvāndamīr, *Tārīkh-i Shāh Ismāʿīl*, 221–23; Junābādī, *Rawzat al-Safaviyyah*, 502–5.
[3] Munshī Qazvīnī, *Javāhir al-Akhbār*, 196; Khvāndamīr, *Tārīkh-i Shāh Ismāʿīl*, 222.
[4] Tahmāsb Safavī, *Tazkirah-yi Shāh Tahmāsb*, 93.
[5] Ibid., 72, 97, 124.

Tahmasb finally asked him to defend himself and respond to the accusations. The khan stood up, walked across the court, and sat down in front of the shah and began:

> When Ibrahim Pasha [the Ottoman grand vizier] sent an emissary stating that if you come over to our side, I will give you the land from Baghdad to Damascus – I have that letter with me – I solemnly swear that I killed the man who brought it, and prepared myself for war with the Ottomans, but they did not arrive [on time] ... When Your Majesty sent word to abandon Baghdad and come hither, 3,000 of my troops were saying, "Stay! For you are [Muhammad Khan] our benefactor; we will keep Baghdad, and neither give it to the Ottomans, nor to the Qizilbash."

He continued, and it is here where he makes his defense, incisive and brief:

> With [only] a thousand ill-fated comrades, I opposed them, and lost all my treasury and home, but I kept the gratitude owed to [my] spiritual master (*murshid*) and benefactor (*valī-yi niʿmat*). These [accusations] are made at the instigation of these chiefs present here. If you believe me [to be culpable] based on their words, then the titles of khan and sultan is not suited for me, for I consider the *minnat* [i.e., obligation-producing favor] of these chiefs as worthless as twigs.[6]

Muhammad Khan stood accused of disloyalty and sedition, and if found guilty he would be disgraced and executed in a brutal fashion. With his life hanging by a thread, he defended his life based on a single plea, that he kept the gratitude owed to his benefactor, his murshid (Sufi spiritual master) and *valī-yi niʿmat* (patron/benefactor).[7]

Muhammad Khan's defense reveals how the obligation of gratitude formed the basis of loyalty to one's patron and was to be vigorously defended when that loyalty was questioned. This was especially true during the initial expansion of the Safavid order, a period of chaos, besiegement, and opportunity, when the chiefs' loyalties were constantly tested.

The key to unlocking the reason why gratitude and loyalty played such a central role in the lives of political men lies in the title that Muhammad Khan used to refer to his patron, Shah Tahmasb: *valī-yi niʿmat* or benefactor (see Figure 5.1). Decoding this title provides the reason why he chose such a line of defense and offers an insight into understanding not

[6] Munshī Qazvīnī, *Javāhir al-akhbār*, 197.

[7] I have opted for the simple term "patron," but it should be clear that the term's origins and designation are spiritually rooted.

FIGURE 5.1 Shah Tahmasb I. A sixteenth-century Persian miniature depicting the monarch in his later years, seated in a tranquil pose within a serene landscape, created toward the end of his long reign.
The Cleveland Museum of Art, Gift of the John Huntington Art and Polytechnic Trust, 1917.1078

only how Safavid political men perceived their Sufi king, but also how in the process they attempted to preserve their bond of loyalty and survive.

In the following I explain how the idea of *valī-yi niʿmat*, an intercessor who in theory passed on the Creator's bounty, came to augment the fading status of the Safavid patriarchs, who no longer functioned as Sufi sheikhs but rather rulers who possessed vast resources and controlled means of collective violence. Shah Tahmasb offers a great case of how a character of a Sufi "sheikh" metamorphosed to a divine patron, what they referred to as *valī-yi niʿmat.*

5.2 THE DIVINE PATRON

One durable type of bond that political men hoped would produce predictable positive loyalties was the obligation of gratitude that consecrated patronage produced, what they called *shukr-i niʿmat.* We observe this concept at work in how Muhammad Khan defended himself when his loyalty came under attack. The significance of this type of obligation bond is magnified further within a tight-knit organization like the Safavid elites, in which such political ties had the potential to strengthen their sense of cohesion and produce a relative organizational advantage.

Another occasion to analyze the nature of chiefs' ties to the Safavid shahs is when the Safavid sacred lineage and their saintly charisma did little to persuade the chiefs to submit to their authority. Such a tense situation was on full display during the foundational period of the dynasty, especially in the struggle for succession of the second Safavid shah, Tahmasb. Lacking his father's military power and spiritual magnetism, Shah Tahmasb, as we discussed, had to rely on other types of bonds to strengthen his power base.

This was an era of political fragmentation when men's loyalty came under immense pressure and the Safavid order nearly disintegrated. Few were the chiefs who understood loyalty like Muhammad Khan and believed that the ten-year-old Tahmasb was their *valī-yi niʿmat*, their patron and divine intermediary.

Valī-yi niʿmat (Ar. *walī al-niʿma*), the title that Muhammad Khan used to refer to Shah Tahmasb, is composed of two interlinking concepts. The first term, "*valīy*" (Ar. *walī*, pl. *awliyāʾ*), in its religiopolitical context, means patron, guardian, benefactor. Many may recognize it when hearing the Shiʿi daily calls for prayer "*ʿAlī walī Allāh*" (ʿAli is the intimate of God), ascribed to the Prophet's cousin and son-in-law, who was the first Shiʿi Imam. *Walī Allāh* is also used as a designation for holy figures and Sufi masters, and *walī al-sajjāda* points to the inheritor of the Sufi master's prayer rug as a form of investiture to lead the order.[8]

[8] See, for example, the definitions of *walī* in early Arabic lexicons such as Muhammad b. Ahmad al-Azharī, *Tahdhīb al-Lugha*, ed. Muhammad ʿAlī al-Najjār and ʿAbd al-Salām Muhammad Hārūn (Cairo: Dār al-Qawmiyya al-ʿArabiyya li-l-Tibāʿa, 1384–87), s.v. "*w-l-y.*"

The term *walī* with connotations of trusted benevolent authority over the centuries has found a multitude of uses in the political sphere. For instance, political men used the epithet *walī al-ʿahd* as a designation for the heir apparent, as we can still observe in today's few remaining monarchies in the Near East. Another important formulation derived from the obligation of *valī-yi fiqh* (guardian of jurisprudence) was reworked and politicized by the first leader of the Islamic Republic of Iran, Ruhollah Khomeini, to construct the concept of *vilāyat-i faqīh* (guardianship by a jurist) in order to restructure the political system of contemporary Iran. Interestingly, Khomeini considered the masses to be his *valī-yi niʿmat*, thereby inverting the pyramid of power, at least in its theoretical conception. Many in Iran and Turkey still allude to the head of their household as their *valī-yi niʿmat* (a person who brings home the life-sustaining daily bread – God's *niʿmat*).[9]

The second part of the compound, "*niʿma*" (Pers. *niʿmat*), generally means favor, benefit, grace. It has a widespread usage and appears so common that it seldom evokes a second thought, as used in such a quotidian phrase as *bi-niʿmat Allāh* (by grace of God) and many proverbs using *niʿma* to signify the bounty of the Creator and the gratitude owed to Him. The spiritual significance of *niʿma*, however, can hardly be overlooked and has its basis in the Qurʾan.

In several passages of the Qurʾan, *niʿma* serves to remind the believers of the Creator's copious benefactions toward humanity. In one passage, for instance, the believer is instructed to "Remember! Moses said to his people: 'Call to mind the favor of God (*niʿmat Allāh*) to you when He delivered you from the people of Pharaoh: They set you hard tasks and punishments, slaughtered your sons, and let your women-folk live'" (Qurʾan 14:6). In another sura, the believer reads:

> And hold fast, all together, by the rope which God [stretches out for you], and be not divided among yourselves; and remember with gratitude God's favor on you (*niʿmat Allāh*); for you were enemies and He joined your hearts in love, so that by His grace, you became brethren. (Qurʾan 3:103)

These verses and others like it reveal that the Creator's *niʿma* incurs a strong obligation of gratitude upon humanity as the beneficiary, an obligation that bound humanity to the Creator and which humanity attempts to sever ceaselessly. The Qurʾan is unequivocal about the rebellious nature of humankind, and its proclivity toward ingratitude. We see that in several

[9] Ruhollah Khomeini, *Sahīfah-yi Imām Khomeini*, vol. 16 (Tehran, 1360), 25.

"covenant passages" of the Qur'an. "When thy Lord drew forth from the Children of Adam – from their loins – their descendants, and made them testify concerning themselves, [saying]: 'Am I not your Lord [who cherishes and sustains you]?'– They said: 'Yea! We do testify!' [This,] lest ye should say on the Day of Judgment: 'Of this we were never mindful'" (Qur'an 7:172).

The sacred bond that exists between the Creator (*Khāliq*) and the created (*makhlūq*) brought about by the obligation of gratitude, *shukr al-ni'ma*, was defended in Islamic ethics, exegesis, political writing, and various forms of didactic literature. In the political sphere, this bond was understood as loyalty between the ruler, chiefs, and government officials, and formed the basis for the Safavid system of patronage. Through the diffusion of the obligation of gratitude in political action and its articulation in political theology, the ruler was hallowed as an intermediary who passed down *ni'mat* from the Creator to the masses. The assumption of this role endowed the Safavid ruler with an aura of unmatched sanctity among the Qizilbash chiefs, and thus loyalty to him became a "sacred obligation." These concepts can be seen in Muhammad Khan's trial where he attempted to first convince the shah (his benefactor) of his consecrated position as the khan's divine intermediary by calling the shah his *valī-yi ni'mat*, and, second, by maintaining that he had maintained the sacred obligation that tied them together.

In medieval and early modern Islamic political thought, *valī-yi ni'mat* carried an aura of spiritual authority that was warranted largely by benefaction and patronage. Thus, those at the apex of political power monopolized the role of a divine intermediary who passes on the Creator's *ni'mat* to others. It was not uncommon for medieval and early modern political actors to describe their clientelist interactions with their overlords, and the rise and fall of their fortunes, in terms of the *ni'mat* that they received from their *valī-yi ni'mat*.[10] This perception explains why the benefits that a divine patron was thought to have passed down from the Creator to his subordinates tended to produce in them a sense of consecrated obligation to him, as well as the expectation of loyalty in return for his patronage. For the Qizilbash chiefs in the early tenth/sixteenth century, patronage that mattered translated materially as governorship of a province, for instance, and protection from rivals, and access to great pastures for their tribe's flocks.

[10] Mottahedeh, *Loyalty and Leadership*, 72–79.

But, beyond its spiritual context in a holy text and the sayings of a prophet, how did debts of gratitude become a sacred bond in the Islamic political theology? The answer may reside in philosophy of ethics. In the classical period, gratitude to the Creator (*shukr al-niʿma*) was regarded as a virtue (*fadīla*), and it was not uncommon for theologians to write extensively about the obligation that it incurs. Due to the expansive exploration of the subject in medieval and early modern ethical treatises and exegetical writings, it may even be called the science of gratitude. These treatments make use of traditional sources of authority, the Qurʾan and the Sunni/Shiʿi hadith corpus.[11]

Abu Hamid al-Ghazali (d. 505/1111), the great jurist and mystic, for instance, explored the nature of obligation of gratitude in his magnum opus *Ihyāʾ ʿUlūm al-Dīn* (*Revival of the Religious Sciences*) and restated it in Persian in the *Kīmīyā-yi al-Saʿādat* (*Alchemy of Happiness*). He presents gratitude as an element of the "savior virtues" (*munjīyāt*) and explains that unlike repentance, patience, fear of God, and asceticism, which are means to the attainment of spiritual elevation, gratitude, similar to love, contentment, and the belief in the unity of God (*tawhīd*), is an end in itself and therefore eternal.

Like many thinkers of the era, al-Ghazali views gratitude as essential for the fulfillment of higher levels of spirituality and naturally relies on the Qurʾan as well as hadith to explore its hidden meanings. He recounts a hadith transmitted by the Prophet's wife ʿAʾisha:

> One night he was with me and said: "O ʿAʾisha, leave me alone so I may devote this night to my Lord." I replied: "O Messenger of God – by God – verily I love to be close to you, and I love that which makes you happy." He stood and began to pray, then he began to cry until his beard became wet, then he cried until his garment became wet, then he cried until the ground became wet. Then Bilal came to call him for the prayer and found him crying, and said: "Messenger of God, you undergo this while you have been forgiven for your past and future faults?" He replied: "Shouldn't I love to be a grateful servant [of God]? Surely tonight a

[11] The Safavid jurist ʿAbd al-Hasib ʿAmuli (d. 1121/1709) summed up this attitude well: "Know that just as the science of knowing God is a necessity, so is the science of gratitude. Whoever disputes the gratitude owed to his benefactor, treds the desert of ignorance and becomes the desert-dweller of ungratefulness as he transforms gratitude into ingratitude and thus will be forever miserable, afflicted, and destined to be vanquished like the armies of infidels." Muhammad ʿAbd al-Hasīb ʿAlavī ʿĀmulī, *Qavāʿid al-Salātīn*, ed. Rasūl Jaʿfariyān (Tehran: Kitābkhānah, Mūzah va Markaz-i Asnād-i Majlis-i Shūrā-yi Islāmī, 1384), 118–20. ʿAbd al-Hasib was a descendant of the famed jurist Muhaqqiq Karaki discussed in the Introduction.

verse was revealed to me – 'woe to the one who recites it but does not reflect upon it' [Qur'an 2:165]."[12]

In another instance, al-Ghazali relates that the Prophet said, "On the Day of Judgment, they will call out, 'Where are the grateful ones?' No one will arise except those who have been grateful to God in every condition."[13] Al-Ghazali has judiciously chosen these two hadith: one archetypal and affective, the other redemptive. In the former, a prophet is so overwhelmed by his grateful love to his Creator that he weeps uncontrollably, and in the latter, the soul's deliverance in the afterlife is assured by gratitude.[14]

The ubiquitous presence of the obligation of gratitude owed to the Creator in great works of medieval Persian literature such as Firdawsi's *Shāhnāmah*, Saʿdi's *Gulistān*, Nizami Ganjavi's *Khamsah*, and Jami's *Haft Awrang* reveals its importance as part of a larger Perso-Islamicate discourse on ethics in governance. By the seventh/thirteenth century, the discourse of gratitude was well integrated into the political ethos, which early modern thinkers appropriated into their works. These didactic expositions in addition to the Qur'an, hadith, and exegetical writings provided men like Muhammad Khan with a rich corpus of spiritual concepts with which to understand their political ties and defend themselves when, for example, their loyalty came under question.[15]

The idea was that the sacred obligation that binds humankind in gratitude to the Creator for the innumerable *niʿmat* He provides them

[12] al-Ghazālī, *Kīmīyā-yi Saʿādat*, 2:357. Different versions of this hadith exist; see, for instance, al-Bukhārī, *Sahīh al-Bukhārī*, vol. 6, book 60, hadith 361 (Arabic version, book 65, hadith 4837).

[13] al-Ghazālī, *Kīmīyā-yi Saʿādat*, 2:356–71.

[14] There are many Shiʿi hadith about this topic. For example, ʿUbayd Allah b. Valid relates that the sixth Shiʿi Imam, Jaʿfar al-Sadiq (d. 148/765), once said that "there are three things through which no harm will set forth: prayer in time of crisis; to seek God's forgiveness in time of sin; and offering gratitude in time of receiving benefit." Muhammad b. Yaʿqūb Kulaynī, *Usūl-i Kāfī*, ed. Javād Mustafavī (Tehran: Kitābfurūshī-i ʿIlmiyyah-i Islāmiyyah, 1378), 4:291.

[15] See, for instance, the downfall of King Jamshid in Abū al-Qāsim Firdawsī, *Shāhnāmah-i Firdawsī*, ed. Mustafā Jayhūnī (Isfahan: Gurūh-i Intishārāt-i Shāhnāmah'pizhūhī, 2001), 1:35–43; the legend of Darius in Nizāmī Ganjavī, *Kulliyyāt-i Nizāmī Ganjavī*, ed. Hasan Vahīd Dastgirdī (Tehran: Intishārāt-i Zavvār, 1388), 280–85; Muslih al-Dīn Saʿdī Shīrāzī, *Gulistān-i Saʿdī*, ed. Ghulāmhusayn Yūsufī (Tehran: Khwārazmī, 1368), 49–50; variation: *Kulliyyāt-i Saʿdī*, ed. Hasan Anvarī (Tehran: Nashr-i Qatrah, 1383), 230; ʿAbd al-Rahmān Jāmī, *Masnavī-i Haft Awrang*, ed. Āghā Murtazā Mudarris Gīlānī (Tehran: Kitābfurūshī-i Saʿdī, 1337), 943–46.

also binds kings in gratitude to the Creator for the *niʿmat* of sovereignty. Al-Ghazali inaugurates his famed treatise *Nasīhat al-Mulūk* (*Counsel for Kings*) – most likely composed for the young Saljuqid ruler Sultan Sanjar (d. 552/1157-8) – with, "Know, O King of the East, that God Almighty has bestowed upon you many benefits, and its gratitude is incumbent upon you, and whoever does not give gratitude for God's benefit, [his] benefit will diminish; and he will be met with shame and disgrace on the Day of Judgment."[16] Al-Ghazali points to faith (*īmān*) as the greatest *niʿmat* in sovereignty, which he describes as the seed of everlasting bliss that needs care and nourishment to flourish. He explains that the foremost branch of the tree of faith "is for a sovereign (*vālī*) to know the value of sovereignty (*vilāyat*), and to know that sovereignty is a *niʿmat* that whoever undertakes it truthfully will attain bliss unlike any other. And if he falls short, such misfortune may befall him that besides blasphemy (*kufr*) is unmatched by any other."[17] Just as man's ingratitude to the Creator leads to him being forsaken, a king's ingratitude to God is condemned and depicted as the leading cause of chaos and the loss of sovereignty. The gratitude for the *niʿmat* of sovereignty, al-Ghazali explains, is the dispensation of justice.

Some among al-Ghazali's intellectual descendants in the Safavid period also tied the survival of the state to gratitude. "One of the principal reasons for the decline of the realm is the abandonment of gratitude to the Creator," writes the jurist Mulla Muhammad Sabzavari (d. 1090/1679) in his *Rawzat al-Anvār-i ʿAbbāsī*, written for Shah ʿAbbas II in the same genre of *specula principum* as that of *Nasīhat al-Mulūk*. Sabzavari attempts to fully incorporate the obligation of gratitude into his political theology by positioning its sacred value within principles that strengthen and preserve sovereignty. The Safavid realm in Sabzavari's time was not as prosperous as it once was and his connecting of political decay and economic woes to the lack of gratitude to the Lord of Bounty bespeaks the socioeconomic contraction of the later eleventh/seventeenth century.

In a cascading fashion, just as kings incur an obligation of gratitude to the Creator in lieu of the *niʿmat* of sovereignty, government officials also incur an obligation of gratitude to their king in exchange for his patronage and protection. One of the prominent proponents of this interpretation that influenced Safavid-era thinkers was Nasir al-Din al-Tusi (d. 672/1274), who underscored the importance of gratitude in

[16] Abū Hāmid Muhammad al-Ghazālī, *Nasīhat al-Mulūk*, ed. Jalāl al-Dīn Humāʾī (Tehran: Chāpkhānah-i Majlis, 1317), 1–2.

[17] Ibid., 14–27.

such works as *Akhlāq-i Muhtashamī*, *Akhlāq-i Nāsirī*, as well as in *Awsāf al-Ashrāf*. In *Akhlāq-i Nāsirī*, for instance, al-Tusi collocates gratitude as a precept in religious ethics with that in politics, and like al-Ghazali, presents the concept as a sacred obligation within broader ideals of justice. However, he goes further and shows how the obligation that gratitude incurs informs political dealings in a manner that we may interpret as clientelistic. Thus, according to al-Tusi, in exchange for the protection and justice that subjects receive from their ruler, they are obliged to offer him sincere prayers, obedience, and renouncement of sedition, based on the dictum that "taking without giving falls outside of the fundamental law of fairness."[18] This line of thought leads him to reveal the religious ethics ensconced in the political obligation of gratitude. According to al-Tusi, if failing to acknowledge gratitude within the king-subject relation is disgraceful, "consider how reprehensible it would be to fail to fulfill the obligation to the True Sovereign (*Mālik al-mulk-i bi-haqīqat*) from whose generosity, every moment, such limitless benefits and bounties reach our souls and bodies that it is beyond the bounds of reckoning."[19]

In the early modern political discourse, the sacrosanct spiritual tie between the Creator and the created about which al-Tusi and al-Ghazali postulated reflects what was understood by political agents as a principle; just as their benefactor was bonded to the Creator by the obligation of gratitude in exchange for the *niʿmat* of sovereignty, they as his servants were bonded to their king by the obligation of gratitude for God's *niʿmat* with which he patronized them. While the obligation of the bond in the spiritual sense is faithfulness to the Creator, in politics it is the obligation of unwavering loyalty (*ikhlās*) to the ruler.

A notable example of this view is offered by Hakim al-Din Idris Bitlisi (d. 926/1520), a scholar and historian who fled to the Ottoman court after the Safavid rise to power. In his advice treatise, *Qānūn-i Shāhanshāhī*, Bitlisi reasons that the obligation incurred toward the Creator generates a similar obligation by subjects toward the ruler who passes down God's bounty. Not surprisingly, he refers to the ruler as "*valī-yi al-niʿmat*" and finds confirmation in the Qurʾan, explaining that

> since sultan means the shadow of God, in the same manner that God demands loyalty from His creation which is commanded in Qurʾan 2:40 ["O Children of

[18] Nasīr al-Dīn al-Tūsī, *Akhlāq-i Nāsirī*, ed. Mujtabā Mīnuvī and ʿAlī Rizā Haydarī (Tehran: Intishārāt-i Khwārazmī, 1978), 138–40.

[19] Ibid.

Israel! Call to mind My [special] favor (*niʿmatī*) which I bestowed upon you, and fulfill your covenant with Me as I fulfill My Covenant with you, and fear none but Me"], the ruler too demands loyalty from his subjects and the continuous expression of *shukr al-niʿmat*, which is in lieu of the obligation to the *valī-yi al-niʿmat*. In return [subjects may] expect fidelity in [the ruler's] pledges and promises.[20]

Bitlisi's interpretation explains why disloyalty to a ruler was equated with ingratitude, *kufr al-niʿmat*. Disloyalty, Bitlisi suggests, was construed as the severance of the earthly manifestation (i.e., the political tie) of the divine covenant (i.e., the spiritual tie). This equivalence produced a powerful instrument of religiopolitical domination for the order's leader vis-à-vis his chiefs.

5.3 DISLOYALTY AS INGRATITUDE

Muhammad Khan's trial showed that treason, a politically motivated act, was not separated from its spiritual underpinning, for one's political loyalty to the order's patriarch also entailed spiritual loyalty. Once a chief turned his back against the Safavid shah in the form of defection or rebellion, he also rejected his spiritual authority. This was partly rooted in the Sufi ideation of legitimacy inherent in the master-disciple relationship to which members of the Safavid order adhered (e.g., it may be recalled that Muhammad Khan also referred to the shah as his murshid or Sufi guide), and partly in the master's position within the cosmology of power. Because the shah was perceived to be a transmitter of God's *niʿmat*, he held the title of *valī-yi niʿmat*, one who facilitates the spreading of the divine benefaction. One who denied the obligation owed to such an intermediary was thus labeled *kāfir al-niʿma* (Pers. *kāfar-i niʿmat*), the denier of benefit (i.e., an ungrateful infidel). Likewise, the act of disloyalty was labeled *kufr al-niʿma* (Pers. *kufrān-i niʿmat*) or, simply stated, ingratitude. In the following, I show the ways in which the concept of spiritual ingratitude entered political theology and was used as an instrument of domination by patrons to maintain political ties with their clients and inhibit disloyalty.

The notion of ingratitude is not foreign to human communities, whether political or not. In our own time, the notion of ingratitude has found expression, for instance, in the Persian sayings "eating salt and

[20] Hakīm al-Dīn Idrīs Bitlīsī, *Qānūn-i Shāhanshāhī*, ed. ʿAbd Allāh Masʿūdī Ārānī (Tehran: Markaz-i Pizhūhishī-i Mīrāṣ-i Maktūb, 1387), 58–59.

breaking the salt-shaker" (*namak khūrdan va namak-dān shikastan*); "may this hand break for it has no [obligation producing] salt" when ingratitude is manifested; and in Turkish by the expression "to bite a hand that provides bread" (*ekmek veren eli ısırmak*).[21] The oft-evoked English proverb "to bite the hand that feeds you" carries a similar meaning. Contemporaneous European intellectuals in the Enlightenment had similar attitudes toward gratitude and condemned its omission. Hume, for instance, wrote that "of all crimes that human creatures are capable of committing, the most horrid and unnatural is ingratitude." Kant was equally unforgiving and states that ingratitude, along with envy and malice, is "the essence of vileness and wickedness."[22] Sufficiently ubiquitous, the obligation that gratitude creates permeates throughout societies, and is a major facet in the formation of sociopolitical ties. On the other hand, ingratitude and the denial of this obligation is a great source of political tension often leading to interpersonal enmity and group conflict.

The term *kufr*, which connoted unbelief and rejection of the obligation owed to the Creator for His bounty, was a powerful tool for suppressing and nullifying opposition to the dominant power because it derives from precepts found in the Qurʾan, the ultimate source of authority in Islam. There are many instances of warning against the folly of ingratitude in the holy book. For instance:

And He hath made subject to you the sun and the moon, both diligently pursuing their courses; and the night and the day hath He [also] made subject to you. And He giveth you of all that ye ask for. But if ye count the favors of God (*niʿmat Allāh*) never will ye be able to number them: Verily, man is given up to injustice and ingratitude (*kaffār*). (Qurʾan 14:33–34)

The close association of *kufr* (disbelief, heresy) with that of ingratitude toward the Creator's *niʿma* is further demonstrated in the Qurʾan in the story of Saba:

There was, for Saba, aforetime, a sign in their homeland – two gardens to the right and to the left. Eat of the Sustenance [provided] by your Lord, and be grateful to Him: a territory fair and happy, and a Lord Oft-Forgiving! But they turned away from God and We sent against them the flood released from the dams, and

[21] Salt and bread are often symbols of gratitude in many Eurasian cultures and a common component in initiation rituals of several Sufi orders and brotherhoods (*futuwwas*).

[22] David Hume, *Moral Philosophy*, ed. Geoffrey Sayre-McCord (Indianapolis: Hackett, 2006), 132–46; Immanuel Kant, *Lectures on Ethics*, trans. Louis Infield (London: Methuen Press, 1979), 218.

We converted their two garden rows into gardens producing bitter fruit, and tamarisks, and some few stunted lote-trees. That was the requital We gave them because they ungratefully rejected Faith (*kafarū*): And never do We give such requital except to such as are ungrateful rejecters (*al-kafūr*). (Qurʾan 34:15–17)

In the classical period, prominent thinkers expounded on the connection between *kufr* and lack of gratitude to the Creator. Al-Ghazali, for example, whose works were read across the Islamic world, alludes in his *Alchemy of Happiness* to a well-known passage in the Qurʾan, the account of Satan's banishment from paradise and his plans to lead humankind astray: "He [Satan] said: 'Because Thou hast thrown me out of the way, lo! I will lie in wait for them on Thy straight way: Then will I assault them from before them and behind them, from their right and their left: Nor wilt Thou find, in most of them, gratitude [for Thy mercies]'" (Qurʾan 7:16–17). Al-Ghazali presents us with Satan's view that humankind has a disposition toward ingratitude with implications that it may lead to deviancy and the rejection of faith. The significance of gratitude for warding off *kufr* and strengthening one's faith is further elaborated in Qurʾan 2:152. Al-Ghazali highlights this sura by stating that there are no clearer signs of gratitude's centrality to Islam than when the Creator raises it self-referentially: "Then do ye remember Me; I will remember you. Be grateful to Me, and reject not Faith." Even though gratitude has such a central position, however, al-Ghazali references Quʾran 34:13 to show that not many will attain it, "Work ye, sons of David, with thanks! But few of My servants are grateful."[23]

[23] al-Ghazālī, *Kīmīyā-yi Saʿādat*, 356. We find similar expressions, for instance, in Timurid histories such as the *Zafar-nāmah* of Sharaf al-Din ʿAli Yazdi. An example of *kufrān-i niʿmat* for Sharaf al-Din ʿAli is when he narrates the tale of Timur's betrayal by his protégé Tuqtamish – one of the highlights of the chronicle: Sharaf al-Dīn ʿAlī Yazdī, *Zafarnāmah: Tārīkh-i ʿUmūmī-i Mufassal-i Īrān dar Dawrah-yi Tīmūrīyān: Az Rū-yi Nusakhī kih dar ʿAsr-i Musannif Nivishtah Shudah*, ed. Muhammad ʿAbbāsī (Tehran: Amīr Kabīr, 1336), 1:358–62. I am grateful to John Woods for this reference. The gravity of this concept is also demonstrated in the classical period, for example in the *Sīyāsat-nāmah* (*Book of Governance*), composed by the famed Saljuq chief minister Nizam al-Mulk. In this treatise, he tells the story of the ʿAbbasid caliph al-Muʿtamid and his confrontation with Yaʿqub Layth, the founder of the Saffarid dynasty, where al-Muʿtamid apparently charges Yaʿqub with *kufrān-i niʿmat* in order to divest his cause of any form of legitimacy. Nizām al-Mulk, *Siyāsat-nāmah*, ed. Hubert Darke (Tehran, 1976), 19–26. We also see this in Mughal politics; for example, in the case of Prince Kamran's rebellion, see Abū al-Fazl b. Mubārak, *Akbarnāmah*, vol. 1, ed. Mulavī Aghā Ahmad ʿAlī (Calcutta: Royal Asiatic Society of Bengal, 1877, 321–25; for an Ottoman example, see Aşıkpaşazade, *Tevarih-Al-i Osman*, ed. ʿAlī Bey (Istanbul: Matbaʿa-i ʿĀmira, 1332), 17.

Mankind's fickle nature and general inclination toward ingratitude as attested to in the Qur'an is perhaps the reason why gratitude occupied a special locus in ethics among theologians as well as Sufi sheikhs. "However much I search to find why humankind has become adrift, the privileged and the multitudes alike," writes the sixth/twelfth-century mystic Ahmad Jam,

> and having considered every path and studied a plethora of opinions – all is due to the abandonment of gratitude and the falling into the depths of ingratitude. And every community that God Almighty condemned with calamity, it was precisely for this . . . now, behold what [the Creator] has done to ingrates, and what He has done for thankful ones! When you perceive the truth, all the goodness rests in gratitude, and all harm is in ingratitude . . . most people are unaware of these two truths: They do not know gratitude for God's benefit, nor abstinence from ingratitude.[24]

Given the severity with which ingratitude to the True Benefactor of humankind was interpreted, medieval political theology used the concept of *kufr al-niʿma* to the Creator and equated it to disloyalty to a patron-king. In the Safavid political context, this meant the denial of the ruler as the purveyor of benefits to his chiefs. The way political theology justified this move was built on the long-held belief that as the Creator's regent on earth, part of the ruler's divine mandate was to eliminate ingrates (*kuffār*) in the same manner as he would, in principle, eradicate unbelief (*kufr*). For ingratitude meant disloyalty, and disloyalty is what leads to chaos and disorder. This powerful idea endowed the Safavid shahs with a ready ideological means to disgrace the actions of clients who severed their political ties as *kufr*, and to denigrate dissenters as ingrates.

Much of Islamic political thought is prescribed to avoid social chaos, and kings, who often viewed themselves in theophanic forms, were tasked to prevent the emergence of chaos by imposing order through the implementation of the divine law (i.e., justice). This ethos is sufficiently common in ancient Near Eastern sacral kingships as well as medieval and early modern religiopolitical thought that it needs little elaboration. What should be emphasized, however, is the interpretation of ingratitude as a force shaping the communal power of a political organization. As noted, the code equated disloyalty with ingratitude, and disloyalty to the ruler was construed as a force behind chaos for its direct link to rebellion (*fitnah*), which disrupts the divinely established cosmic order.

[24] Abū al-Fath Muhammad b. Mutahhar Ahmad Jām, *Rawzat al-Muznibīn va Jannat al-Mushtāqīn*, ed. ʿAlī Fāzil (Tehran: Bunyād-i Farhang-i Īrān, 1976), 98–101.

This had the effect of granting moral authority to he who held power, while restricting the agency of chiefs and subsuming their political interest to that of their overlord.

5.4 THE INGRATE PRINCE

By relying on the belief that maintaing gratitude toward his patron would ward off the charge of *kufr*, Muhammad Khan in his trial avoided being perceived as an agent of chaos, an infidel deserving a dishonorable death. He was fortunate in that he made a convincing argument and proved his loyalty. Others were not so lucky. One of the most threatening rebellions of the tenth/sixteenth century that demonstrates what happens when a political agent refuses to submit to the Safavid shah was the revolt of Prince Alqas, second in line to the Safavid crown. The high-ranking Qizilbash commander and court historian Hasan Rumlu refers to the event as "the opposition of Alqas the Ingrate," and reveals how the code of obligation of gratitude was used to dishonor and delegitimize the uprising. "With utmost effort," Rumlu writes, "[Alqas] gathered forces of rebellion and transgression and endeavored to annul the gratitude of the benefactor (*valī-yi niʿmat*) [as he] became impervious to the maxim *al-kufrān ashshad min al-kufr* [ingratitude is more severe than blasphemy]."[25]

Rumlu reports that initially when Alqas came under suspicion of treason in 953/1546, the prince sent his son Sultan Ahmad and mother, Khan Begi Khanum, to convey a message to the shah: "That prince [i.e., Tahmasb] is my *valī-yi niʿmat*, and [it is] from wicked deeds and unwarranted hostility, and because of dark fortune, that I have become in line with the corruption of evildoers, and for that I am ashamed and regretful."[26] Hasan Rumlu attempts to show that Alqas acknowledges the authority of Tahmasb as his *valī-yi niʿmat*, for the opprobrium of ingratitude toward a benefactor would tarnish Alqas's quality as a leader and divest him of honor and legitimacy. As it turned out, Alqas's regret was ephemeral, for soon thereafter, his plans for regional autonomy in Shirvan became clear to Tahmasb. "The truth is that," writes Tahmasb in his memoir pointing to the dual religiopolitical nature of his house's authority, "[even] if the Qizilbash heads' get detached, they wouldn't separate the *tāj* [i.e., the Safavid red headgear, a symbol of loyalty] from themselves,

[25] Rūmlū, *Ahsan al-Tavārīkh*, 3:1299–1301.
[26] Ibid., 1299–1300.

and when Alqas wore the *tāj* no one followed him, for in the path of Sufism they recognize only one spiritual master, and if there were a hundred thousand princes, they would not gaze upon them."[27]

"He who is not steadfast in loyalty, his existence is in no place other than the realm of extinction," writes Ruhallah Lari, the secretary to the Safavid governor of Shiraz in a victory letter (*fath-nāmah*) to inform the provinces of the news of Prince Alqas's defeat before his flight to seek refuge with the Ottoman Sultan Suleyman. "The meaning of these words," he continues, "is to relate the state of circumstances of Abul Ghazi known as Alqas the Ingrate (*Alqās-i nā-sipās*). He became chained for his lack of gratitude (*kufrān-i niʿmat*) toward the bountiful royal favors, [thus] the farmland of his fortune became deprived of the raindrops of the infinite clouds of beneficence."[28]

Ruhallah echoed the widely accepted idea that *valī-yi niʿmat* was an intercessor that transmitted the Creator's *niʿmat*, and obedience to him was necessary if *niʿmat* was to persist, as he points to the famous saying "*wa-bi-l-shukr tadūm al-niʿam*" (and through gratitude do benefits endure). In imagery reminiscent of the Qurʾanic story of Saba mentioned above regarding *niʿmat*, Prince Alqas's life, due to his ingratitude toward his benefactor, is made analogous to a desolate field dispossessed of divine beneficence where nothing grows. After his capture in 957/1550, Tahmasb dispatched him to the prison castle of Qahqahah where he was thrown off its citadel.

In 969/1561, years after Alqas's rebellion had been quashed, when Prince Bayazid, the renegade son of the Ottoman Sultan Suleyman (to whose court Alqas had fled), sought refuge in the Safavid court, Tahmasb recorded his deliberation as to whether turn him in or not: "I said to myself, this man has betrayed his father, his *valī-yi niʿmat*, and has not observed the duties toward [his] parents, whose reverence is obligatory by

27 Tahmāsb Safavī, *Tazkirah-i Shāh Tahmāsb*, 110.

28 From the MS 494, ff. 1a–1b, John Rylands Library, authored by Ruh Allah Lari Shirazi Futuhi, in reference to Prince Alqas, who rebelled against his brother Shah Tahmasb. Ruh Allah was a secretary in the provincial court at Shiraz in the mid-tenth/sixteenth century. His *Munshaʾāt* has been published under *Sharafnāmah: Mukātibāt-i Dīvānī-i Iyālat-i Fārs va Lāristān dar Dawrah-i Safaviyyah*, ed. Muhammad Bāqir Vuşūqī (Tehran: Kitābkhānah, Mūzah va Markaz-i Asnād-i Majlis-i Shūrā-yi Islāmī, 1389). However, the *fath-nāmah* in which the poem quoted above appears was not in the manuscripts used by Vuthuqi in his edition. See also John R. Walsh, "The Revolt of Alqās Mīrzā," *Wiener Zeitschrift für die Kunde des Morgenlandes* 68 (1976): 61–78, for a discussion on the manuscript in John Rylands Library.

the message of the revelation and the traditions. While I am in peace with Sultan Suleyman, is it right to do him ill and assist a disloyal [man]?"[29]

No doubt, Prince Bayazid's disloyalty was a painful reminder of his own brother's betrayal, and his decision to hand him over to the Ottoman delegation who had arrived to fetch him was politically motivated. Yet, Tahmasb, who was in a constant struggle against treacherous men around him, framed Bayazid's rebellion as ingratitude to his *valī-yi niʿmat*, and thus attempted to wash his hands clean of his blood. He knew that Bayazid's opponents would vilify the renegade prince as *kāfar-i niʿmat*, an ingrate, undeserving of any degree of sympathy. The delegation soon thereafter strangled the prince along with his four sons.[30]

5.5 COSMOLOGICAL HIERARCHY

As was shown, the reformulation of *kufrān-i niʿmat* as political disloyalty was legitimized by the perceived obligation owed to the Creator for His beneficence. The Safavid political theology reflected this understanding, and those in power frequently exploited it to impress upon their subordinates that the obligation of gratitude that is owed to the Creator is also owed to a ruler. Once the order's shahs were perceived to be divine patrons, the existing political theology positioned him in the cosmological hierarchy. This placement endowed him with the ideological power over the dispensation of the Creator's *niʿmat*. We see this association clearly established, for instance, with Tahmasb's grandson ʿAbbas I.

Shah ʿAbbas I, arguably the greatest of the Safavid rulers and often credited for inaugurating the Safavid "golden age," like his grandfather suffered a similar fate against treacherous chiefs and Ottoman invasions, when he ascended the throne at the closing of the tenth/sixteenth century. However, by then the patronage dynamics that produced the inhibitive theology of loyalty were well-established in their political culture. The following two cases reveal how his court framed the severance of their sacred ties.

Qazi Ahmad Qummi, the Safavid minister and historian, who narrates the fall of a prominent Safavid chief, offers a striking example of the parallelism. He reports on Yaʿqub Khan, a powerful Qizilbash amir of the Zu al-Qadr tribe in control of the wealthy province of Fars, with the

[29] Tahmāsb Safavī, *Tazkirah-i Shāh Tahmāsb*, 159.
[30] Shīrāzī, *Takmilat al-Akhbār*, 120.

city of Shiraz as his seat of power. This event is considered a turning point in the reign of Shah ʿAbbas I when he tried to assert his royal authority after the succession struggle that erupted at his grandfather's death. "No tyrant and oppressor lived in this world who did not receive its equivalence in retribution," Qazi Ahmad begins the account, "and no ingrate lived decently and didn't at the end taste the poison of annihilation." He condemns ingratitude in a short poem:

> The companion who became ungrateful,
> Deduce his downfall from his deed;
> Whatever evil emerges of humankind,
> It wouldn't be worse than ingratitude;
> In ingratitude don't be brave, for
> From the cosmos harm will visit you.[31]

Qazi Ahmad tells us that Yaʿqub Khan fortified himself in the impenetrable castle of Istakhr "unaware that God Almighty because of his ingratitude would bring him out of that castle in shackles," for "with *valī-yi niʿmat* if you fall out of favor, you will fall even if you're as high as the heaven."[32] He then quotes a Qurʾanic verse to cast a somber hue on his account, "Wherever you may be, death will overtake you, even if you are in high towers" (Qurʾan 4:78), and sketches a metaphor of Yaʿqub Khan's imminent doom:

> But at the end, from the ever-revolving perfidious fortune
> The moon of Zu al-Qadr waned into a sliver.

Qazi Ahmad's account reads like a cautionary tale, a kind of parable for other chiefs to weigh the consequences of disloyalty to their *valī-yi niʿmat*, and he is not inhibited from reporting the punitive outcome. When Yaʿqub Khan finally surrendered, he was hung from a tree and beaten with canes all night long. He was then brought down and cut to pieces and his flesh was eaten by the companions of those whom he had killed as a ritualistic form of vengeance.[33]

[31] Qummī, *Khulāsat al-Tavārīkh*, 2:915–16.

[32] Iskandar Beg Turkman, in his chronicle *Tārīkh-i ʿĀlam'ārā-yi ʿAbbāsī*, 2:428, borrows this line from Qazi Ahmad to relate another instance of treason.

[33] Qummī, *Khulāsat al-Tavārīkh*, 2:915–19; Mahmūd b. Hidāyat Allāh Afūshtah'ī, *Nuqāwat al-Āṣār fī Zikr al-Akhyār*, ed. Ihsān Ishrāqī (Tehran: Bungāh-i Tarjumah va Nashr-i Kitāb, 1350), 351–61; Munshī, *Tārīkh-i ʿĀlam'ārā-yi ʿAbbāsī*, 2:431–37. For a discussion on various aspects of Persian court poetry and historical writings prior to the early modern era, see Julie Scott Meisami, "History as Literature," *Iranian Studies* 33, no. 1–2 (2000): 15–30; Julie Scott Meisami, *Persian Historiography to the End of the Twelfth Century*

There are several examples in this period of how the Safavid political men recognized the rigid hierarchy of power. One occurs in the account of the downfall of ʿAli Khan Garayali, a provincial governor during the early years of Shah ʿAbbas I's reign. "[ʿAli Khan] had gone astray from the path of loyalty and devotion (*ikhlās va yak-dilī*)," explains the historian and royal secretary Iskandar Beg Turkman, "and became rebellious . . . in truth, because ʿAli Khan was not grateful for the [royal] patronage, he undertook the offense of *kufrān-i niʿmat*, which is the worst of transgressions, and became deserving of a series of punishments." Iskandar Beg recounts the gruesome outcome that befell the amir because of his treachery:

> In the same manner that royal beneficence had become veiled from the discerning eye of his intellect, [Shah ʿAbbas I] removed his eyes from their sockets and deprived him of the *niʿmat* of sight, and cut off his limbs and abandoned him in the desert. The camp moved on, and from the fear of arousing the shah's anger, no one from the troops or servants in hopes of collecting rewards for the hereafter dared to help him.

Iskandar Beg composes a verse to titivate his account:

> In ingratitude famous he became;
> And the spirit abandoned his body in tormenting shame.

Iskandar Beg envisions his patron, the shah, as having jurisdiction over one of the Creator's primary benefits to humankind, the gift of sight. He relates that because ʿAli Khan did not see the benefits that his *valī-yi niʿmat* had extended toward him, the shah deprived him of the *niʿmat* of his eyes. What Iskandar Beg seems to suggest is that the *valī-yi niʿmat* is endowed with the authority to dispense the Creator's own *niʿmat*, and if ingratitude is manifested, he may divest the ingrate of benefits on God's behalf. The chronicler comes to this conclusion because, like many in his milieu, he operates with the code that equates disloyalty with ingratitude or *kufr*, the vilest of blasphemies. "Fortunate are those," he later reflects, "who have opened [their] guidance-seeing eyes and have observed these consequences, acknowledged gratitude for blessings, and have not become

(Edinburgh University Press, 1999). For the practice of cannibalism, see Bashir, "Shah Ismaʿil and the Qizilbash"; for the significance of Yaʿqub Khan's surrender to the assertion of Shah ʿAbbas's royal authority, see Sholeh A. Quinn, *Historical Writings during the Reign of Shah ʿAbbas: Ideology, Imitation, and Legitimacy in Safavid Chronicles* (Salt Lake City: University of Utah Press, 2000), 95–121.

forsaken in this and the next world by defaming themselves with the offense of ingratitude."[34]

In a remarkable example of how gratitude was now viewed as part of a universal system of obligations cascading down from the Creator to patron-kings, then onto their clients, Iskandar Beg even alludes to divine intervention. When Yuli Beg, a provincial amir, tried to carve out an independent territory near the city of Isfahan in the third year of Shah ʿAbbas I's reign, he fortified himself in a castle with troops and rations in an act of direct challenge to the young shah. After a short siege, Iskandar Beg tells us that Yuli Beg realized that "this disgraceful ruse is *kufrān-i niʿmat* and will result in him being forsaken in this world and the hereafter."

The royal secretary then records the shah's indignation at his chief's treachery: "The august prince for appearance's sake showed him due respect, but inwardly he was deeply offended, and how could he not be? To rebel against the *valī-yi niʿmat* and to commit such offenses in this manner, and to have hope of being saved! What impudence and foolishness!" Yuli Beg quickly abandoned the hope of ever ruling Isfahan and became content that his life would be spared. Assured by the shah's assurance that no harm would come to him, he surrendered. Harm, nevertheless, did visit him, but not from the shah, we are told. "The consequence of ingratitude followed him," Iskandar Beg chillingly reports, "and before long the twine of his life was cut by the blade of fortune's wrath," as he makes clear that even if his *valī-yi niʿmat* would not punish him for his ingratitude, the Creator certainly would. Yuli Beg died under mysterious circumstances.[35]

Shah ʿAbbas I had inherited his place as a divine benefactor in a dynasty that was nearly a century old by then. His grandfather, Shah Tahmasb, on the other hand, had to forge it through decades of bloodshed and politicking with the elites. The result of Tahmasb's transformation in the eyes of his chiefs as a *valī-yi niʿmat*, a title not usually associated with Sufi leaders, marked a watershed in their history – an indication that a transition from spiritual Sufi origins to one of temporal power, with all the trappings of kingship, had taken firm root. This perception granted the new generation of Sufi kings authority as the transmitters of the Creator's *niʿmat* in material patronage, and endowed them with an unassailable claim to legitimacy beyond what their holy Shiʿi-Sufi lineage offered.

34 Munshī, *Tārīkh-i ʿĀlam'ārā-yi ʿAbbāsī*, 542.
35 Ibid., 426–28.

By the early eleventh/seventeenth century, the Safavid shah and his family had vast material resources to create a court society soaked in ease and contentment in a new capital, the city of Isfahan. It was around this time that the Qizilbash began to lose their military prestige and political power. If Ibn Khaldun had observed the Safavids' ideological transition (see the Introduction), he undoubtedly would have warned that the seed of their disintegration just sprouted.

6

Devotional Loyalty at the Epicenter of Power

As shown in Chapters 4–5, a host of political, religious, and military challenges confronted the Safavids when Tahmasb ascended the throne and struggled to rule amidst foreign invasions and the shattered Qizilbash confederacy. In this era of severe instability strengthening his tie with the Qizilbash chiefs through deliberate cultivation of patronage relationships was framed as sacred, as we saw in the form of high administrative and provincial appointments. The court's hope that such perception would convince many of the chiefs to remain loyal produced substantial results that manifested in the reunification of the Qizilbash confederacy by the mid-tenth/sixteenth century that effectively countered the Ottoman invasion and forced the Peace of Amasya.

Unlike consecrated ties of loyalty in broad political associations, the type of relationship explored in this chapter concerns the personal ties between Tahmasb and members of his inner circle. This was the heart of the Safavid political power – the decision-making nucleus and the cohort behind many of the political gains and losses discussed in Chapter 5.

6.1 *MUQARRABĀN*: TAHMASB'S INNER CIRCLE

Several Qizilbash chiefs resided close to court (*umarā-yi dargāh*) in contrast to most of the provincial commanders (*umarā-yi sar-hadd*). The chiefs and ministers who were part of the itinerant Safavid court naturally occupied a physical proximity that enabled them to form fuller

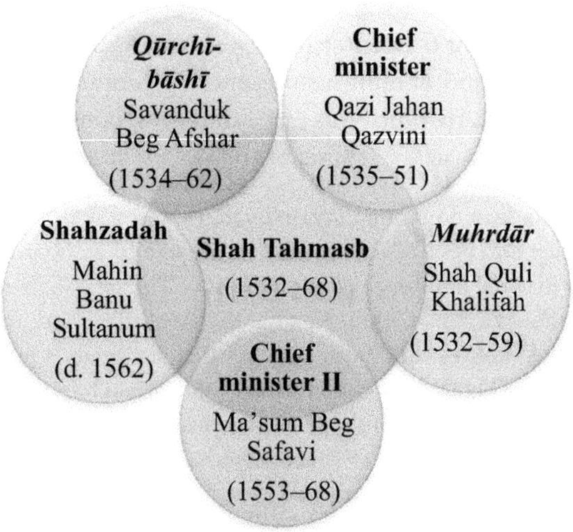

FIGURE 6.1 Shah Tahmasb's inner circle

connections with one another. They were there because of their personal friendship and proven loyalty to Tahmasb and the Safavid house.[1]

Tahmasb's inner circle was known at court as the *muqarrabān* (i.e., "those who have gained proximity to the holy"; see Section 6.2), his most trusted advisors and confidants. They were Savinduk Beg (d. 969/1562) from the Afshar tribe, the head of Tahmasb's elite bodyguards (*qūrchī-bāshī*); Shah Quli Khalifah (d. 965/1557) of the Zu al-Qadr tribe, the keeper of the royal seal (*muhrdār*); Qazi Jahan Qazvini (d. 960/1553), the chief minister (*vizīr*) from a family of scholars of Qazvin; and Mahin Banu Shahzadah Sultanum (d. 969/1562), Tahmasb's younger sister (see Figure 6.1).[2] In order to focus the discussion, I have chosen the above three senior officials among the cohort of trusted courtiers precisely for

[1] Other members of the court society known by the categories of *musāhib*, *mulāzim*, and *mu'tamad* (generally a "trusted retainer") served the ruler's various needs and indeed developed personal attachments to their patron and vice versa that were deep and often lifelong such as the intimate relationship between Princess Mahin Banu and her attendants discussed in Section 6.6. They also served as close attendants of the royal household and powerful chiefs. Their function, however, was distinct from those of the *muqarrabān* and did not constitute "decision-making power." For various duties of the *mulāzims*, see Floor, *Government Institutions*, 144–49. A clear example is Munshi Qazvini's usage of *mulāzim* in reference to the governor of Baghdad Muhammad Khan Sharaf al-Din's newly acquired companions (*Javāhir al-Akhbār*, 196–97).

[2] For a description of Tahmasb's inner circle, see the recently discovered document in José Cutillas Ferrer, "War and Diplomacy: A Letter Describing Shah Tahmasb I and His Ministers," in *The Spanish Monarchy and Safavid Persia in the Early Modern Period:*

the reason that they occupied the highest military and bureaucratic offices of the emerging state at the center of power, and Mahin Banu for her vast patronage activities and ubiquitous presence in Tahmab's political life.

A Venetian emissary who was at Tahmasb's court in 946/1539-40 provides a rare eye-witness account of the shah's *muqarrabān*:

> The King was thus seated upon a *takya-namad*, that is, a felt of Khurasan, which was of great price; and beside him was his sword, with its scabbard depicted like a lion's skin, and his bow and four or five arrows ... The said Shah entrusted me to the hands of the said Shah Quli Khalifa the Muhrdar, and the whole time I frequented the houses of those Lords, that is Shah Quli Khalifa, the Qurchibashi, Qara Khalifa ... Qadi-yi Jahan [and others] ... Thus, all of these used to take pleasure in talking with me and used to take me freely to their houses, and allow me to stay sometimes 15 or 20 days.[3]

There was a growing number of influential officials serving the Safavid court who contributed to building a viable political system. For nearly three tumultuous decades, however, these four individuals stand out in the sources when Tahmasb attempted to consolidate his power, roughly from the first Ottoman invasion in 940/1532-3 to 969-70/1562 when Tahmasb imprisoned his son Ismail Mirza, the future Shah Ismail II.[4]

Politics, War and Religion, ed. Enrique García Hernán, José Cutillas Ferrer, and Rudi Matthee (Valencia: Albatros, 2016), 29–41. This generation of *muqarrab*s under Tahmasb paved the way for the institutionalization of the position for subsequent shahs. Toward the end of the Safavid period *muqarrab*s included senior officers of the heram, the chief astrologer, and the holder of the royal seal. Mīrzā Rafīʿā Jābirī Ansārī, *Dastur al-Moluk: A Safavid State Manual*, ed. and trans. Willem M. Floor and Mohammad Hassan Faghfoory (Costa Mesa: Mazda Publishers, 2007), 162–68. There were two categories in this group: those titled *ʿālī-jāh muqarrab al-khāqān*, who were considered the pillars of state (*arkān-i dawlat*) and occupied the highest echelon of the court, and the other assembly, the *muqarrab al-khāqān*, without the special appellation of *ʿālī-jāh*. These latter officials were of a lower rank than the seven "pillars of the state." For details on their various functions, see the three late Safavid state manuals *Tazkirat al-Mulūk*, *Dastūr al-Mulūk*, and *Alqāb va Mavājib-i Dawrah-yi Salātīn-i Safaviyyah*, written between 1137/1725 and 1143/1731. Roger M. Savory, "The Principal Offices of the Safawid State during the Reign of Ismaʿīl I (907–30/1501–24)," *Bulletin of the School of Oriental and African Studies* 23, no. 1 (1960): 91–105; Roger M. Savory, "The Principal Offices of the Safawid State during the Reign of Tahmāsp I (930–84/1524–76)," *Bulletin of the School of Oriental and African Studies* 24, no. 1 (1961): 65–85; Roger M. Savory, "Some Notes on the Provincial Administration of the Early Safawid Empire," *Bulletin of the School of Oriental and African Studies* 27, no. 1 (1964): 114–28; Floor, *Government Institutions*, 28–34, 40–41.

3 Membré, *Mission to the Lord Sophy of Persia*, 21, 31.

4 Other powerful members of Tahmsb's coterie included Maʿsum Beg Safavi, Badr Khan Ustajlu, and Hasan Beg *yūzbāshī*. Maʿsum Beg was a distant cousin of Shah Tahmsb. His grandfather was Shaykh Haydar's brother. According to *Tārīkh-i Qizilbāshān*, 23, he was a *qūrchī* at the time of Shah Tahmasb's accession; then became *yūzbāshī*, and after that was

Savinduk Beg, Shah Quli Khalifah, and Qazi Jahan rose together and their association with Tahmasb began during the dire situation of the Ottoman invasion of 940/1533-4. Over the next three decades, their camaraderie deepened and was continually renewed by their participation in the politics of power that engulfed their lives. Their long careers (Savinduk Beg as the head of the royal guards (*qūrchī-bāshī*), twenty-eight years; Shah Quli as the royal seal bearer (*muhrdār*), twenty-six years; and Qazi Jahan, the chief minister (*vazīr*), fifteen years) underline their firm loyalty to Tahmasb and commitment to the survival of the order. Another person in Tahmasb's inner circle was his sister and confidant Mahin Banu (d. 969/1562), a powerful political figure at court, and a great patron of the era's intellectual activities. As an intimate of the brother, she was uniquely positioned to advise him on all matters, political and personal (see Section 6.6).

In one respect, these four represented four crucial elements of Tahmasb's struggle to strengthen his hold on power: the military (Savinduk Beg who later became the *amīr al-umarā*, chief of the army); political Sufism (Shah Quli Khalifah, a spiritual deputy and military commander); the administration and finance (Qazi Jahan, his chief minister); and the family (his sister Mahin Banu).

Tahmasb's coterie served a similar function as that of his father, Shah Ismail, and his small band of devotees known as the *ahl-i ikhtisās* (Sufis of Lahijan), a group whose devotional loyalty and political skills helped secure crucial alliances in the initial phase of the Safavid insurrection in the 890s/1490s. Tahmasb's inner circle belonged to that generation of devotees, intensely loyal, and now committed in helping Ismail's son survive.[5]

The trio were members of the *dīvān-i aʿlā* (the high council), and part of a more exclusive inner court, the *dīvān-i jānqī* (royal privy council). Many of the political gains and failures discussed in Chapter 5 were due to the role this group played during the formative period of the dynasty. Several court officials orbited the Safavid shah and were considered his *muqarrabs*. These three, however, were regarded as the 'pillars of the

elevated to the head custodian of the Ardabil shrine. He finally became the *vakīl* of the shah but was killed years later in 976/1568 on a journey to Mecca on the orders of Sultan Selim II. Badr Khan and Hasan Beg were among Tahmasb's trusted generals and they are frequently mentioned in major political events of the period.

5 Aubin, " Révolution chiite et conservatism." The chronicler Qummī describes them as *ahl-i ikhtisās*. Qummī, *Khulāsat al-Tavārīkh*, 435; Shīrāzī, *Takmilat al-Akhbār*, 36.

state' (*arkān-i dawlat*) and occupied senior positions at the heart of the Safavid political system.[6]

Their title, *muqarrab*, was a spiritually laden descriptor meaning "he who is brought near [to the Sacred]." When examined closely, the term helps explain the hermeneutics that brought it to the thresholds of the Safavid political theology and aided political men in defining their ties to the Sufi king at the center of power. The lives and careers examined below demonstrate how spiritual ties of this sort were generated over time and maintained as the Safavid order began to assume the political structures of dynastic kingship by the mid-tenth/sixteenth century.

6.2 QURBA

The title of *muqarrabān* (Pers. pl.) was traced to *al-muqarrabūn* of the Qur'an, meaning those who have gained proximity to the Creator through their remarkable faith as found in the famous apocalyptic verses of Surat al-Waqiʿa (The Event) 56:1–12, 56:88; Surat al-Mutaffafin (The Defrauding) 83:13–28; and the coming of the Prophet Jesus son of Mary in Surat Al ʿImran (The House of ʿImran) 3:42–46.[7] For sheikhs and disciples submerged in Sufi practices and ruminations on the holy book, *qurba* and *taqarrub* became technical terms central to understanding their spiritual progression on the path to the Creator. Sufi sheikhs such as

[6] According to the late administrative manual *Tazkirat al-Mulūk*, seven members comprised the *dīvān-i jānqi*: the *qūrchī-bāshī* (head of the royal guards, and commander in chief of the army); the *vizīr* (chief minister); the *qullar-āqāsī* (commander of cavalry); the *īshīk-āqāsī-bāshī* (master of ceremony); the *tufangchī-āqāsī* (commander of firearms); the *dīvānbegī*; and the *majlis-nivīs* (chancery secretary). Minorsky, trans., *Tadhkirat al-Mulūk*, 44. The comptroller general (*mustawfī al-mamālik*) Khvajah Qasim Natanzi, for example, was a member of the inner circle and served Tahmasb for nearly three decades (938–68/1532–61). The record regarding his life and career, however, is scarce.

[7] From the Arabic root *q-r-b*, meaning "nearness, closeness"; the verbal noun *taqarrub* means "approach, approximation," which in Persian turned into the compound verbs *taqarrub yāftan/justan/varzīdan*, "to gain/seek proximity." For further philological details, see "*q-r-b*" in early lexicons Ismāʿīl b. Hammad al-Jawharī, *Tāj al-Lugha wa-Sihāh al-ʿArabiyya*, ed. Ahmad al-Ghafūr ʿAttār (Beirut: Dar al-ʿIlm, 1987); Abū al-Qāsim Ismāʿīl b. ʿAbbād Sāhib al-Tālqānī, *al-Muhīt fī al-Lugha*, ed. Muhammad Hasan Āl Yāsīn (Beirut: ʿĀlam al-Kutub, 1994); al-Azharī, *Tahdhib al-Lugha*, 9:122–27. For medieval/early modern periods, see "*q-r-b*" in Muhammad b. Mukarram Ibn Manzūr, *Lisān al-ʿArab* (Riyadh: Markaz al-Turāth li-l-Barmajiyyāt, 2013); Abū Tāhir Majīd al-Dīn Muhammad b. Yaʿqūb Fayrūzābādī, *al-Qāmūs al-Muhīt*, ed. Nasr al-Hurini (Beirut: Dār al-Fikr, 1978). Court designation as such became ubiquitous in the political language of the other early modern states such as the Ottomans and the Mughals who shared with the Safavids the common reservoir of sacred language found in the Qur'an.

Sarraj al-Tusi, Nur al-Din Isfarayini, Haj Bektash Vali, and others viewed *qurba* as one of the psychological states (*ahvāl*) sought by their disciples.[8]

The concept, for instance, served the Safavid order's political needs to signify the disciples' (i.e., the officials') journey to attain proximity to the Sufi king. This was yet another manner by which the Safavids inscribed mystical meaning into their sociopolitical ties. The concept thus reveals how loyalty was safeguarded at the epicenter of Safavid power. *Taqarrub varzīdan* in the context of political Sufism required a prolonged face-to-face interaction. Shah Tahmasb's relationship with his *muqarrab*s, as explored below, formed over many years, under extremely perilous circumstances, and was only severed by death.[9]

6.3 THE HEAD OF THE KING'S GUARDS (*QŪRCHĪ-BĀSHĪ*)

"Ninety years old, tall and lean ... He rides with great magnificence, surrounded by about two hundred servants, some walking, others on horseback. And they carry his sceptre, bow and arrows, and a rug in a broadcloth bag, and a small silver pitcher."[10] This description of Savinduk Beg is found in a report by an anonymous Italian emissary in the early 1560s. Decades earlier, the Venetian envoy Michele Membré, who stayed with Savinduk Beg upon his visit to the court, describes him in this manner: "[Savinduk Beg has] a white beard, who also goes with a *tabarrā'ī* crying out before him, his dwelling in Tabriz is to the west, by a bath, and in his courtyard, there is a truly beautiful garden. All these great Lords too, each one of them has one or two of those *tabarrā'ī*s who curse the Ottomans." He further reported that Savinduk Beg's chambers at court in Tabriz were adjacent to the royal quarters, signifying his proximity to the shah.[11]

[8] al-'Abbādī, *al-Tasfiyah*, 195–96; Isfarāyinī, *Kāshif al-Asrār*, 119–20, 113–14, 151–52; Abū Nasr Sarrāj al-Tūsī, *al-Lum'a fī al-Tasawwuf*, ed. Reynold Nicholson, trans. Mahdī Muhabbatī (Tehran: Asātīr, 1381), 26–27; Kāshānī, *Misbāh al-Hidāya*, 417–19; Veli, *Maqālāt-i Ghaybiyyah*, 73.

[9] One's *qurba* to a patron may on rare occasions be passed on to one's son, as was the case with Shah 'Abbas I's *sipahsālar*, Murshid Quli Khan, and his son, Imam Quli Khan. See also the other usage of *taqarrub* in the chancellery document collection *Sharafnāmah* (322–33) by the mid-tenth/sixteenth-century court secretary Ruh Allah Lari Shirazi.

[10] Ferrer, "War and Diplomacy," 33n19.

[11] The *tabarrā'ī* that he mentions is a person in charge of cursing the first three caliphs publicly, much to the fury of the Ottoman court and 'ulema. Aside from the shah and the princes, only the highest-ranking members of the Safavid elite had these men in their service. Membré, *Mission to the Lord Sophy of Persia*, 21–29.

As was previously noted, the execution of Hussein Khan, the chief of the Shamlus, was a turning point in Tahmasb's reign. Hussein Khan's end thus marked a new beginning for Savinduk Beg, who had plunged his dagger into Hussein's side in the royal tent. From that moment on, Savinduk Beg became the most powerful military commander in the realm, in charge of the elite of the Safavid forces, the *qūrchī*s (royal bodyguards), while possessing the added leverage of having Tahmasb's ear. Unlike some of the chiefs of the Ustajlus, Shamlus, and Takallus, Savinduk Beg and other Afshar chieftains managed to avoid the deadly factional politics of the civil war in the late 930s/early 1530s, which might have helped his climb.[12]

As the head of the royal guards, Savinduk Beg's position entailed certain administrative duties. In theory, the appointment, dismissal, and welfare of the *qūrchī*s were under his purview.[13] It seems, however, that he had delegated most of these administrative tasks to his bureaucratic underling, the minister Khvajah Mirza Beg,[14] who was in charge of the *daftar-i qūrchī* (registers of the guards) and their respective staff. Savinduk Beg appears to have devoted his time more to military and political affairs than to administration.[15]

In the late 960s/1550s, when the capital was transferred to Qazvin, Savinduk Beg was among the few Safavid grandees who built his home in

[12] Haneda posits that the office of *qūrchī-bāshī* was secondary to other prominent stations such as *khānī*. He cites a case where an amir abandons his position as a *qūrchī-bāshī* in favor of becoming a *khān* (chief). This case might very well have been a personal decision based on that amir's political maneuvering at the time and should not be taken as definite indication of the subordinate position of *qūrchī-bāshī* in the Safavid politico-military organization. Aside from the three state manuals of the later Safavid period, there is more than ample evidence in the chronicles attesting to the primacy of this office at the center of the Safavid political structure. Haneda, *Le Châh et les Qizilbāš*, 182–84.

[13] The *qūrchī*s were drawn from various Qizilbash tribes such as the Ustajlu, Rumlu, Takallu, and Afshar. They were most likely those who had proven themselves in battle. Some were also recruited from among the troops of defeated provincial rulers. In the later Safavid period, Georgians and Circasians also entered the ranks of the *qūrchī*s in greater numbers. Haneda, "L'Évolution de la Garde Royale des Safavides."

[14] Qummī, *Khulāsat al-Tavārīkh*, 2:987.

[15] Floor, *Government Institutions*, 152–53. The *qūrchī* corps was subdivided into three divisions under the *qūrchī-bāshī*'s command. They consisted of (a) *qūrchīyān-i mulāzim* (guards-in-waiting), who attended the shah; (b) *qūrchīyān-i yarāq* (guards of the royal arsenal), who were responsible for the shah's sword, dagger, bow and arrow, musket, mace, shield, and armor; and (c) *qūrchīyān-i ʿizām* (regulars), who were permanently stationed in the palace and charged with the shah's safety. These subdivisions were most pronounced in the later eleventh/seventeenth century, as reflected in *Dastūr al-Mulūk*. See Floor, *Government Institutions*, 138–47, for details of these divisions.

the royal precinct in the Chahar Bagh district. The Tahmasbian poet and bureaucrat ʿAbdi Beg Shirazi in his *Rawzat al-Safāt* describes the gardens and palaces of these individuals alongside members of the royal family such as Bahram Mirza and Mahin Banu. A patriarchal city, the royal quarter of the new capital reflected Tahmasb's perception of his inner circle as members of his extended household.[16]

We first hear of Savinduk Beg as the governor of a small frontier town of Sarakhs on the Safavid-Uzbek border in the east. In 927/1521, he warned Durmish Khan Shamlu, the late governor of Herat and the elder brother of Hussein Khan Shamlu (whom he helped execute), that he was facing a massive invasion. This was the Uzbek army of ʿUbayd Khan, 30,000 strong, that had crossed Amudarya and entered Safavid territory.[17]

Savinduk Beg must have earned a fierce reputation as an Afshar commander during the brutal Uzbek wars in the eastern frontiers of Khurasan, where he was stationed in the decade following the death of Shah Ismail in 930/1524. Within five years of the decisive Battle of Jam in 935/1528-9 against the Uzbeks, he had climbed the military ranks to become a *muqarrab* and one of the shah's most trusted men. The sources are silent concerning this period of his rise. We only begin to get to know him after he succeeds Khalifah Muhammad Shamlu as the head of the royal guards in 940/1534.[18]

Savinduk Beg's climb was in no way meteoric, however. He had been a devotee of the Safavid order from the onset of Shah Ismail's insurrection. He was one of the *ahl-i ikhtisās* or Sufis of Gilan. This highly exclusive designation during the early years of Shah Ismail's uprising was reserved only for the most die-hard devotees who were closest to the Safavid house in its most vulnerable period. He must have strongly believed in the sanctity of Shah Ismail's mission as a young man, fighting for the Safavid cause along with his Afshar tribesmen.[19]

[16] ʿAbdī Beg Shīrāzī, *Rawzat al-Safāt* (Moscow: Idārah-i Nashr-i Dānish, 1974), 40–59. For a discussion on a patriarchal city in the Islamicate context, see Stephen P. Blake, *Shahjahanabad: The Sovereign City in Mughal India, 1639–1739* (Cambridge University Press, 2002).

[17] Khvāndamīr, *Tārīkh-i Shāh Ismāʿīl*, 103. Sarakhs remains a frontier town today on the Iran-Afghanistan border.

[18] The sources are not clear as to Savinduk Beg's immediate predecessors. In 940/1533-4 we read of three different individuals holding the office of the *qūrchī-bāshī*: Khalifah Muhammad Shamlu, Ughlan Khalifah Shamlu (who might very well be the same person as Khalifah Muhammad Shamlu), and Shir Hasan Zu al-Qadr. Floor, *Government Institutions*, 141.

[19] Qummī, *Khulāsat al-Tavārīkh*, 1:435; Shīrāzī, *Takmilat al-Akhbār*, 36. This group (Sufīyan-i Jilani or Gilani) is sometimes referred to as the "Sufis of Lahijan," in reference to the capital of Gilan province.

Savinduk Beg was in his late twenties when the young Ismail entered Tabriz triumphant in the summer of 906/1501 and was crowned the shah. He exemplified a young Qizilbash warrior filled with passion and enthusiasm for his charismatic leader, for whom he was willing to lay down his life. Now, more than thirty years later, he was in a position to devote himself to Ismail's son in a perilous time. No doubt, his personal qualities had helped him along the way to eventually gain *qurba* in a most trusted position in the order in charge of Tahmasb and his family's security.[20]

Since his succession to the throne, the young Tahmasb had been fighting enemies from abroad and disloyal kinsmen at home who did not expect him to survive. By 940/1534, when Tahmasb reached twenty years of age, Savinduk Beg was in his late fifties, a seasoned warrior and a widely respected veteran who embodied *ikhlās* to the Safavid house. This strong bond of loyalty is demonstrated by the fact that he retained his post until his death twenty-eight years later in 969/1562. In fact, the only *qūrchī-bāshī* in the history of the Safavids that came close to having as long a tenure as that of Savinduk Beg was Shah ʿAbbas I's *qūrchī-bāshī* Allah Quli Beg of the Qajar tribe, who served for twenty-one years.[21]

Absolute loyalty to Tahmasb was sometimes extremely burdensome, however. When, for example, Savinduk Beg's brother Mahdi Quli Sultan Afshar, the governor of Shushtar, rebelled in 946/1540, Tahmasb sent him and another Afshar chief, Haydar Quli Sultan, to suppress the rebellion. They crushed the revolt and Savinduk Beg brought his brother's severed head back to Tahmasb, demonstrating that his loyalty and obedience to the king transcended even filial ties.[22]

6.4 SAVINDUK BEG'S POLITICAL IMPACT

According to later Safavid sources, one had to be a member of the *qūrchī* corps to become its leader. With the suspension of the position of the *amīr al-umarā* (commander of the army) after Hussein Khan's execution, the office of the *qūrchī-bāshī* took on the duties of the former, as Tahmasb increasingly relied on Savinduk Beg for political and military advice. As a

[20] Qummī states that Savinduk Beg was more than ninety years old at the time of his death in 969/1562. He therefore must have been born in the 870s/1470s (Qummī, *Khulāsat al-Tavārīkh*, 1:435).

[21] Ghaffārī, *Tārīkh-i Jahān'ārā*, 307; Qummī, *Khulāsat al-Tavārīkh*, 1:435. See the details related to the office of the *qūrchī-bāshī* in Floor, *Governmnet Institutions*, 140–43.

[22] Qummī, *Khulāsat al-Tavārīkh*, 1:289; Ghaffārī, *Tārīkh-i Jahān'ārā*, 294.

result of merging the top-two military offices into the hands of a man deeply loyal to him, Tahmasb increased his own power and clout vis-à-vis Rumlu, Takallu, and certainly the Shamlu chiefs at a crucial time.[23]

The importance of the office of *qūrchī-bāshī* to the person of the shah is evident in that the first and third Safavid *qūrchī-bāshī*s (Abdal ʿAli Beg Dadah and Saru Pirah Ustajlu) were chosen from the *ahl-i ikhtisās*. In the decade following the death of Shah Ismail in 930/1524, the post of *qūrchī-bāshī* changed hands no less than eight times, but Savinduk Beg was able to maintain his position for nearly three decades. Those who occupied the post prior to Savinduk Beg, such as Tatar Ughli Takallu and Durah Beg (Dahdah Beg), were caught up in the maelstrom of the civil war and unable to steer clear of factionalism to retain their sensitive position. Tatar Ughli, for instance, was put to death in 935/1528-9 apparently for his opposition to the chief Chuha Sultan's ascendency and hard-earned *qurba* to Tahmasb. Durah Beg was killed for his role in the Takallu rebellion of 938/1531 and the violent clash that ensued near the royal encampment that directly placed Tahmasb's life in jeopardy.[24]

In the shaping of Safavid foreign relations, Savinduk Beg's role was crucial, especially in his negotiations with the Ottoman governor Ayas Pasha. In a letter dated 951/1544, for instance, Savinduk Beg spells out the Safavid position on the disputed Georgian territories that Tahmasb had annexed, iterates a protocol for exchange of defectors, and insists on promotion of diplomacy between the two powers.[25] Later that year, when the Mughal Prince Humayun had lost the upper hand to his brother Kamran for the throne and had to flee the subcontinent, Savinduk Beg

[23] Floor, *Government Institutions*, 138–39, citing the late eleventh/seventeenth-century European travelers' observations. There is, however, no evidence to support that this regulation was in place during the tenth/sixteenth century. Certainly, there is no mention of Savinduk Beg as a member of the *qūrchī* corps prior to his appointment as its head.

[24] Shīrāzī, *Takmilat al-Akhbār*, 70–71; Khvurshāh b. Qubād Husaynī, *Tārīkh-i Īlchī-i Nizām Shāh: Tārīkh-i Safavīyah az Āghāz tā Sāl-i 972 Hijrī Qamarī*, ed. Muhammad Rizā Nasīrī and Koichi Haneda (Tehran: Anjuman-i Āsār va Mafākhir-i Farhangī, 2000), 101; Qummī, *Khulāsat al-Tavārīkh*, 214–15.

[25] Fekete and Hazai, eds., *Einführung in die Persische Paläographie*, 411–23; cf. the Ottoman grand minister Iskandar Pasha's communications with the Safavid *muqarrab*s in ʿAbd al-Husayn Navāʾī, *Shāh Tahmāsb Safavī: Majmūʿah-i Asnād va Mukātibāt-i Tārīkhī* (Tehran: Bunyād-i Farhang-i Īrān, 1350), 240–44; see also their exchanges with the Ottoman court in the 960s/1560s, especially with Rustam Pasha, Muhammad Pasha, and ʿAli Pasha in ibid., 437–41; Feridun Bey, *Mecmua-ı Münşeât-i Feridun Bey*, vol. 2 (Istanbul: Takvimhane-i Amire, 1858), 59–61. Another major event of the time involving the Mughals of India was Prince Humayun's flight to Tahmasb's court which they helped arrange (Rūmlū, *Ahsan al-Tavārīkh*, 3:1291).

was among the Safavid dignitaries who welcomed him to court in 951/1544.[26]

In 967/1560, when the Ottoman Prince Bayezid sought refuge with Tahmasb, he inevitably pulled the Safavids into the Ottoman war of succession that nearly destroyed the hard-won Peace of Amasya between the two states.[27] When Bayezid reached the vicinity of the Safavid capital at Qazvin, Shah Tahmasb dispatched Savinduk Beg to escort him and his troops to court.[28] One of Bayezid's sons, Sultan Muhammad, was entrusted to Savinduk Beg's personal care. After a series of lengthy diplomatic maneuverings, Tahmasb agreed to surrender the renegade prince along with his household. Savinduk Beg's men made the arrests and handed them over to the Ottoman imperial delegate who had recently arrived at court. They executed the prince along with his family shortly thereafter. Tahmasb bartered their lives in exchange for preserving the peace accord.[29]

In addition to handling sensitive state matters, military campaigning was part of Savinduk Beg's duties. In 945/1538, for example, the large force that Tahmasb dispatched to subdue Shahrukh b. Sultan Farrukh of Shirvan was under his command along with two prominent Ustajlu chiefs, Mantasha Sultan and Badr Khan;[30] he led a force of *qūrchī*s to pacify the province of Shakki during the third Ottoman invasion in 955/1548; and played a leading role in the campaigns of 957–60/1550–53 in the northeastern frontier.[31] His death in 969/1562 no doubt left a void in Tahmasb's court and among his inner circle that was not easily filled. In fact, Tahmasb did not officially appoint another *qūrchī-bāshī* for more than a decade, until 982/1574.[32]

6.5 THE POLITICAL CAREER OF A SUFI DEPUTY (*KHALĪFAH*)

One of Membré's hosts at the royal encampments and later in Tabriz was Shah Quli Khalifah of the Zu al-Qadr tribe, the *muhrdār* (keeper of the

[26] Rūmlū, *Ahsan al-Tavārīkh*, 3:1289–91; Wheeler M. Thackston, trans., *Three Memoirs of Homayun: Gulbadan Begims Humáyunnáma; Jawhar Áftábachí's Tadhkiratul-Wáqíát; Báyazid Bayáts Táríkh-i Humáyún* (Costa Mesa: Mazda Publishers, 2009), 141.

[27] Svanidze, "The Amasya Peace Treaty," 192.

[28] Rūmlū, *Ahsan al-Tavārīkh*, 3:1415; Ghaffārī, *Tārīkh-i Jahān'ārā*, 304–6.

[29] Shīrāzī, *Takmilat al-Akhbār*, 117; Ghaffārī, *Tārīkh-i Jahān'ārā*, 306.

[30] Rūmlū, *Ahsan al-Tavārīkh*, 3:1261–63.

[31] Ibid., 1323; Munshī, *Tārīkh-i 'Ālam'ārā-yi 'Abbāsī*, 120.

[32] Qummī, *Khulāsat al-Tavārīkh*, 1:435; Floor, *Government Institutions*, 137–41. Savinduk Beg's body was taken to the holy city of Mashhad and interred within the mausoleum precinct of Imam Riza, between the sepulcher of the chief minister Qazi Jahan and the *sadr* Mir Asad Allah.

royal seal). Membré describes him as "a rather fat man, with a slight defect in his eye and a short beard. He has a son who is the Shah's *parvanchi* [a courtier in charge of the royal umbrella]. His dwelling in Tabriz is to the east, near a bath, facing the river, on the right bank."[33]

Shah Quli Khalifah and Savinduk Beg entered Tahmasb's inner circle around the same time, between 939/1532-3 and 940/1533-4, and over the years formed a close friendship. Shah Quli had initially been a *qūrchī* (a royal guard) at court. He most likely served in the upper echelon of the *qūrchī*s in close attendance to the Safavid household. It is unclear how long he served in that capacity before becoming a *muqarrab*. The anonymous author of the *Tārīkh-i Qizilbāshān* tells us that he was elevated to the post of the *īshīk āghāsi-bāshī* (chief chamberlain) after his role in the execution of a certain Dilushaikhi, which must have occurred sometime before 937-8/1531.[34] At that time, Kabah Khalifah Takallu was the *muhrdār*, but he was caught up in the Takallu rebellion during the civil war and executed in 938/1531.[35] For the following two years, the office of the *muhrdār* was in the hands of Mahmud Beg Zu al-Qadr. After his death in 939/1533, Tahmasb appointed Shah Quli as the new *muhrdār-i muhr-i humāyūn*, which he held for the next twenty-six years (939–65/1532–59) until his final days.[36]

Even though he was a high-ranking *qūrchī*, he was also a "*khalīfah*" (deputy), a member of the spiritual guides of the order who oversaw the relations between the Safavid shahs and their disciples across Anatolia and other provinces as discussed in Chapter 2. The Italian visitor Membré recounts two occasions in which ordinary Safavid devotees, one from Adana in Anatolia, the other from Khurasan, came to Shah Quli seeking a personal article belonging to Shah Tahmasb to use as a holy amulet.[37]

As a *muqarrab* and a *khalīfah*, Shah Quli participated in patronage activities, especially in the religious sphere. A record of one of his charitable bequests has survived: a contribution to the endowment (*vaqf*) of the

[33] Membré, *Mission to the Lord Sophy of Persia*, 31.
[34] *Tārīkh-i Qizilbāshān*, 50.
[35] He was involved in the violent clash between Shamlu and Takallu factions at the royal encampment (Qummī, *Khulāsat al-Tavārīkh*, 214–15). There is conflicting information in the sources as to the holder of this office prior to Shah Quli. Munshī Qazvīnī, *Javāhir al-Akhbār*, 161, names Karajlu Ahmad Takallu as the *muhrdār*.
[36] Qummī, *Khulāsat al-Tavārīkh*, 1:223; Ghaffārī, *Tārīkh-i Jahān'ārā*, 287.
[37] Membré, *Mission to the Lord Sophy of Persia*, 41–42; Savory, "The Office of Khalīfat Al-Khulafā"; Floor, "The Khalifeh al-Kholafa."

shrine of the Imam ʿAbd al-ʿAzim in Ray.[38] Moreover, Tahmasb appointed him governor of Qum underlying Shah Quli's spiritual function, for the town held a special place for Shiʿis. It had long been considered a center of their learning and Hazrat-i Maʿsumah's mausoleum added to its sanctity and importance for she was the revered sister of the eighth Shiʿi Imam, ʿAli al-Riza, buried in Mashhad. Her shrine was lavishly patronized by the Safavid family and became a major pilgrimage destination that has continued to this day. As pilgrimage towns usually do, they attract commerce and Qum's revenues boosted the economic and political influence of an empowered Shiʿi clerical class. Shah Quli Khalifah exemplified the hybrid character of militarized Sufis that inhabited the early Safavid governing body.[39]

Tahmasb's confidence in Shah Quli had been established long before his official appointment in 940/1533.[40] During the army's march back from Khurasan, when news reached Tahmasb that Sultan Suleyman himself had crossed into Safavid territory at the head of the main army, they all realized that a full-scale invasion was underway. The threat of a disaster like what occurred after the Battle of Chaldiran in 920/1514, when part of the Safavid household fell into the hands of the Ottoman army, was entirely plausible. Tahmasb, avoiding his father's mistake, sent the royal household from Qum south to Isfahan under Shah Quli's care.[41]

Tahmasb's trust in Shah Quli continued over the years. When in 956/1549, Mahin Banu, Tahmasb's beloved sister, decided to go on a pilgrimage to the shrine of Imam Riza in Mashhad, he chose him to accompany her and made the arrangements. Tahmasb might have even endorsed his

38 Muhammad ʿAlī Hidāyatī, ed., *Āstānah-i Ray: Majmūʿah-i Asnād va Farāmīn* (Tehran: Shirkat-i Sahāmī Ufsit, 1344), 83–92.

39 Qummī, *Khulāsat al-Tavārīkh*, 1:394. Around 960/1553 he held the governance of the province of Darabjird, the easternmost district of Fars (Nasīrī, *Titles and Emoluments*, 174, 263–64). Because of Shah Quli's constant presence at court, he had delegated the city's administration to the cleric Asif Jah Mirza ʿAtaʾ Allah (Qummī, *Khulāsat al-Tavārīkh*, 1:332–33).

40 Around the same time that Tahmasb appointed Shah Quli as the main *muhrdār*, he also appointed Suleyman Beg Kamunah as the keeper of a smaller seal (*muhrdār-i muhr-i sharaf-nifāz*), another highly trusted amir whose office at the time seems to have been a bureaucratic innovation. The information regarding their duties, however, comes from state manuals composed at the end of the Safavid period and may not reflect accurately the responsibilities of these two *muhrdārs*. In the second quarter of the tenth/sixteenth century, when official duties were not clearly demarcated, *muhrdārs* participated in military as well as administrative duties at court (Jābirī Ansārī, *Dastur al-Moluk*, 77; Floor, *Government Institutions*, 68–69).

41 Shīrāzī, *Takmilat al-Akhbār*, 77–78.

marriage to a Safavid princess, the highest form of royal patronage and honor.[42]

Shah Quli's position as the keeper of the great seal gave him immense political power. Membré, who stayed with him, reports that he carried the royal "seals on his breast on golden chains with many jewels." The Safavid seal, aside from serving major administrative functions, was a symbol of power and prestige for its bearer and worn conspicuously at court. In 915/1510, a Venetian traveler who saw Shah Ismail's *muhrdār* Amir Beg Khan Mawsulu reports that he was "a great adherent of Ismael's, who wore two gold chains, covered with rubies and diamonds, round his neck, to which was attached the seal of Ismael, a mark of his greatest confidence."[43]

Like many among the Safavid inner circle, Shah Quli's position crossed the bureaucratic, military, religious boundaries. According to a late Safavid administrative manual, *Dastūr al-Mulūk*, a *muhrdār* "had to seal all *tiyul-nāmah*s for amirs and governors as well as appointment diplomas for viziers, *kalāntar*s, *mustawfī*s, and local tax officials (*ʿummāl*), as well as documents granting various tax exemptions (*suyurghāl*s, *maʿāfī*s, *musallamis*, and *iqtāʾ-yi tamlīk*)." These interventions gave the keeper of royal seal immense influence, but it is uncertain if the early *muhrdār*'s position was this bureaucratic.[44]

Shah Quli's presence alongside Savinduk Beg in the frontlines during the Ottoman wars (939–61/1533–54), and his role in the suppression of several local rebellions, explains why he was perceived primarily as a military leader. For instance, in 946/1539, Tahmasb sent him to Astara as the head of a large contingent to crush Amirah Qubad.[45] Between 957/1551 and 965/1558, Shah Quli was involved in several key campaigns: in Targur and Margur (Kurdish regions) in 957/1551 along with Maʿsum Beg Safavi and a Takallu chieftain, ʿAlu Sultan; a year later, he directed a siege at Saqnaq castle, while Savinduk Beg and Badr Khan assaulted the castle of Kish, which resulted in the subjugation of Darvish Muhammad Khan, the powerful governor of Shakki;[46] in 961/1554, when the Ottomans invaded Safavid territory for the last time under Sultan Suleyman, Shah Quli, along

42 Munshī Qazvīnī, *Javāhir al-Akhbār*, 206; Shīrāzī, *Takmilat al-Akhbār*, 103; Membré, *Mission to the Lord Sophy of Persia*, 26.

43 Membré, *Mission to the Lord Sophy of Persia*, 29; Barbaro and Contarini, *Travels to Tana and Persia*, pt. 2, 109, 197.

44 Jābirī Ansārī, *Dastur al-Moluk*, 76–77; *Tārīkh-i Qizilbāshān*, 4; Floor, *Government Institutions*, 69.

45 Qummī, *Khulāsat al-Tavārīkh*, 1:288; Rūmlū, *Ahsan al-Tavārīkh*, 3:1269.

46 Rūmlū, *Ahsan al-Tavārīkh*, 3:1337–41.

with Maʿsum Beg Safavi and the heir apparent Ismail, were put in charge of raids and counterattacks in the Ottoman territories with significant success, which offered the Safavids some leverage in the ensuing peace negotiations of Amasya; a few months later, we find him leading Safavid troops into Georgia.[47]

Alqas's lengthy uprising against his brother Tahmasb that began in 953/1546 (see Section 5.4) was yet another threat to the survival of the order, and Shah Quli and Savinduk Beg played a central role in its unfolding. Shah Quli was the general who engaged Alqas's forces in the final clash before the latter's flight to the Ottoman court. Prior to the clash, Tahmasb had dispatched a delegation led by Shah Quli and Savinduk Beg to persuade him to abandon his plans for regional autonomy in Shirvan, where he was the governor. An agreement was only to be accepted by the assurance of his oath of loyalty to Tahmasb.[48]

They failed to persuade him. This proved to be their crowning diplomatic failure. Alqas fled to the court of Ottoman Sultan Suleyman, the Safavid's archenemy, only to return at the head of a large army supplied by the sultan leading to nearly a decade of brutal conflict. In 955/1548, his forces attacked the cities of Hamadan, Qum, Kashan, and Isfahan. Unable to compel other Qizilbash chiefs to support him, his failures quickly swelled. Abandoned by his Ottoman benefactor and hotly pursued by Tahmasb's forces, he finally surrendered in Marivan on 9 Ramazan 956 (October 1, 1549). Shah Quli, along with Prince Bahram and Ibrahim Khan of the Zu al-Qadr tribe (the long-time governor of Shiraz), detained and brought him back to court.[49]

The Alqas affair was one among several highly sensitive matters concerning members of the Safavid house that Tahmasb entrusted to Shah Quli. Not long after his appointment to the office of *muhrdār* in 939/1533, Sam Mirza, Tahmasb's other brother, and his royal guardian (*lalah*) Aghzivar Khan came under suspicion of treason. They soon fled eastward. By 943/1536, when they failed to take the frontier town of Qandahar and were defeated by Mughal forces under the command of Prince Kamran, they retreated and held up at the castle of Tabas. Tahmasb soon dispatched

47 Qummī, *Khulāsat al-Tavārīkh*, 1:367–68; Rūmlū, *Ahsan al-Tavārīkh*, 3:1371–72; Shīrāzī, *Takmilat al-Akhbār*, 107.

48 Munshī Qazvīnī, *Javāhir al-Akhbār*, 199–200; Rūmlū, *Ahsan al-Tavārīkh*, 3:1299–1306; Qummī, *Khulāsat al-Tavārīkh*, 1:316; Ghaffārī, *Tārīkh-i Jahān'ārā*, 296.

49 Rūmlū, *Ahsan al-Tavārīkh*, 3:1306, 1330–31; Qummī, *Khulāsat al-Tavārīkh*, 1:338. For a chronology of events, see Cornell Fleischer, "Alqās Mīrzā," *Encyclopædia Iranica*, www.iranicaonline.org/articles/alqas-alqasb-alqas-mirza-safawi.

Shah Quli to the castle to negotiate his surrender. He assured the prince of Tahmsab's pledge for his safety and escorted him back to court. Tahmasb honored his words, but Sam Mirza's companions did not fare so well. They were put to the sword on Tahmasb's orders.[50]

Michele Membré, who arrived at the royal camp three years later and stayed with Shah Quli, unaware of what had transpired, writes how they teased him at court: "Sām Mīrzā, only enjoys himself with his falcons; for the King does not give power to the said Sām Mīrzā; he only has the title, that they call him Emperor of Constantinople and he has no beard. He is a young man of twenty-eight years, stout and short." The chiefs mocking Sam Mirza as the "Emperor of Constantinople" was based on the allegation that he had sought Sultan Suleyman's patronage and protection, and the sultan had in return called him "his son." Later when Sam Mirza at last realized that he could not rebuild his trust with Tahmasb, he asked permission to take up residence in their ancestral town of Ardabil so that he might "devote himself to prayer and intellectual activities" – a pretext at the time for retirement from politics due to fear for one's life. Tahmasb eventually acquiesced.[51]

In 965/1558, while leading an army to crush a Turkmen incursion into Astarabad, Shah Quli fell ill with colic. Shortly thereafter he died on 18 Ramazan 965 (July 4, 1558). Because of the summer heat, his companions could not carry his body far. They thus separated his bones from the flesh and took them for burial to the hallowed grounds of Imam Riza's mausoleum in Mashhad. Shah Quli had the longest tenure as the *muhrdār* in the history of the dynasty, that is, twenty-six years. Before his death, Tahmasb promised him that the office would remain in his family ad infinitum – a gesture that bespoke his deep sense of gratitude to him during the harrowing period of his reign.[52]

6.6 "THE SECOND MARY"

One of the most influential people at court was Tahmasb's younger sister Mahin Banu Shahzadah Sultanum (d. 969/1562). She was the youngest daughter of Shah Ismail and only four years Tahmasb's junior. Their

[50] Rūmlū, *Ahsan al-Tavārīkh*, 3:1247–48; Qummī, *Khulāsat al-Tavārīkh*, 1:266.

[51] Husaynī, *Tārīkh-i Īlchī-i Nizām Shāh*, 126; for rumors of Sam Mirza's defection to the Ottomans, see Tahmāsb Safavī, *Tazkirah-i Shāh Tahmāsb*, 88.

[52] Rūmlū, *Ahsan al-Tavārīkh*, 3:104; Munshī Qazvīnī, *Javāhir al-Akhbār*, 213; Qummī, *Khulāsat al-Tavārīkh*, 1:394–96.

mother, Tajlu Khanum of the Mawsulu tribe, had been a dominant force at court for many years. Tahmasb had four other sisters: Khanish Khanum, Pari-khan Khanum, Farangiz Khanum, and Shah Zainab Khanum. Unlike Tahmasb's other sisters, who had married prominent chiefs and lived away from him, Mahin Banu never married and resided at court with Tahmasb. An intimate bond thus grew between them, especially given their shared experiences of living through the difficult two decades following Tahmasb's accession.[53]

Mahin Banu was deeply involved in the main political events of the period. She exchanged letters, for example, with Khurram Sultan, Sultan Suleyman's beloved wife and a dominant figure at the Ottoman court; she seems to have been instrumental in compelling Tahmasb to assist the dispossessed Mughal prince Humayun to regain his throne;[54] and she was in council during her nephew Ismail Mirza's counterattacks against the Ottomans in the borderlands in 960/1553.[55] One chronicler relates that once when Tahmasb was overcome he placed "all matters of state and finance to be contingent upon her evaluation, and he would not act without her consultation, discretion, and knowledge."[56]

She used her power to protect members of her family from the revenge and fratricide rampant in her midst. When news reached the court that her brother Alqas Mirza had revolted, reports spread that Bahram Mirza, Tahmasb's other brother, had joined him in the rebellion. Mahin Banu quickly dispatched an emissary and urged Bahram to come to court at once so that his loyalty to Tahmasb would not fall under suspicion. Bahram Mirza, who was in Shushtar, wasted no time, and traveled a great distance to arrive at court, bearing gifts. Tahmasb having experienced several betrayals was by now a highly suspicious man. Mahin Banu knew this and by acting quickly managed to prevent what might have turned into a devastating tragedy.[57]

Four years later when Alqas was finally captured on 9 Ramazan 956 (October 1, 1549), Tahmasb prepared a humiliating public spectacle for his brother's homecoming. A degrading costume, bulky and laden with

53 Qummī, *Khulāsat al-Tavārīkh*, 1:155.

54 Navāʾī, ed., *Majmūʿah-i Asnād va Mukātibāt*, 343–47; Thackston, trans., *Three Memoirs of Homayun*, 139–46; Riazul Islam, *Indo-Persian Relations: A Study of the Political and Diplomatic Relations between the Mughal Empire and Iran* (Tehran: Iranian Culture Foundation, 1970), 36–37.

55 Munshī Qazvīnī, *Javāhir al-Akhbār*, 208.

56 Qummī, *Khulāsat al-Tavārīkh*, 1:430.

57 Munshī Qazvīnī, *Javāhir al-Akhbār*, 198.

loads of cotton, was waiting for him. He was made to wear it while riding in on a little sickly horse, one of his hands tied to the neck by means of a "v-shaped" tree branch (known as *du-shākhah*, a type of cangue). When Mahin Banu learned of Tahmasb's plan, she intervened and convinced him to spare Alqas the agony and allow her to instead send him a simple coat (*qabā-yi sādah*) and food.[58]

He was taken to the infamous castle of Qahqahah soon thereafter on the shah's orders. Everyone at court, including Mahin Banu, knew that his fate was sealed, and that she would not see him again. On 21 Rabiʿ I 957 (April 9, 1550), he was thrown down from Qahqahah's high walls to his death.[59] Her decision to undertake a long pilgrimage to the shrine of Imam Riza in Mashhad precisely at this time bespeaks her state of mental health. She chose Shah Quli Khalifah to lead the retinue.[60]

A remarkable record exists regarding Mahin Banu's final days before her death, her will addressed to Tahmasb, preserved by the meticulous pen of the courtier Qazi Ahmad Qummi. The will excerpted here provides a rare glimpse into the special bond that these two siblings shared. Composed in the melancholia of her deathbed, it is deeply poignant. Her informal tone in expressing her final wishes to her brother (she uses the casual second-person singular pronoun "*tu*" and singular personal suffixes) conveys a level of intimacy with the ruler not seen in other sources.

I, Mahin Banu, make a [last] will to Lord Shah Tahmasb that you are my brother, I swear to you; to the sovereignty of Almighty God, that besides Him there is no other god; [I swear] by the spirits of the Immaculate Fourteen that you first send me [i.e., my body] to Karbala. Secondly, abide to all that I have said of ritual prayers [for my spirit], pilgrimage to Mecca, Islamic charitable tax and donations, and reparation for injustices as written in a separate scroll ...

Obey [my] recommendation for Mulla ʿImad [al-Din ʿAli Qari]. [Next,] my stewardess, who has served me for forty-three years; she is an old woman. Protect whatever property I have given her and relinquished [at my death]. Her property at court, I beg of you to give to her: Khan Begi Khanum's horse and Zainal's mule are hers; and give her the mule of Jam and the horse of Gulvarn Sufiyan. Appoint her as Prince Sultan Suleyman's stewardess and send her to Mashhad, for she is a virtuous woman. If she [wishes] to accompany me [i.e., my corpse] to Karbala, permit her. After she returns, of course, send her to Holy Mashhad to Sultan Suleyman [the Safavid prince] so that she would remain there.

58 Ibid., 204–5.
59 Ghaffārī, *Tārīkh-i Jahān'ārā*, 299; Rūmlū, *Ahsan al-Tavārīkh*, 3:339–40.
60 Shīrāzī, *Takmilat al-Akhbār*, 103; Munshī Qazvīnī, *Javāhir al-Akhbār*, 205–6.

> What more shall I write? Absolve me, [and] if I have behaved impolitely, forgive me. Do not forget me, for other than you, who are my father as well as my brother, I have no beneficiary. After [my] death, I have arranged for the freedom of my servants and have paid them; and I have freed Iqbal. After me, I leave them to you to look after, for they are strangers and without a lord.[61]

The obligation she carried for the welfare of her servants after her death points to the intimate patron-client bond that carried into the afterlife. She died on 14 Jumadi I 969 (January 20, 1562), at the age of forty-four.[62]

She remained unmarried throughout her life – an unusual occurrence for a Safavid princess, as one way that the Safavids expanded their power was by absorbing other influential houses through marriage.[63] Tahmasb, in a procession led by her teacher Mawlana ʿImad al-Din Qari and the *sadr* Mir Taqi al-Din Muhammad, carried her lifeless body to Imamzadah Shahzadah Hussein for the ritual prayer (*namāz-i miyyat*). From there she was taken to the city of Qum for burial near Hazrat-i Maʿsumah's mausoleum, of which she was a patroness. Years later in 993/1585, her remains were at last transferred to Karbala in accordance with her will, where they were interred in their final resting place.[64] The poet Muhtasham Kashani in his elegy extols her piety and saintliness, immortalizing her as "the Second Mary" (*Maryam-i thānī*).[65]

Tahmasb seems to have remained preoccupied with her memory years after her death. Concerned about her afterlife, he did the only thing a religious man could do for a deceased loved one – implore God for her salvation. In a royal decree dated 972/1564, for instance, he instructs six Qurʾan reciters to continuously read the holy book upon "the grave of my blessed departed sister Sultanim."[66]

The years 968–69/1561–62 were tragic for the Safavid court. One chronicler wrote, "the perfidious fortune removed an assembly who in their own way were without equal . . . this group was the adornment of the [royal] camp." He was referring to a series of deaths that occurred at court

[61] Qummī, *Khulāsat al-Tavārīkh*, 2:983–84; Munshī Qazvīnī, *Javāhir al-Akhbār*, 220–21.

[62] Ghaffārī, *Tārīkh-i Jahān'ārā*, 307; Qummī, *Khulāsat al-Tavārīkh*, 1:429; Rūmlū, *Ahsan al-Tavārīkh*, 3:1427.

[63] There are speculations that Tahmasb did not permit her to marry because he wanted to await the arrival of the hidden Imam and marry her to him. This claim, however, cannot be fully substantiated.

[64] Qummī, *Khulāsat al-Tavārīkh*, 1:428–31.

[65] Rūmlū, *Ahsan al-Tavārīkh*, 3:1426; Muhtasham Kāshānī, *Dīvān-i Muhtasham-i Kāshānī*, ed. Akbar Bihdarvand (Tehran: Nigah, 1401), *qataʿāt* no. 117.

[66] The decree is preserved in the British Museum. See Farhang Jahānpūr, "Farāmīn-i Pādishāhān-i Safavī dar Muzah-yi Brītāniyyā," *Barrasīhā-yi Tārīkhī* 4, no. 4 (1348).

during this time. Two weeks prior to Mahin Banu's death, on 1 Jumadi I 969 (January 7, 1562), Savinduk Beg passed away. Qazi ʿImad Isfahani, the steward of the royal household (*nāzir-i buyūtāt*), and Mir Faiz Allah Baghdadi, the army judge (*qāzī muʿaskar*), also passed away at this time. In the previous year, the court's prayer leader (*pīsh-namāz*) Sayyid Muhammad, comptroller general (*mustawfī al-mamālik*) Khvajah Qasim, and Hasan Beg *yūzbāshī*, who was Savinduk Beg's right-hand man, had also died.[67]

Within the span of two years, Tahmasb had lost most of his old comrades. Affected by these intimate losses and awakened to the brevity of life, it is during this time that he pens his memoirs.[68]

6.7 THE CHIEF MINISTER IN THE TIME OF TROUBLES

Qazi Jahan Syafi Hasani Qazvini, Tahmasb's chief minister (*vizīr*), came from an established bureaucratic family of Qazvin that traced its lineage back to Imam Hasan b. ʿAli, the eldest grandson of the Prophet and the second Shiʿi Imam.[69] His father had served as the chief justice of Qazvin, and no doubt helped him secure his judgeship in the city before entering the royal service at the court of Shah Ismail. They were among the *aʿyān* (notables) of the city. An astute politician with a knack for survival, he returned to court in 942/1535, having spent the last ten years of his life in prison in Gilan in the north. He had been ensnared by an old rival – Shah Qavam al-Din Tarashti, the minister of Muzaffar Sultan, the ruler of Rasht, whose loyalty Tahmasb had long suspected.[70]

67 Munshī Qazvīnī, *Javāhir al-Akhbār*, 220; Qummī, *Khulāsat al-Tavārīkh*, 1:435; Ghaffārī, *Tārīkh-i Jahān'ārā*, 307.

68 Tahmasb's memoirs cover the years between 930/1524 and 969/1561 and appear to have been written or dictated in a short period of time. Tahmāsb Safavī, *Tazkirah-i Shāh Tahmāsb*.

69 Safavid scholars writing in the West have consistently misread his name and attached an *izāfah* to the title Qazi before the proper noun Jahan, thus rendering the name to mean "judge of the world." This is incorrect. The name should be read without the genitive case just as one reads the name of the Mughal ruler Shah Jahan (it is not Shah-i Jahan – "the shah of the world"), or the name of Mahmud Shah Deccani's minister Khvajah ʿImad al-Din Mahmud Gavan, known as Khvajah Jahan (and not Khvajah-yi Jahan). Moreover, a learned minister whose political education would have taught him the benefits of upholding the appearance of humility in the political arena would not have misapplied his name as "judge of the world." Lastly, Jahan was a common name (and sometimes a nickname) in the Safavid era much as it is now in today's Persian-speaking communities.

70 Qummī, *Khulāsat al-Tavārīkh*, 1:162–63, 272–73. Muzaffar Sultan was previously known as Amira Dubbaj before submitting to Shah Ismail in 925/1519. He managed to solidify his

In terms of administrative importance, the office of chief minister (*vizārat*) was at the apex of power and therefore exceptionally precarious for the holder as seen by its high rate of violent deaths. Prior to Tahmasb's accession, for instance, Qazi Jahan had served as the undersecretary to Shah Ismail's chief minister Mirza Shah Hussein, who according to one account, while strolling with the nine-year-old Tahmasb, was brutally cut down by a resentful chieftain, Mihtar Shah Quli, in the *hasht-bihisht* palace of Tabriz.[71]

The move that made Qazi Jahan a *muqarrab* came in 930/1524, when the warrior king Ismail died. Qazi Jahan and the powerful queen mother, Tajlu Begum, formed an alliance with Kupik Sultan, the chief of the Ustajlus, and Div Sultan, the chief of the Rumlus, to secure Tahmasb's throne from the other chiefs. Qazi Jahan earned his promotion to the office of chief minister in place of Khvajah Jalal al-Din, who fell out of favor with Div Sultan, who later had him burnt alive. Such was the power of the Qizilbash chiefs vis-à-vis the young shah, which demonstrated for all to see his diminished political power and religious authority.[72]

Qazi Jahan must have made a deep impression on the young shah, who was under tremendous pressure and in need of a trustworthy minister. The close affinity between Qazi Jahan and the prince is demonstrated in a pocket-sized copy of ʿArifi's *Gūy u Chawgān* (*The Ball and the Polo Stick*), inscribed by Tahmasb and dedicated to the minister.[73]

Qazi Jahan may be said to be the only chief minister in this period who escaped an ignoble downfall and untimely death, though he came very close. Soon after he took office, for example, the intertribal rivalry among the Qizilbash factions intensified, and he found himself unable to disassociate from the Ustajlu camp because of his kinship ties with their chief, Kupik Sultan; one of his daughters was married to Kupik Sultan's son. He was captured by the governor of Isfahan and chief of the Ustajlus,

alliance with the Safavid house through marriage with Shah Ismail's daughter Khanish Khanum (d. 971/1564).

[71] Munshī Qazvīnī, *Javāhir al-Akhbār*, 138; Floor, *Government Institutions*, 35–40.

[72] Qummī, *Khulāsat al-Tavārīkh*, 1:155–56; Shīrāzī, *Takmilat al-Akhbār*, 60; Munshī Qazvīnī, *Javāhir al-Akhbār*, 147.

[73] This MS is dated 1523-4, and is kept in the Leningrad Public Library, D. N. CDXLI. I was unable to see the MS in person, but examined the image provided by Stuart Cary Welch, *A King's Book of Kings: The Shahnameh of Shah Tahmasp* (New York: Metropolitan Museum of Art, 1972), 51–53, where the calligraphy is unrefined, reflecting Tahmasb's rudimentary skills. See also ʿĀrifī-i Harawī, *The Ball and Polo Stick or The Book of Ecstacy: Gūy va chawgān, yā, Hālnāmah*, ed. and trans. Wheeler M. Thackston and Hossein Ziai (Costa Mesa: Mazda Publishers, 1999).

Mantasha Sultan, and nearly executed were it not for the intervention of the queen mother, Tajlu Begum. Qazi Jahan's property, nonetheless, was seized and his household taken to Qazvin in disgrace.[74]

The fortunes of the Ustajlu tribe did not improve much since the start of the hostilities, and finding little reassurance, Qazi Jahan fled to Gilan with the rest of the Ustajlu renegades. It must have been after the Ustajlus suffered a final defeat at Sharur against the other confederates that Qazi Jahan was captured and imprisoned by Muzaffar Sultan.

As dismal as the situation might have been to Qazi Jahan at the time, he fared much better than his immediate successor, Mirza Jaʿfar Savuji. His appointment to the vizierate coincided with the rise of Hussein Khan, the chief of the Shamlus, after the latter had disposed of his rival, the Takallu chief Chuha Sultan (see Section 4.6 for Hussein Khan's dreadful death for betraying Tahmasb). Hussein Khan wanted to choose a minister loyal to him and in line with his political goals, and Mirza Jaʿfar, who had served Chuha Sultan, did not exactly inspire trust. Not long after Hussein Khan took control, orders for Mirza Jaʿfar's execution were handed out to his Shamlu commanders. They caught up to Mirza Jaʿfar in his estate of Ribat-i Nik near Zanjan in Muharram 938/1531 and strangled him with a bowstring.[75]

Khvajah Saʿd al-Din ʿInayat Khuzani, who had a reputation for being a competent administrator, was next to fill the vacant seat of the *vizarat*, a post he briefly shared with Qazi Jahan upon the latter's return from

[74] Shīrāzī, *Takmilat al-Akhbār*, 211–13, based on details provided by Qummī, *Khulāsat al-Tavārīkh*, for the year 960/1553; Munshī Qazvīnī, *Javāhir al-Akhbār*, 149; Tahmāsb Safavī, *Tazkirah-i Shāh Tahmāsb*, 52. Immediately before the start of the civil war, Mantasha Sultan Ustajlu undertook a series of diplomatic maneuvers to prevent the outbreak of military clashes between the tribes. In an effort to appease Chuha Sultan and Div Sultan, the chiefs of Takallus and Rumlus, respectively, Mantasha Sultan charged a number of high-ranking men such as Qaranjah Bahadur of his own clan, Narin Beg of the Qajars, and Qazi Jahan the minister with inciting discord among the tribes. He executed the first two, and if it were not for the intervention of Tajlu Begum the queen mother, Mantasha Sultan would have done the same with Qazi Jahan. The chronicler Qazi Ahmad Qumi, on the other hand, states that it was Div Sultan who ordered the execution of these men (Qummī, *Khulāsat al-Tavārīkh*, 1:169). See Savory, "Principal Offices during the Reign of Tahmasp I," 66.

[75] Qummī, *Khulāsat al-Tavārīkh*, 1:218; Ghaffārī, *Tārīkh-i Jahān'ārā*, 286; Munshī Qazvīnī, *Javāhir al-Akhbār*, 162; Rūmlū, *Ahsan al-Tavārīkh*, 3:1210. Rūmlū, *Ahsan al-Tavārīkh*, 3:1210; Munshī Qazvīnī, *Javāhir al-Akhbār*, 160, 162, states that Ahmad Beg's brother Mir Ghiyath al-Din Mahmud was also appointed as "vizier." Hussein Khan's execution three years later (see Sections 4.1 and 4.6) in turn brought misfortune upon many of his clients, including his new minister, Ahmad Beg, who was imprisoned and had his property plundered, along with two of his brothers (Qummī, *Khulāsat al-Tavārīkh*, 2:948).

captivity. The khvajah's career, however, was even shorter and more tragic than his predecessors. Soon after his appointment, it was rumored that the minister had indecent relations with a young courtier, a certain ʿIsa son of Basliq Beg. When his enemies at court got wind of this, they informed the shah, whom they hoped would react harshly to the news. Tahmasb fell for their machinations and ordered the minister's execution.[76]

The order was to be carried out on the day that Muzaffar Sultan of Rasht (Qazi Jahan's captor) was to be executed, as well. Muzaffar Sultan was charged with disloyalty for seeking allegiance with the Ottoman Sultan Suleyman during his first invasion of Iran.[77] After being captured, Muzaffar Sultan was brought into Tabriz in a great public spectacle of humiliation. Tahmasb had him wear an embarrassing garment and paraded through the city in an iron cage, which his tormentors finally suspended from a minaret in the Qaysariyyah. The minister, on the other hand, they suspended from the cage by his genitals, apparently to account for the "indecency portion" of his crime. Shortly thereafter, they both were set ablaze. The khvajah's chronogram was devised to read: "for the love of Basliq's son."[78]

Public executions, especially for transgressing divine law, provided an opportunity for Tahmasb to display his piety in the public eye, as implementer of divinely sanctioned justice. Burning Muzaffar Sultan alive was political and served to convey to his military elite the price of disloyalty. After this ghastly spectacle, Qazi Jahan became the chief minister with full independence, leaving many to wonder why he would accept such a perilous position.

When he took up office in 942/1534-5, he must have found the emerging bureaucracy and administration of resources in complete disarray. The Qizilbash chiefs such as Chuha Sultan Takallu and Hussein Khan Shamlu, who had fomented the civil war, had reallocated to their respective clientages many of the Ustajlu land assignments (*iqtās*). In fact, the discontinuation of land grants to the Ustajlu tribe was one of the main reasons for their continued resistance in joining the confederation.[79]

In addition to managing the court's financial crises and streamlining the administration throughout the 940s/1530s, Qazi Jahan had to deal with

[76] Rūmlū, *Ahsan al-Tavārīkh*, 3:1245.

[77] Munshī Qazvīnī, *Javāhir al-Akhbār*, 182–83.

[78] Shīrāzī, *Takmilat al-Akhbār*, 84–85; Qummī, *Khulāsat al-Tavārīkh*, 1:256; Munshī Qazvīnī, *Javāhir al-Akhbār*, 184; Rūmlū, *Ahsan al-Tavārīkh*, 3:1245–46.

[79] See Floor's discussion on the functions of royal chancellery and the administrative procedures in this period in *Government Institutions*, 40–64.

the logistics of war against the Ottomans, the Uzbeks, and campaigns in the Caucasus. He was greatly assisted, no doubt, by his comptroller-general (*mustawfī al-mamālik*) Khvajah Qasim Natanzi, who oversaw the kingdom's finances and served in that capacity for nearly thirty years (938–60s/1531–60s). Together, they helped develop the Safavid bureaucratic practices in the two decades following the civil war and put the nascent state administration on solid footing.[80]

Tahmasb developed a great affinity for the old minister during these years, so much so that he once swore that as long as Qazi Jahan was alive, he would not dismiss him from office. He also patronized him extravagantly. For example, when Tahmasb transferred the capital from Tabriz to Qazvin, the construction of the royal pavilions had not been completed so the court lodged in Qazi Jahan's estate, which must have been large enough to host the royal family with their many retainers.[81] Membré meticulously describes the qazi's wealth and fine gifts that he presented to Tahmasb, followed by a sumptuous banquet in his house for the occasion of *bairām* (*ʿīd al-fitr*, commemoration of the end of Ramazan) of 947/1540:

> And the next day, the King's Minister, Qazi-yi Jahan, gave a very great present to the Shah, which was, if I remember correctly, 9 fine horses with brocade horse-cloths and saddles of massy gold and with the threads of gold in the middle of their hair; and 18 fine mules, and 36 very fine camels; and velvets, satins, many turban-cloths and cups of silver, bottles, gilded belts and I know not how much money in cash; so much so that I heard it said that the present was worth 1,000 tūmāns, which is 40,000 ducates ... After that day had passed, the Shah went to eat in the house of his Minister, Qāzī-yi Jahān, and he remained there for three days and then returned to his own house. And all the charges were paid by the said Minister, and I believe that more than 3,000 people ate in his house each day for certain.[82]

80 Qummī, *Khulāsat al-Tavārīkh*, 1:428. In particular, he was responsible for the economic affairs of the *mamālik* lands (state domains), while the *mustawfī-yi khāssah* (somewhat lower in rank) oversaw the crownlands (*khāssah*). For a discussion on these offices, see Floor, *Government Institutions*, 40–46.

81 Qummī, *Khulāsat al-Tavārīkh*, 1:337, 379; see also Stephen P. Blake, "Shah ʿAbbās and the Transfer of the Safavid Capital from Qazvin to Isfahan," in *Society and Culture in the Early Modern Middle East: Studies on Iran in the Safavid Period* (Leiden: Brill, 2003), 145–64; Michel M. Mazzaoui, "From Tabriz to Qazvin to Isfahan: Three Phases of Safavid History," in *XIX. Deutscher Orientalistentag: Vom 28. Sept. bis 4. Okt. 1975 in Freiburg i. Br: Vorträge* (Wiesbaden: Steiner, 1977), 514–22.

82 Membré, *Mission to the Lord Sophy of Persia*, 36.

Patron-client gift exchange not only served to further cement the bond between the two but also projected an aura of royal power and prestige, as the client's wealth reflected the triumph of the patron. Qazi Jahan further strengthened his ties with Tahmasb in 956/1549, when he succeeded in gaining the shah's approval for a marriage between his granddaughter and Prince Sultan Ibrahim Mirza (d. 985/1577). As noted earlier, creating family ties with the Safavid house was the highest level of patronage and honor for a client.[83]

By 957/1551, after serving the Safavid realm for fifteen years, Qazi Jahan resigned, expressing fatigue and old age as the reason. Tahmasb, who was about thirty-seven years old and in full command of the state affairs, accepted his resignation. Finding a worthy successor for Qazi Jahan does not appear to have been easy, for the office changed hands no less than five times following his departure (between 957/1551 and 960/1553). Tahmasb finally decided to delegate the post to one of his cousins, Maʿsum Beg Safavi, who went on to hold the office for the next sixteen years (960–76/1553–68).[84]

Two years after Qazi Jahan's withdrawal, his old rivals at court informed the shah that he had appropriated vast properties that were part of irrevocable pious endowments (*awqāf*). Tahmasb immediately took measures to retrieve the properties and all their accumulated dividends. Upon hearing the news, Qazi Jahan returned to court to address the charges. By that time, he was an old man in his eighties, and seemed concerned with his legacy and wanted to prevent the defaming of his family's reputation. The charge of misappropriation of religious endowments was not only a serious transgression, but it also carried public condemnation that would have a lasting effect. Tahmasb, seeing the frail old minister in a state of angst, dismissed the charges, and instead gifted him a land grant.[85]

Qazi Jahan died on his return home, on 11 (or 17) Dhul Hijjah 960 (November 24 (or 30), 1553). When the news of his death reached

[83] Khvāndamīr, *Tārīkh-i Shāh Ismāʿīl*, 232. Sultan Ibrahim Mirza was beginning to gain a reputation for his interest and support of the arts and learning. A remarkable result of his patronage was a commission of *Haft Awrang* by the poet and mystic ʿAbd al-Rahman Jami (d. 897/1492), considered a masterpiece in the arts of the illuminated manuscript in the early modern era. See Marianna Shreve Simpson and Massumeh Farhad, *Sultan Ibrahim Mirza's Haft Awrang: A Princely Manuscript from Sixteenth-Century Iran* (New Haven, CT: Yale University Press, 1997).

[84] Rūmlū, *Ahsan al-Tavārīkh*, 3:1369–70; Floor, *Government Institutions*, 36.

[85] Rūmlū, *Ahsan al-Tavārīkh*, 3:1370.

Tahmasb, he showed his gratitude for his minister's devoted service by distributing gold to the masses and arranging for his body to be buried in Karbala, like the funeral arrangements of his sister. Unable to proceed to Iraq-i ʿArab because of an outbreak of a plague in the area, the funerary troupe moved on to Mashhad and interred the body in Imam Riza's mausoleum, Iran's holiest site. All three *muqarrab*s were put to rest there.[86]

[86] Qummī, *Khulāsat al-Tavārīkh*, 1:363. Burial near Imam Riza indicated deep reverence for the deceased. Prominent members of the royal family and the ʿulema were buried there throughout the Safavid period.

Conclusion

The Safavid community forged its sense of cohesion through the years by binding the sources of religious and political forces within their reach. Their proselytizing brand of Sufism at the inception of the order channeled the principles of legitimate spiritual leadership to the person of Safi al-Din and epitomized in his life and teachings, a mission that later deputies, elders, and disciples took up and disseminated. The foundation of the Safavid claims to spiritual authority whence they hailed was laid at this stage and is reflected in the birth of the community's sacred history, *Quintessence of Purity* (*Safvat al-Safā*). Having control over the community's history further strengthened the perception that spiritual authority laid in the house of the Safavid family through descent from Sheikh Safi.

Safi al-Din's family proprietorship provided the family social prestige and material capabilities valued by many in their community, as seen, for instance, in the expansion of Safi al-Din's grave site into a vast mausoleum complex with provisions for various "social services." In time, the mausoleum became a major pilgrimage destination in the region. A landowning Sufi order that had navigated the perilous vicissitudes of Ilkhanid and Timurid powers during the eighth/fourteenth and ninth/fifteenth centuries and survived empowered Safi al-Din's progeny like Junayd and Haydar to venture into the political and military realm with legitimacy even though those claims were contested by established military houses like the Aqquyunlus under the chief of chiefs Uzun Hasan. Junayd had accumulated enough political and military clout that Uzun Hasan accepted him as an ally and facilitated his marriage to one of his sisters, Khadijah Khatun – a turning point in the militarization of the order.

By the later ninth/fifteenth century, the armed wing of the Safavid community was infused with considerable military capability, since their union with the Aqquyunlus and Junayd son Haider (an Aqquyunlu prince) meant better organizational abilities and means of communication, which enabled it to yoke the community's political potential. Political Sufis of the ninth/fifteenth century like Junayd and Haydar led politically motivated communities. A Sufi order is the perfect organization to militarize for it embodies the ideological capacity to create and preserve group solidarity among its members long term – key to a viable political venture. As noted in Chapter 2, the master-disciple dynamics of power at the heart of Sufi piety, for instance, when examined microscopically, harbored latent powers in shaping the perceptions of Sufi sheikhs as legitimate political and military leaders. A new, all-encompassing force engulfed the community during the ninth/fifteenth century with dynamism unlike any other – that of Shiʿism, or more correctly put, ʿAlevism.

The Safavid community's turn to the unconditional veneration of Imam ʿAli in the later ninth/fifteenth century with a range of antinomian and fringe beliefs that accompanied it had a long journey through the pathways of popular legends, holy texts, and sacred histories to reach the community's core beliefs. Once ʿAlevism found a foothold in the community's political ideology, it became a catalyst for a host of political solicitations. Imam ʿAli had become by the end of the ninth/fifteenth century, at the time of Ismail's insurrection, the cornerstone of their devotional life and politico-military ideals. For them, ʿAli was the embodiment of the archetypal Sufi king and epitome of virtue and justice in leadership – a belief they dreamed but was now materializing. Many among them perceived the Safavid house as the rightful inheritor of ʿAli's mantle of corporeal sovereignty and guardianship. Their collective exaltation for Imam ʿAli strengthened their faith and deepened their sense of group identity amidst war and bloodshed against enemies. Having the established powers such as the Shirvanshahis and the Aqquyunlus to struggle against cannot be overstated for the Safavid's militarization. While they suffered repeated defeats and loss of leadership, they gained in return experience and a hardened sense of cohesion.

But the sacred ties of loyalty that underpinned their social relations and strengthened the cohesion they had cultivated did not transfer well into power politics. It never seemed to work. This was quickly realized when the community ascended to power in the opening decade of the tenth/sixteenth century and staked its claim as a dynastic power but began to experience a series of devasting setbacks. Specifically, the unraveling of the

Safavid community's political and military cohesion began after their defeat against the Ottomans in 920/1514 and Shah Ismail's loss of the divine aura of invincibility. When he died ten years later at the age of thirty-seven, and his loyalist placed his ten-year-old son Tahmasb on the throne, the disunity was on display for all to see. A decade-long civil war among the tribes engulfed the nascent Shiʿi kingdom, with powerful external enemies like the self-proclaimed champions of Sunnis, the Ottoman Empire in the west and the Uzbek confederation from the east, determined to bring about his demise.

Chapters 4–6 explored the ways in which this young and uncharismatic shah, who very few people expected to survive, tried to recreate with his ministers and allies his family's dynastic power and rekindle the Safavid community's loss of cohesion that had been key to their ascent to power a generation ago. By the time Tahmasb's camp gained the upper hand and ended the civil war around 941/1534, the superpower of the early modern world, the Ottoman Empire, with which his father, Ismail, had picked a fight, was now marching toward Tabriz under its most impressive emperor, Sultan Suleyman. The Ottomans captured the Safavid capital while Tahmasb retreated with his beleaguered forces, many of whom he could not trust, like his cousin Hussein Khan Shamlu, whom they slew in the royal tent. They scorched the earth, poisoned the wells, hit the Ottoman lines in guerilla warfare in attempts to demoralize and starve the Ottoman army. It was during this period that the fissures in the Safavid cohesion manifested themselves most starkly, in the series of high-level betrayals and defections at the heart of the Safavid order that nearly caused its collapse. And it was in this period that the notion of loyalty took center stage in their communications.

Knowing well their fickle nature, political actors usually devise ways to preserve their fragile ties. During hard times the Safavid court, for instance, highlighted the consecrated nature of their political ties in an attempt to inhibit their severance and ward off disloyalty. They defamed tiebreakers as infidels and ingrates and buttressed the role of the Safavid shah as the purveyor of divine benefit and patronage. Crafting a new public aura for Tahmasb as distinct from that of his father, Ismail, who basked in the halo of charismatic warrior kings, was not an easy and simple process, for what emerged along the way was the recasting of the Sufi king as a preserver of faith and a purveyor of God's bounty – as a divine patron, a *valī-yi niʿmat*.

The Safavid ministers coupled this strategy in the 940s/1530s by strengthening the young shah's ties with the powerful Qizilbash chiefs through patronage activities and a series of key appointments to govern major hubs of economic and political activity like Shiraz, Kirman, Mashhad, Isfahan, Yazd, and Herat. The effects of such policies reverberated on several fronts. One result in particular was substantial. They helped regenerate the military class's sense of group cohesion, a sign of which manifested itself in their performance combating the final Ottoman invasion under Sultan Suleyman. The Safavids were finally able to force a costly stalemate with the Ottomans, which culminated in the historic Peace of Amasya in 962/1555.

Tahmasb moved his capital from Tabriz further east to Qazvin around this time away from Ottoman reach. Tabriz had been the hub of political and commercial life of the region for centuries. Tahmasb's decision radically altered the political dynamic of the deep-rooted nobility and power brokers as a new generation of military elite, the descendants of the early "state-builders," began to forge new ties of loyalty and patronage in what could now rightfully be called a state.

C.1 THE MANTLE

The *khirqa* (mantle worn by Sufis) was thrown over Tahmasb's shoulder at the age of ten when he succeeded his father, "the perfect guide" Shah Ismail (*murshid-i kāmil*), as the nominal head of the Safavid order. His community over the years patched onto it the insignia of temporal sovereignty with threads of the divine law (*sharīʿah*) in the red hue of Shiʿism. Over time, the mantle felt heavy. It reeked of roasted flesh and exotic fragrances from beyond the southern seas, stained with death and disfigured by inequities of corporeal sovereignty. Faded and frayed, it became unrecognizable as having ever belonged to a Sufi sheikh by the end of the tenth/sixteenth century.

The Italian traveler Vincentio d'Alessandri in 979/1571 saw Tahmasb in person in the royal palace in Qazvin and left a rare glimpse of the Sufi king toward the end of his life. "More than anything else," d'Alessandri records, "he is of melancholy disposition, which is visible in many signs, but principally be the fact that he has not come out of his palace for the duration of ten years, not even once to hunt or to engage in any other kind of amusement, to the great dissatisfaction of his people." Tahmasb died five years later in his capital Qazvin on 15 Safar 984 (May 14, 1576) and joined the other three *muqarrab*s in their final resting place in Mashhad.[1]

Soon after Tahmasb exhaled his last breath, his chiefs and kinsmen competed to pick up what remained of the mantle and place it on their own candidates, either the palace-raised Haydar, Tahmasb's young son, or Ismail Mirza, whom Tahmasb had imprisoned for the last twenty years. The Qizilbash chiefs showed their renewed power when they defeated the court faction behind Haydar and murdered him. They then brought out the confined prince from captivity to be their next shah, a decision they soon regretted. Years of confinement, it seemed, had made him extremely anxious and distrustful. Soon after enthronement, he began executing Safavid royals, chiefs and their ministers, courtiers, and those whose loyalty he doubted.

It did not take the chiefs long to realize Ismail was too unpredictable and ruthless to even ensure their safety let alone keep the confederacy from fracturing. They also knew that his supporters were not bound by the sacred loyalty and the patronage relationship that sustained it like that of his father. So, they poisoned his opium one night without fear of consequence. The regicide demonstrated that the mantle was now nothing but a jeweled royal robe, bereft of its spiritual substance, coveted by power-hungry men, and incapable of upholding the symbol of their Sufi order's spiritual authenticity.

It appeared that Tahmasb's achievements during his fifty-two-year reign – a lasting peace with the Ottoman Empire (the Ottomans invaded Iran not long after Tahmasb's death), unification of the Qizilbash confederation, and relative political stability – were all but lost. Yet, the bureaucracy whose bedrock Qazi Jahan and his chancellery laid, the principles of Safavid legitimacy that Shah Tahmasb's loyal Shiʿi clerics broadcasted, and the network of clients that depended on the patronage of the court

[1] Vincentio d'Alessandri, "Narrative of the Most Noble Vincentio d'Alessandri," in *A Narrative of Italian Travels in Persia*, 211–29; Vincentio d'Alessandri, "Documento XXVI, Relazione presentata al Consiglio dei Dieci il 24 settembre 1572 e letta l'll ottobre da Vicenzo Alessandri, Veneto legato a Thamasp re di Persia," in *La Repubblica di Venezia e la Persia: Nuovi Documenti e Regesti*, ed. Guglielmo Berchet (Venezia: Antonelli, 1866), 169–70. For another interesting firsthand account by a European traveler about Tahmasb in his later life in Qazvin, see the report of Anthony Jenkinson of the English Muscovy Company who had an audience with him on November 20, 1562: Edward Delmar Morgan and Charles Henry Coote, eds., *Early Voyages and Travels to Russia and Persia by Anthony Jenkinson and Other Englishmen*, vol. 1 (London: Hakluyt Society, 1886), 141–47.

merged to produce a political system that had grown sufficiently hardened to absorb the turmoil of succession and provisional governance.

The communities that gravitated toward the Safavid house for their leadership in the course of the ninth/fifteenth century carried the beliefs of political Sufism to its maturation and forged a type of kingship whose authority rested on a series of ideological monopolies: the Shiʿi Sufi principle of temporal sovereignty, the belief in absolute obedience to the now Shiʿi Sufi shahs of the order, and the ability to control greater means of collective violence relative to the tribal chiefs, held together by a matrix of patrons and clients. Tahmasb and his court managed these monopolies, ideological and material, which served to convince enough of them to believe that their power and privilege, their *niʿmat*, depended solely on the Safavid shahs, a crowning political breakthrough in their attempt to levy stability. Thus transformed, the Safavid order emerged in the mid-tenth/sixteenth century in control of adequate sources of social power to foster enough cohesion to edge itself over and into the realm of political equilibrium and relative stable governance.

Bibliography

PRIMARY SOURCES

al-ʿAbbādī, Qutb al-Dīn Muzaffar b. Ardashīr. *al-Tasfiyah fī Ahwāl al-Mutasawwifah: Sūfī-nāmah*. Edited by Ghulāmhusayn Yūsufī. Tehran: Intishārāt-i Bunyād-i Farhang-i Īrān, 1347.

Abū al-Fazl b. Mubārak. *Akbarnāmah*. Vol. 1. Edited by Mulavī Aghā Ahmad ʿAlī. Calcutta: Royal Asiatic Society of Bengal, 1877.

Afūshtah'ī, Mahmūd b. Hidāyat Allāh. *Nuqāwat al-Āsār fī Zikr al-Akhyār*. Edited by Ihsān Ishrāqī. Tehran: Bungāh-i Tarjumah va Nashr-i Kitāb, 1350.

Ahmad Jām, Abū al-Fath Muhammad b. Mutahhar. *Hadīqat al-Haqīqah*. Edited by Muhammad ʿAlī Muvahhid. Tehran: Bungāh Tarjumah va Nashr-i Kitāb, 1343.

Rawzat al-Muznibīn va Jannat al-Mushtāqīn. Edited by ʿAlī Fāzil. Tehran: Bunyād-i Farhang-i Īrān, 1976.

Ahmadī, Nuzhat. *Ruʾyā va Sīyāsat dar ʿAsr-i Safavī*. Tehran: Nashr-i Tārīkh-i Īrān, 1388.

ʿĀlam'ārā-yi Shāh Ismāʿīl. Edited by Asghar Muntazir Sāhib. Tehran: Shirkat-i Intishārāt-i ʿIlmī va Farhangī, 1384.

ʿĀlam'ārā-yi Shāh Tahmāsb: Zindagī-i Dāstānī Duvvumīn Pādishāh-i Dawrah-i Safavī. Edited by Īraj Afshār. Tehran: Dunyā-i Kitāb, 1370.

ʿAlavī ʿĀmilī, Muhammad ʿAbd al-Hasīb b. Ahmad. *Qavāʿid al-Salātīn*. Edited by Rasūl Jaʿfariyān. Tehran: Kitābkhānah, Mūzah va Markaz-i Asnād-i Majlis-i Shūrā-yi Islāmī, 1384.

Amīnī Haravī, Ibrāhīm b. Mīrak Jalāl al-Dīn. *Futūhāt-i Shāhī: Tārīkh-i Safavī az Āghāz tā Sāl-i 920 H. Q*. Edited by Muhammad Rizā Nasīrī. Tehran: Anjuman-i Āsār va Mafākhir-i Farhangī, 1383.

ʿĀmulī, Haydar b. ʿAlī. *Jāmiʿ al-Asrār wa-Manbaʿ al-Anwār*. Beirut: Dār al-Muhajja al-Baydāʾ, 2007.

ʿĀmulī, Shams al-Dīn Muhammad. "Risālah-i Futuvvatiyyah." In *Rasāʾil-i Javānmardān: Mushtamil bar Haft Futuvat'nāmah*. Edited by Murtazā

Sarrāf, 58–88. Tehran: Qismat-i Īrānshināsī-i Anstitū-yi Pizhūhish'hā-yi ʿIlmī dar Īrān, 1352.

Ardabīlī, Muhammad b. Sultān Muhammad. *Tazkirat al-Zākirīn; Risālah-i Sūfiyyah-i Safaviyyah; Munājāt*. Kāshān: Hamgām bā Hastī, 1391.

ʿĀrīfī-i Harawī. *The Ball and Polo Stick or The Book of Ecstasy: Gūy va chawgān, yā Hālnāmah*. Edited and translated by Wheeler M. Thackston and Hossein Ziai. Costa Mesa: Mazda Publishers, 1999.

al-Arrajānī, Farāmurz b. Khudādād. *Samak Ayyār*. Edited by Parvīz Nātil Khānlar. Tehran: Intishārāt-i Bunyād-i Farhang-i Īrān, 1347.

Aşıkpaşazade. *Tevarih-i Al-i Osman*. Edited by ʿAlī Bey. Istanbul: Matbaʿa-i ʿĀmira, 1332.

"Tevarih-i Al-i Osman." In *Osmanlı Tarihleri*, edited by Nihal Atsız, 79–294. Istanbul: Türkiye Yayınevi, 1949.

ʿAttār, Farīd al-Dīn. *Dīvān-i Sheikh Farīd al-Dīn ʿAttār*. Edited by Mahmud Darvish. Tehran: Javid, 1402.

Ayan, Hüseyin. *Nesîmî Hayatı, Edebî Kişiliği, Eserleri ve Türkçe Divanının Tenkidli Metni*. Ankara: Türk Tarih Kurumu Basım Evi, 2002.

ʿAyyāshī, Muhammad b. Masʿūd. *Kitāb al-Tafsīr*. Edited by Hāshim Rasūlī Mahallātī. Qum: Chāpkhānah-i ʿIlmiyyah, 1380–81.

al-Azharī, Muhammad b. Ahmad. *Tahdhīb al-Lugha*. Edited by Muhammad ʿAlī al-Najjār and ʿAbd al-Salām Muhammad Hārūn. Cairo: Dār al-Qawmiyya al-ʿArabiyya li-l-Tibāʿa, 1384–87.

Bābā Faghānī Shīrāzī. *Dīvān-i Ashʿār-i Bābā Faghānī Shīrāzī*. Edited by Ahmad Suhaylī Khvānsārī. Tehran: Iqbāl, 1362.

Barbaro, Josafa, and Ambrogio Contarini. *Travels to Tana and Persia*. Translated by William Thomas. London: Hakluyt Society, 1873.

Beckwith, Ryan Teague. "Read the Transcript of James Comey's Testimony." *Time*, June 8, 2017. https://time.com/4810345/james-comey-testimony-real-time-transcript/.

Bey, Feridun. *Mecmua-ı Münşeât-i Feridun Bey*. Vol. 2. Istanbul: Takvimhane-i Amire, 1858.

al-Bukhārī, Muhammad b. Ismāʿīl. *Sahīh al-Bukhārī: The Translation of the Meanings of Sahīh al-Bukhārī: Arabic–English*. Translated by Muhammad Muhsin Khan. Riyadh: Dār al-Salām, 1997.

Burrill, Kathleen R. F. *The Quatrains of Nesimī, Fourteenth-Century Turkic Hurufi, with Annotated Translations of the Turkic and Persian Quatrains from the Hekimoğlu Ali Paşa MS*. The Hague: Mouton, 1972.

Chahārdah Risālah dar Bāb-i Futuvvat va Asnāf. Edited by Mihrān Afshārī and Mahdī Madāyinī. Tehran: Nashr-i Chishmah, 1388.

D'Alessandri, Vincentio. "Documento XXVI, Relazione Presentata al Consiglio dei Dieci il 24 settembre 1572 e letta l'll ottobre da Vicenzo Alessandri, Veneto legato a Thamasp re di Persia." In *La Repubblica di Venezia e la Persia: Nuovi Documenti e Regesti*, edited by Guglielmo Berchet, 169–70. Venezia: Antonelli, 1866.

"Narrative of the Most Noble Vincentio d'Alessandri." In *A Narrative of Italian Travels in Persia, in the Fifteenth and Sixteenth Centuries*, translated and edited by Charles Grey, 211–29. London: Hakluyt Society, 1873.

Darvīsh ʿAlī b. Yūsuf. "Zubdat al-Tarīq ilā Allāh." In *Rasāʾil-i Javānmardān: Mushtamil bar haft Futuvvat'nāmah*, edited by Murtazā Sarrāf, 218–326. Tehran: Qismat-i Īrānshināsī-i Anstitū-yi Pizhūhish'hā-yi ʿIlmī dar Īrān, 1352.

al-Dhahabī, Muhammad b. Ahmad. *Maʿrifat al-Qurrāʾ al-Kibār ʿalā al-Tabaqāt wa-l-Aʿsār*. Edited by Tayyar Altıkulaç. Istanbul: Türkiye Diyanet Vakfı, Islam Araştırmaları Merkezi, 1995.

Dihgān, Ibrāhīm. "Du Farmān-i Safavī." *Rāhnamā-yi Kitāb* 12 (1348): 179–81.

Fayrūzābādī, Abū Tāhir Majīd al-Dīn Muhammad b. Yaʿqūb. *al-Qāmūs al-Muhīt*. Edited by Nasr al-Hurini. Beirut: Dār al-Fikr, 1978.

Fekete, Lajos, and György Hazai, eds. *Einführung in die Persische Paläographie: 101 Persische Dokumente*. Translated by Manfred Lorenz. Budapest: Akadémiai Kiadó, 1977.

Firdawsī, Abū al-Qāsim. *Shāhnāmah-i Firdawsī*. Edited by Mustafā Jayhūnī. Isfahan: Gurūh-i Intishārāt-i Shāhnāmah'pizhūhī, 2001.

Futuvvat'nāmah'hā va Rasāʾil-i Khāksāriyyah: Sī Risālah. Edited by Mihrān Afshārī. Tehran: Pizhūhishgāh-i ʿUlūm-i Insānī va Mutāliʿāt-i Farhangī, 1382.

Ghaffārī, Ahmad b. Muhammad. *Tārīkh-i Jahān'ārā*. Edited by Mujtabā Mīnuvī. Tehran: Kitābfurūshī-i Hāfiz, 1343.

al-Ghazālī, Abū Hāmid Muhammad. *Kīmīyā-yi Saʿādat*. Edited by Husayn Khadīvjam. Tehran: Markaz-i Intishārāt-i ʿIlmī va Farhangī, 1371.

Nasīhat al-Mulūk. Edited by Jalāl al-Dīn Humāʾī. Tehran: Chāpkhānah-i Majlis, 1317.

Hākim al-Nīsābūrī, Muhammad b. ʿAbd Allāh. *al-Mustadrak ʿalā al-Sahīhayn*. Edited by Mustafā ʿAbd al-Qādir ʿAtāʾ. Beirut: Dār al-Kutub al-ʿIlmiyya, 1411.

Hatâyî Dîvâni. Edited by Muhsin Macit. Istanbul: Türkiye Yazma Eserler Kurumu Başkanlığı, 2017.

Hātifī Kharjirdī. *Shāhnāmah-i Hātifī Kharjirdī: Hamāsah-i Futūhāt-i Shāh Ismāʿīl Safavī*. Edited by ʿAlī Āl-i Dāvūd. Tehran: Farhangistān-i Zabān va Adab-i Fārsī, 1387.

Hayātī Tabrīzī, Qāsim Beg. *A Chronicle of the Early Safavids and the Reign of Shah Ismail*. Edited by Kioumars Ghereghlou. New Haven, CT: American Oriental Society, 2018.

Herrmann, Gottfried. "Ein Erlass des Ǧalāyeriden Soltān Hoseyn aus dem Jahr 780/1378." In *Göttinger Orientforschungen: Syriaca*. Vol. 3, *Erkenntnisse und Meinungen*, edited by Gernot Wießner, 135–63. Wiesbaden: Harrassowitz, 1973.

Hidāyatī, Muhammad ʿAlī, ed. *Āstānah-i Ray: Majmūʿah-i Asnād va Farāmīn*. Tehran: Shirkat-i Sahāmī Ufsit, 1344.

al-Hilālī, Sulaym b. Qays. *Kitāb Sulaym b. Qays al-Hilālī*. Edited by Muhammad Bāqir al-Ansārī. Qum: Nashr al-Hādī, 1415.

Horst, Heribert. "Zwei Erlasse Šāh Tahmāsps I." *Zeitschrift Der Deutschen Morgenländischen Gesellschaft* 110, no. 2 (1960): 301–9.

Hujwīrī, Abū al-Hasan. *Kashf al-Mahjūb*. Edited by Valentin Zhukovski. Leningrad, 1344.

Husaynī, Khvurshāh b. Qubād. *Tārīkh-i Īlchī-i Nizām Shāh: Tārīkh-i Safavīyah az Āghāz tā Sāl-i 972 Hijrī Qamarī*. Edited by Muhammad Rizā Nasīrī and Koichi Haneda. Tehran: Anjuman-i Ās̱ār va Mafākhir-i Farhangī, 2000.

Ibn Abī al-Hadīd, ʿAbd al-Hamīd b. Hibat Allāh. *Sharh Nahj al-Balāgha*. Edited by Muhammad Abū al-Fadl Ibrāhīm. Beirut: Dār Maktabat al-Hayāt, 1965–67.
Ibn Khaldun. *The Muqaddimah: An Introduction to History*. Translated by Franz Rosenthal. Princeton University Press, 1967.
Ibn Manzūr, Muhammad b. Mukarram. *Lisān al-ʿArab*. Riyadh: Markaz al-Turāth li-l-Barmajiyyāt, 2013.
Ibn al-Mughāzilī, ʿAlī b. Muhammad. *Manāqib ʿAlī b. Abī Tālib*. Edited by Muhammad Bāqir Bahbūdī. Tehran: al-Maktabah al-Islāmiyyah, 1403.
Ibn Shahrāshūb, Muhammad b. ʿAlī. *Manāqib Āl-i Abī Tālib*. Edited by Yūsuf al-Baqāʿī. Qum: Intishārāt Dhawī al-Qurbā, 1421.
Ibn Yamīn, Fakhr al-Dīn Mahmūd. *Dīvān-i Ashʿār-i Ibn Yamīn Farnawmadī*. Edited by Husayn ʿAlī Bāstānī'rād. Tehran: Sanāʾī, 1359.
Idrīs Bitlīsī, Hakīm al-Dīn. *Qānūn-i Shāhanshāhī*. Edited by ʿAbd Allāh Masʿūdī Ārānī. Tehran: Markaz-i Pizhūhishī-i Mīrāṣ-i Maktūb, 1387.
Irbilī, ʿAlī b. ʿĪsā. *Kashf al-Ghummah fī Maʿrifat al-Aʾimmah*. Edited by Ahmad Ishkavari, Qum, 1421.
Isfarāyinī, Nūr al-Dīn ʿAbd al-Rahmān b. Muhammad. *Kāshif al-Asrār: bi-Inzimām-i Pāsukh bih Chand Pursish. Risālah dar Ravish-i Sulūk va Khalvat'nishīnī*. Edited by Hermann Landolt. Tehran: Intishārāt-i Muʾassasah-i Mutāliʿāt-i Islāmī, Dānishgāh-i Makgīl, Shuʿbah-i Tehran, bā Hamkārī-i Markaz-i Bayn al-Milalī-i Guftugū-yi Tamaddunhā, 1383.
Isfarāyinī, Nūr al-Dīn ʿAbd al-Rahmān b. Muhammad, and Ahmad b. Muhammad Simnānī. *Murshid va Murīd: Mukātibāt-i ʿAbd al-Rahmān Isfarāyinī bā ʿAlāʾ al-Dawlah-i Simnānī*. Edited by Hermann Landolt. Tehran: Qismat-i Īrānshināsī, Anstītū-yi Faransavī-i Pizhūhish'hā-yi ʿIlmī dar Īrān, 1351.
Jābirī Ansārī, Mīrzā Rafīʿā. *Dastūr al-Molūk*. Edited by M. T. Dānešpažūh. MDAT 16/5-6. Tehran, 1347/1968.
Dastur al-Moluk: A Safavid State Manual. Edited and translated by Willem M. Floor and Mohammad Hassan Faghfoory. Costa Mesa: Mazda Publishers, 2007.
Jaʿfariyān, Rasūl, ed. *Tārīkh-i Qizilbashān-i Safavī dar Chand Matn-i ʿArabi-yi Dawrah-yi Othmānī*. Qum, 1397.
Jahānpūr, Farhang. "Farāmīn-i Pādshāhān-i Safavī dar Mūzah-yi Brītāniyyā." *Barrasīhā-yi Tārīkhī* 4, no. 4 (1348).
Jāmī, ʿAbd al-Rahmān. *Dīvān-i Kāmil-i Jāmī*. Edited by Hashim Razi. Tehran: Chāpkhānah-i Pīrūz, 1341.
Lawā'ih: A Treatise on Ṣūfism. Translated by E. H. Whinfield and Mīrzā Muḥammad Ḳazvīnī. London: Royal Asiatic Society, 1906.
Masnavī-i Haft Awrang. Edited by Āghā Murtazā Mudarris Gīlānī. Tehran: Kitābfurūshī-i Saʿdī, 1337.
al-Jawharī, Ismāʿīl b. Hammād. *Tāj al-Lugha wa-Sihāh al-ʿArabiyya*. Edited by Ahmad al-Ghafūr ʿAttār. Beirut: Dar al-ʿIlm, 1987.
Junābādī, Mīrzā Bayg. *Rawzat al-Safaviyyah*. Edited by Ghulām Rizā Tabātabāʾī Majd. Tehran: Bunyād-i Mawqūfāt-i Duktur Mahmūd Afshār, 1378.
Kasāʾī Marvazī, Abū al-Hasan. *Ashʿār-i Hakīm Kasāʾī Marvazī va Tahqīqī dar Zindagānī va Āsār-i ū*. Edited by Mahdī Dirakhshān. Tehran: Intishārāt-i Dānishgāh-i Tehran, 1364.

Kāshānī, ʿIzz al-Dīn Mahmūd b. ʿAlī. *Kitāb Misbāh al-Hidāya wa-Miftāh al-Kifāya*. Edited by Jalāl al-Dīn Humāʾī. Tehran: Intishārāt-i Sukhan, 1394.

Kāshānī, Muhtasham. *Dīvān-i Muhtasham-i Kāshānī*. Edited by Akbar Bihdarvand. Tehran: Nigah, 1401.

Kāshānī Samarqandī, ʿAbd al-Razzāq. "Tuhfat al-Ikhwān." In *Rasāʾil-i Javānmardān: Mushtamil bar Haft Futuvvat'nāmah*. Edited by Murtazā Sarrāf, 1–57. Tehran: Qismat-i Īrānshināsī-i Anstitū-yi Pizhuhish'hā-yi ʿIlmī dar Īrān, 1352.

Kāshifī, Husayn Vāʿiz. *Akhlāq-i Muhsinī*. MS, Cambridge University Library, add 748, fols.5a–182b.

Futuvvat'nāmah-i Sultānī. Edited by Muhammad Jaʿfar Mahjūb. Tehran: Bunyād-i Farhang-i Īrān, 1350.

Mawāhib ʿĀliyya yā Tafsīr-i Husaynī. 4 vols. Edited by Muhammad Rizā Jalālī Nāʾīnī. Tehran: Iqbāl, 1317–29.

Rawzat al-Shuhadā. Edited by Hasan Zulfaqari. Tehran, 1390.

Khāmahyār, Ahmad. "Maktūbi-i Sultān Junayd-i Safavī bih Ibn Shammāʿ-i Halabī." *Payām-i Bahāristān*, D2, S5, SH20 (1392): 130–39.

"Mazār-i Du Tan az Mashāyikh-i Safavīyah dar Lubnān va Filistīn." In *Shamʿ-i Jādū-yi Umīd: Vīzha'nāmah-i Marāsim-i Nikūdāsht-i Ustād Duktur Muhammad ʿAlī Muvahhid*, edited by Muhammad Khusruwshāhī. Tabriz: Dānishgāh-i Tabrīz, 1393.

Khunjī, Fazl Allāh b. Rūzbahān. *Tārīkh-i ʿĀlam'ārā-yi Amīnī: Sharh-i Hukmrānī-i Salātīn-i Āq Qūyūnlū va Zuhūr-i Safaviyān*. Edited by Muhammad Akbar ʿAshīq. Tehran: Mīrās-i Maktūb, 1382.

Khūsifī Bīrjandī, Muhammad b. Husām. *Khāvarān'nāmah*. Edited by Farhād Naqqāsh. Tehran: Vizārat-i Farhang va Irshād-i Islāmī, 1381.

Khvājū-yi Kirmānī, Mahmūd b. ʿAlī. *Dīvān-i Kāmil-i Khvajū-yi Kirmānī*. Edited by Hasan Anvari. Tehran: Behzād, 1374.

Khvāndamīr, Amīr Mahmūd. *Tārīkh-i Shāh Ismāʿīl va Shāh Tahmāsb-i Safavī: Zayl-i Tārīkh-i Habīb al-Sīyar*. Edited by Muhammad ʿAlī Jarrāhī. Tehran: Nashr-i Gustarah, 1370.

Khvāndamīr, Ghiyās al-Dīn b. Humām al-Dīn al-Husaynī. *Tārīkh-i Habīb al-Sīyār fī Akhbār-i Afrād-i Bashar*. Edited by Jalāl al-Dīn Humāʾī. Tehran: Kitābfurūshī-i Khayyām, 1362.

Kiyāʾ Gīlānī, Ahmad b. Muhammad. *Sirāj al-Ansāb*. Edited by Mahdī Rajāʾī. Qum: Kitābkhānah-i ʿUmūmī-i Āyat Allāh al-ʿUzmā Marʿashī Najafī, 1367.

Kubrā, Najm al-Dīn. *Fawāʾih al-Jamāl wa Fawātih al-Jalāl*. Translated by Muhammad Bāqir Sāʿidī Khurāsānī. Edited by Husayn Haydarkhānī Mushtāq ʿAlī. Tehran: Marvī, 1407.

Kulaynī, Muhammad b. Yaʿqūb. *Al-Kafi*. 8 vols. Translated by Muhammad Sarwar. New York: The Islamic Seminary, 2004.

Usūl-i Kāfī. Edited by Javād Mustafavī. Tehran: Kitābfurūshī-i ʿIlmiyyah-i Islāmiyyah, 1378.

al-Usūl min al-Kāfī. Edited by ʿAlī Akbar Ghaffārī. Tehran: Dār al-Kutub al-Islāmiyyah, 1362–63.

Lāhījī, ʿAlī b. Shams al-Dīn. *Tārīkh-i Khānī: Shāmil-i Havādis̱-i Chihil Salah-i Gīlān az 880 tā 920 Qamarī.* Edited by Manūchihr Sutūdah. Tehran: Bunyād-i Farhang-i Īrān, 1973.

Lārī Shīrāzī, Rūh Allāh. *Sharafnāmah: Mukātibāt-i Dīvānī-i Iyālat-i Fārs va Lāristān dar Dawrah-i Safaviyyah.* Edited by Muhammad Bāqir Vus̱ūqī. Tehran: Kitābkhānah, Mūzah va Markaz-i Asnād-i Majlis-i Shūrā-yi Islāmī, 1389.

Lings, Martin. *Muhammad: His Life Based on the Earliest Sources.* 2nd ed. Rochester, VT: Inner Traditions, 2006.

Majlisī, Muhammad Taqī. *Risālah-i Tashvīq al-Sālikīn.* Tehran: Nūr-i Fātimah, 1362.

Marāghāhʾī, Awhadī. *Dīvān-i Kāmil-i Awhadī Marāghāhʾī.* Edited by Amīr Ahmad Ashrafī. Tehran: Intishhārāt-i Pīshraw, 1362.

al-Masʿūdī, ʿAlī b. al-Husayn. *Murūj al-Dhahab wa-Maʿādin al-Jawhar.* Edited by Charles Pellat. Beirut: al-Jāmiʿa al-Lubnāniyya, 1965–79.

Maybudī, Rashīd al-Dīn Ahmad b. Ahmad. *Kashf al-Asrār va ʿUddat al-Abrār, Maʿrūf bi-Tafsīr-i Khvājah ʿAbd Allāh Ansārī.* 10 vols. Edited by ʿAlī Asghar Hikmat. Tehran: Intishārāt-i Dānishgāh-i Tehran, 1331–39.

Membré, Michele. *Mission to the Lord Sophy of Persia (1539–1542).* Edited by A. H. Morton. Warminster: E. J. W. Gibb Memorial Trust, 1999.

Menāḳib. Istanbul Belediyesi Atatürk Kitaplığı, MS 27.

Menavino, G. A. *Trattato de' costume et vita de' Turchi.* Florence, 1548.

Minadoi, Giovanni. *The History of the Vvarres betvveene the Turkes and the Persians.* Written in Italian by John Thomas Minadoi and translated into English by Abraham Hartwell. London: John Woolf, 1595.

Minorsky, Vladimir. "A Mongol Decree of 720/1320 to the Family of Shaykh Zāhid." *Bulletin of the School of Oriental and African Studies* 16, no. 3 (1954): 515–27.

"The Poetry of Shāh Ismāʿīl I." *Bulletin of the School of Oriental and African Studies* 10, no. 4 (1942): 1006–29.

Minorsky, Vladimir, trans. *Tadhkirat al-Mulūk: A Manual of Ṣafavid Administration (circa 1137/1725): Persian Text in Facsimile (B.M. Or. 9496).* Cambridge: Trustees of the E. J. W. Gibb Memorial, 1943.

Mīr Jaʿfarī, Husayn, and Majīd Hāshimī Ardakānī. "Farmān-i Shāh Tahmāsb-i Safavī bih Mawlānā Razī al-Dīn Muhammad." *Barrashī'hā-yi Tārīkhī* 9, no. 51 (1353/1974): 97–106.

Morgan, Edward Delmar, and Charles Henry Coote, eds. *Early Voyages and Travels to Russia and Persia by Anthony Jenkinson and Other Englishmen.* Vol. 1. London: Hakluyt Society, 1886.

Muʾazzin Sabzavārī, Shaykh Muhammad ʿAlī. *Tuhfah-yi ʿAbbāsī: The Golden Chain of Sufism in Shiʿite Islam.* Translated by Mohammad Hassan Faghfoory. Lanham, MD: University Press of America, 2008.

Mufīd Mustawfī Bāfqī, Muhammad. *Jāmiʿ-i Mufīdī.* 3 vols. Edited by Īraj Afshār. Tehran: Asātīr, 1385.

Muhammad b. Husām al-Dīn. *Dīvan-i Mawlanā Muhammad b. Husām.* Edited by Ahmad Birjandi. Mashhad, 1366.

Muhammadī Ray'shahrī, Muhammad, Muhammad Kāzim Tabātabā'ī, and Mahmūd Tabātabā'ī, eds. *Mawsū'at al-Imām 'Alī b. Abī Tālib fī al-Kitāb wa-l-Sunnah wa-l-Tārīkh*. Qum: Mu'assasat Dār al-Hadīth, 1421.

Munsha'āt-i Sulaymānī. Edited by Rasūl Ja'farīyān. Tehran: Kitābkhānah, Mūzih va Markaz-i Asnād-i Majlis-i Shūrā-yi Islāmī, 1388.

Munshī, Iskandar Beg. *Tārīkh-i 'Ālam'ārā-yi 'Abbāsī*. 2 vols. Edited by Īraj Afshār. Tehran: Amīr Kabīr, 1382.

Munshī Qazvīnī, Būdāq. *Javāhir al-Akhbār: Bakhsh-i Tārīkh-i Īrān az Qarāqūyūnlū tā Sāl-i 984 H. Q.* Edited by Muhsin Bahrām'nizhād. Tehran: Mīrās̱-i Maktūb, 1378.

Musha'sha'ī, 'Alī b. 'Abd Allāh. *al-Rihlah al-Makkiyyah: Tārīkh-i Siyāsī va Ijtimā'ī-i Musha'sha'īyān*. Edited by 'Ārif Nasr. Tehran: Markaz-i Pizhūhishī-i Mīrās̱-i Maktūb, 1396.

Mushīrī Bardsīrī, Mīr Muhammad Sa'īd. *Tazkirah-i Safavī-i Kirmān*. Edited by Muhammad Ibrāhīm Bāstānī Pārīzī. Tehran: Nashr-i 'Ilm, 1369.

Mustawfī Qazvīnī, Hamd Allāh. *Tārīkh-i Guzīdah*. Tehran: Amīr Kabīr, 1364.

Naba'ī, Abū al-Fazl. *Awzā'-i Sīyāsī va Ijtimā'ī-i Īrān dar Qarn-i Hashtum-i Hijrī*. Mashhad: Intishārāt-i Dānishgāh-i Firdawsī-i Mashhad, 1375.

Najm al-Dīn Rāzī, 'Abd Allāh b. Muhammad. *Mirsād al-'Ibād min al-Mabda' ilā al-Ma'ād*. Edited by Husayn al-Husaynī Ni'mat Allāh. Tehran: Dār Matba'ah-i Majlis bi-Tab' Rashīd, 1312.

The Path of God's Bondsmen from Origin to Return = (Mirsād al-'Ibād min al-Mabda' ilā al-Ma'ād): A Sufi Compendium. Translated by Hamid Algar. Delmar: Caravan Books, 1982.

Nasīrī, 'Alī Naqī. *Alqāb va Mavājib-i Dawrah-i Salātīn-i Safavīyah*. Edited by Yūsuf Rahīm'lū. Mashhad: Dānishgāh-i Firdawsī, 1993.

Nasīrī, Mīrzā Naqī. *Titles and Emoluments in Safavid Iran: A Third Manual of Safavid Administration*. Edited and translated by Willem Floor. Washington, DC: Mage Publishers, 2008.

Nāsirī, Muhammad Rizā. "Chand Sanad-i Tārīkhī." *Barrasī'hā-yi Tārīkhī* 9, no. 5 (1353/1974–75): 113–36.

Navā'ī, 'Abd al-Husayn. *Asnād va Mukātibāt-i Tārīkhī-i Īrān az Tīmūr tā Shāh Ismā'īl*. Bungāh-i Tarjumah va Nashr-i Kitāb, 2536/1977.

Shāh 'Abbās: Majmū'ah Asnād va Mukātibāt-I Tārīkhī. Tehran: Bunyād-i Farhang-i Īrān, 1352.

Shāh Ismā'īl Safavī: Asnād va Mukātabāt-i Tārīkhī Hamrāh bā Yadāshtaha-yi Tafsīlī. Tehran: Bunyād-i Farhang-i Īrān, 1347.

Shāh Tahmāsb Safavī: Majmū'ah-i Asnād va Mukātibāt-i Tārīkhī. Tehran: Bunyād-i Farhang-i Īrān, 1350.

al-Nawawī, Yahyā. *Tahdhīb al-Asmā' wa-l-Lughāt*. Beirut: Dār al-Kutub al-'Ilmiyya, 1996.

Nishātī Shīrāzī, Muhammad. *Tarjumah-i Nuskhah-i Khattī-i Tazkirah-i Shaykh Safī al-Dīn Ardabīlī: Mahfūz dar Kitābkhānah-i Sāltīkūf Shichidrīn San Pitirzbūrg Rūsiyyah*. Translated by Dāvūd Bahlūlī. Qum: Nashr-i Adyān, 1388.

Nizām al-Mulk, Abū 'Alī Hasan. *Siyāsat-nāmah*. Edited by Hubert Darke. Tehran, 1976.

Siyāsat'nāmah. Edited by Muhammad Qazvīnī and Murtazā Mudarrisī Chahārdahī. Tehran: Zavvār, 2537/1978.

Nizāmī Ganjavī. *Kulliyyāt-i Nizāmī Ganjavī*. Edited by Hasan Vahīd Dastgirdī. Tehran: Intishārāt-i Zavvār, 1388.

Paşazade, Kemal. *Tevârih-i Âl-i Osman: I. Defter*. Edited by Serafettin Turan. Ankara: Türk Tarih Kurumu Basımevi, 1991.

Qā'im-Maqāmī, Jahāngīr. "Farmān Mansūb bih Sultān Ahmad Jalāyir." *Barrasī'hā-yi Tārīkhī* 17 (1347): 273–90.

Yak Sad va Panjāh Sanad-i Tārīkhī az Jalāyirīyān tā Pahlavī. Tehran: Sitād-i Buzurg-i Artishtārān, 1348.

Qarīb, Mīrzā 'Abd al-'Azīm. "Futuvvat'nāmah-yi Mīrzā 'Abd al-'Azīm Khān-i Qarīb." In *Chahārdah Risālah dar Bāb-i Futuvvat va Asnāf*, edited by Mihrān Afshārī and Mahdī Madāyinī. Tehran: Nashr-i Chishmah, 1388.

Qavāmī Rāzī, Badr al-Dīn. *Dīvān-i Sharaf al-Shu'arā' Badr al-Dīn Qavāmī Rāzī*. Edited by Jalāl al-Dīn Husaynī Muhaddis Urmavī. Tehran: Chāpkhānah-i Sipihr, 1334.

Qazvīnī, Yahyā b. 'Abd al-Latīf. *Lubb al-Tavārīkh*. Edited by Mīr Hāshim Muhaddith. Tehran: Anjuman-i Āsār va Mafākhir-i Farhangī, 1386.

Qissah-yi Sultān Junayd. Istanbul, Sulaymaniya Library, MS Fatih 4354; Paris, Bibliothèque Nationale de France, MS Supplément Turc 636.

Qummī, Qāzī Ahmad b. Sharaf al-Dīn. *Die Chronik Ḫulāsat At-tawārīḫ Des Qāzī Ahmad Qummī: Der Abschnitt Über Schah 'Abbās I*. Akademie Der Wissenschaften Und Der Literatur – Veröffentlichungen Der Orientalischen Kommission Bd. 14. Wiesbaden: F. Steiner, 1964.

Sharaf al-Dīn. *Die Frühen Safawiden Nach Qāzī Ahmad Qummī*. Islamkundliche Untersuchungen Bd. 5. Freiburg i. Berlin: Schwarz, 1970.

Sharaf al-Dīn. *Khulāsat al-Tavārīkh*. 2 vols. Edited by Ihsān Ishrāqī. Tehran: Intishārāt-i Dānishgāh-i Tehran, 1359.

Qushayrī, 'Abd al-Karīm b. Hawāzin. *Tarjumah-i Risālah-i Qushayriyyah*. Edited and translated by Badī' al-Zamān Furūzānfar. Tehran: Bungāh-i Tarjumah va Nashr-i Kitāb, 1345.

al-Qushayri, Abu 'l-Qasim. *Al-Qushayri's Epistle on Sufism: Al-Risala al-qushayriyya fi 'ilm al-tasawwuf*. Translated by Alexander D. Knysh. Reading, UK: Garnet Publishing, 2007.

Rabī'. *'Alī-Nāmah*. Edited by Shafi'i Kadkani. Tehran, 2009.

Rūmī, Jalāl al-Dīn. *Khulāsah-i Masnavī*. Edited by Badī' al-Zamān Furūzānfar. Tehran: Bank-i Millī, 1321.

The Mathnawī of Jalāl al-Dīn Rūmī. Translated by Reynold A. Nicholson. Reprint. Cambridge: Trustees of the E. J. W. Gibb Memorial, 2001.

Rūmlū, Hasan. *Ahsan al-Tavārīkh*. 3 vols. Edited by 'Abd al-Husayn Navā'ī. Tehran: Bungāh-i Tarjumah va Nashr-i Kitāb, 1371–75.

Rycaut, R. *Present State of the Ottoman Empire*. London, 1670.

Sa'dī Shīrāzī, Muslih al-Dīn. *Gulistān-i Sa'dī*. Edited by Ghulāmhusayn Yūsufī. Tehran: Khwārazmī, 1368.

Kulliyyāt-i Sa'dī. Edited by Hasan Anvarī. Tehran: Nashr-i Qatrah, 1383.

Şah, Serap. "Safvetü's-safa'da Safiyyüddin-i Erdebili'nin Hayatı, Tasavvufi Görüşleri ve Menkıbeleri" [The life, Sufic thoughts, and miracles of Safi al-Dīn Ardabili in *Safvat al-Safā*]. 2 vols. PhD diss, Marmara University, 2007.

Sāhib al-Tālqānī, Abū al-Qāsim Ismā'īl b. 'Abbād. *al-Muhīt fī al-Lugha*. Edited by Muhammad Hasan Āl Yāsīn. Beirut: 'Ālam al-Kutub, 1994.

Sanā'ī al-Ghaznavī, Abū al-Majd Majdūd b. Ādam. *Dīvān-i Hakīm Abū al-Majd Majdūd b. Ādam Sanā'ī Ghaznavī.* Edited by Muhammad Taqī Mudarris Razavī. Tehran: Sanā'ī, 1354.

Sarrāf, Murtazā. *Rasā'il-i Javānmardān: Mushtamil bar Haft Futuvvat'nāmah*. Tehran: Qismat-i Īrānshināsī-i Anstitū-yi Pizhuhish'hā-yi 'Ilmī dar Īrān, 1352.

Sarrāj al-Tūsī, Abū Nasr. *al-Lum'a fī al-Tasawwuf*. Edited by Reynold Nicholson. Translated by Mahdī Muhabbatī. Tehran: Asātīr, 1381.

Shāh Ismā'īl b. Haydar Safavī. *Hatayî Divanı; Şah Ismail Safevı, Edebı Hayatı ve Nefesleri*. Edited by Sadeddin Nüzhet Ergun. Istanbul: Maarif Kitaphanesi, 1956.

Khatā'ī, Shāh Ismā'īl Safavī: Kulliyāt-i Dīvān, Nasīhatnāmah, Dahnāmah, Qūshmālār, Fārsjā Shi'rlar. Edited by Rasūl Ismā'īl-zādah. Tehran: al-Hudā, 1380.

Shāh Ni'mat Allāh Valī. *Kullīyāt Dīvān-i Shāh Ni'mat Allāh Valī Kirmānī*. Edited by Muhammad 'Abbāsī. Tehran: Kitābfurūshī-i Fakhr-i Rāzī, 1362.

Sharīf al-Razī, Muhammad b. al-Hussein. *Peak of Eloquence, Nahjul Balagha: Sermons, Letters and Sayings of Imam Ali ibn Abu Talib*. Translated by Sayed Ali Reza. Elmhurst, NY: Tahrike Tarsile Qur'an, 1996.

Shaykh al-Mufīd. *Kitāb al-Irshād*. Translated by I. K. A. Howard. Elmhurst, NY: Tahrike Tarsile Qur'an, 1989.

Shīrāzī, 'Abdī Beg. *Rawzat al-Safāt*. Moscow: Idārah-i Nashr-i Dānish, 1974.

Sarīh al-Mulk: Vaqf-nāmah-i Buq'ah-i Shaykh Safī al-Dīn Ardabīlī. Edited by Mahmūd Hidāyatī. Tehran, 2011.

Takmilat al-Akhbār: Tārīkh-i Safavīyah az Āghāz tā 978 Hijrī Qamarī. Edited by 'Abd al-Husayn Navā'ī. Tehran: Nashr-i Nay, 1369.

Shukrī, Yad Allāh, ed. *'Ālam'ārā-yi Safavī.* Tehran: Bunyād-i Farhang-i Īrān, 1350.

Sibt b. al-'Ajamī, Abū Dharr Ahmad b. Ibrāhīm. *Kunūz al-Dhahab fī Tārīkh Halab*. Edited by Shawqī Sha'ath and Fālih Bakkūr. Aleppo: Dār al-Qalam al-'Arabī bi-Halab, 1418.

Sī Futuvvat'nāmah-i Dīgar: Sī Risālah-i Nāshinākhtah dar Futuvvat va Pīshah'varī va Qalandarī. Edited by Mihrān Afshārī. Tehran: Nashr-i Chishmah, 1391.

Simnānī, Ahmad b. Muhammad. *Chihil Majlis, yā Risālah-i Iqbāliyyah*. Edited by Najīb Māyil Haravī. Tehran: Intishārāt-i Adīb, 1366.

Simnānī, Ahmad b. Muhammad, and Nūr al-Dīn 'Abd al-Rahmān b. Muhammad Isfarāyinī. *Murshid va Murīd: Mukātibāt-i 'Abd al-Rahmān Isfarāyinī bā 'Alā' al-Dawlah-i Simnānī*. Edited by Hermann Landolt. Tehran: Qismat-i Īrānshināsī, Instītū-yi Faransavī-i Pizhūhish'hā-yi 'Ilmī dar Īrān, 1351.

Tabarī, Abū Ja'far Muhammad. *The History of al-Ṭabarī*. Vol. 6, *Muḥammad at Mecca*. Translated by W. Montgomery Watt and M. V. McDonald. Albany: State University of New York Press, 1988.

al-Mustarshid fī Imāmat Amīr al-Mu'minīn 'Alī b. Abī Ṭālib. Edited by Ahmad al-Mahmūdī. Tehran: Mu'assasat al-Thaqāfah al-Islāmiyyah li-Kūshānbūr, 1415.

Tārīkh-i Tabarī, yā, Tārīkh al-Rusul wa-l-Mulūk. Translated by Abū al-Qāsim Pāyandah. Tehran: Intishārāt-i Asāṭīr, 1362.

Tahmāsb Safavī. *Tazkirah-i Shāh Tahmāsb*. Edited by Karīm Fayzī. Qum: Matbū'āt-i Dīnī, 1383.

Tārīkh-i 'Ālam'ārā-yi Safavī. Edited by Yad Allāh Shukrī. Tehran: Bunyād-i Farhang-i Īrān, 1350.

Tārīkh-i Qizilbāshān. Edited by Mīr Hāshim Muhaddith. Tehran: Intishārāt-i Bihnām, 1361.

Tarsūsī, Abū Tāhir. *Abū Muslim Nāmah*. 4 vols. Edited by Hossein Esmaili. Tehran: Anjuman-i Īrānshināsī-yi Farānsah dar Īrān, 2001.

Tawakkul b. Ismā'īl (Ibn Bazzāz Ardabīlī). *Safvat al-Safā: Dar Tarjumah-yi Ahvāl va Aqvāl va Karamāt-i Shaykh Safī al-Dīn Ishāq Ardabīlī*. Edited by Ghulām Rizā Tabātabā'ī Majd. Tehran: Intishārāt-i Zaryāb, 1376.

Thackston, Wheeler M., trans. *Three Memoirs of Homayun: Gulbadan Begims Humáyunnáma; Jawhar Áftábachí's Tadhkiratul-Wáqiát; Báyazid Bayáts Táríkh-i Humáyún*. Costa Mesa: Mazda Publishers, 2009.

al-Tūsī, Nasīr al-Dīn Muhammad. *Akhlāq-i Nāsirī*. Edited by Mujtabā Mīnuvī and 'Alī Rizā Haydarī. Tehran: Intishārāt-i Khwārazmī, 1978.

Awsāf al-Ashrāf. Scribed by Muhammad Husayn 'Imād al-Kuttāb. Tehran: Daftar-i Nashr-i Farhang-i Islāmī, 1368.

Varthema, Ludovico. "Itinerario." In *Navigationi et Viaggi*, vol. 1, edited by Giovanni Baptista Ramusio, folios 159a–188b. Venetia: Giunti, 1550.

Itinerario dallo Egypto alla India. Edited by Enrico Musacchio. Bologna: Fusconi, 1991.

Veli, Hacı Bektaş. *Manakıb-ı Hacı Bektâş-ı Velî "Vilâyet-nâme."* Edited by Abdülbâki Gölpınarlı. Istanbul: İnkılap Kitabevi, 1958.

Maqālāt-i Ghaybiyyah. Edited by Ihsān Allāh Shukr'khudā. Isfahan: I. Shukr'khudā, 1381.

Vilāyat-nāmah. Edited and translated by Esra Dughan and Maryam Sultani. Erbil, 1998.

Ya'qūbī, Ahmad b. Abī Ya'qūb. *Tārīkh-i Ya'qūbī*. Edited by Ebrahim Ayati. Tehran: Bungāh-i Tarjumah va Nashr-i Kitāb, 2536/1977.

Yazdī, Sharaf al-Dīn 'Alī. *Zafarnāmah: Tārīkh-i 'Umūmī-i Mufassal-i Īrān dar Dawrah-yi Tīmūrīyān: Az Rū-yi Nusakhī kih dar 'Asr-i Musannif Nivishtah Shudah*. Edited by Muhammad 'Abbāsī. Tehran: Amīr Kabīr, 1336.

Yemînî, Derviş Muhammed. *Fazîlet'nâme*. Edited by Yusuf Tepeli. Ankara: Atatürk Kültür, Dil ve Tarih Yüksek Kurumu Türk Dil Kurumu, 2002.

Yıldırım, Rıza, ed. *Menâkıb-ı Evliyâ (Buyruk)*. Istanbul: Yapı Kredi Yayınları, 2020.

Zāhidī, Husayn b. Abdāl. *Silsilat al-Nasab-i Safaviyyah: Nasab'nāmah-i Pādshāhān bā 'Azamat-i Safavī*. Berlin: Chāpkhānah-i Īrānshahr, 1343.

Zirke, Heidi, trans. and ed. *Ein hagiographisches Zeugnis zur persischen Geschichte aus der Mitte des 14. Jahrhunderts: Das achte Kapitel des Ṣafwat aṣ-ṣafā in kritischer Bearbeitung*. Berlin: Klaus Schwarz, 1987.

Zeno, Caterino. "Travels in Persia." In *A Narrative of Italian Travels in Persia, in the Fifteenth and Sixteenth Centuries*, translated and edited by Charles Grey, 1–65. London: Hakluyt Society, 1873.

SECONDARY SOURCES

Abisaab, Rula Jurdi. *Converting Persia: Religion and Power in the Safavid Empire*. London: I.B. Tauris, 2015.

"The Ulama of Jabal ʿAmil in Safavid Iran, 1501–1736: Marginality, Migration and Social Change." *Iranian Studies* 27 (1994): 103–22.

Alatas, Farid. *Ibn Khaldun*. Oxford University Press, 2013.

Allouche, Adel. *The Origins and Development of the Ottoman-Safavid Conflict (906-962/1500-1555)*. Berlin: Schwarz, 1983.

Anjum, Tanvir. "Sufism in History and Its Relationship with Power." *Islamic Studies* 45, no. 2 (2006): 221–68.

Anooshahr, Ali. "The Rise of the Safavids according to Their Old Veterans: Amini Haravi's Futuhat-e Shahi." *Iranian Studies* 48, no. 2 (2015): 249–67.

Arjomand, Said A. "The Clerical Estate and the Emergence of a Shiʿite Hierocracy in Safavid Iran: A Study in Historical Sociology." *Journal of the Economic and Social History of the Orient* 28, no. 2 (1985): 169–219.

The Shadow of God and the Hidden Imam: Religion, Political Order, and Societal Change in Shi'ite Iran from the Beginnings to 1890. University of Chicago Press, 1984.

"Two Decrees of Shah Tahmasb concerning Statecraft and the Authority of Shaykh ʿAli al-Karakī." In *Authority and Political Culture in Shiʿism*, edited by Said A. Arjomand, 250–62. Albany: State University of New York Press, 1988.

Asad'pūr, Hamīd, and Husayn Iskandarī. *Artish-i Īrān dar Dawrah-i Safavī va Tahavvulāt-i Ān*. Tehran: Nigāristān-i Andīshah, 1398.

Atcil, Abdurrahman. "Ottoman Religious Rulings concerning the Safavids." in *The Empires of the Near East and India: Source Studies of the Safavid, Ottoman, and Mughal Literate Communities*, edited by Hani Khafipour, 97–107. New York: Columbia University Press, 2019.

Aubin, Jean. "Etudes safavides. I. Shah Ismaʿil et les notables de l'Iraq person." *Journal of the Economic and Social History of the Orient* 2 (1959): 37–81.

"Révolution chiite et conservatisme. Les soufis de Lâhejân, 1500-1514." *Moyen Orient & Océan Indien* 1 (1984): 1–40.

Aytberov, Temur. "The Newly Found Tomb-Stone of Sheikh Haydar the Safavid in Dagestan." *Iran & the Caucasus* 13, no. 2 (2009): 281–84.

al-Azmeh, Aziz. *Ibn Khaldūn in Modern Scholarship: A Study in Orientalism*. London: Third World Centre, 1981.

Baali, Fuad. *The Science of Human Social Organization: Conflicting Views on Ibn Khaldun's (1332–1406) Ilm al-Umran*. Lewiston, NY: Edwin Mellen Press, 2005.

Babaie, Sussan, Kathryn Babayan, Ina Baghdiantz-McCabe, and Massumeh Farhad. *Slaves of the Shah: New Elites of Safavid Iran*. London: I.B. Tauris, 2004.

Babayan, Kathryn. *The City as Anthology: Eroticism and Urbanity in Early Modern Isfahan*. Stanford University Press, 2021.

Mystics, Monarchs, and Messiahs: Cultural Landscapes of Early Modern Iran. Cambridge, MA: Center for Middle Eastern Studies at Harvard University, 2003.

Badawī, ʿAbd al-Rahman. *Muʾallafāt Ibn Khaldūn*. Cairo, 1962.

Baddar, Maha. "The Education of Male Slaves in the Ottoman Empire and the Restructuring of Ottoman Social Hierarchy." In *Incarceration and Slavery in the Middle Ages and the Early Modern Age: A Cultural-Historical Investigation of the Dark Side in the Pre-Modern World*, edited by Albrecht Classen, 327–46. Lanham, MD: Lexington Books, 2021.

Baltacıoğlu-Brammer, Ayşe. "Neither Victim nor Accomplice: The Kızılbaş as Borderland Actors in the Early Modern Ottoman Realm." In *Historicizing Sunni Islam in the Ottoman Empire, c. 1450–c. 1750*, edited by Tijana Krstić and Derin Terzioğlu, 423–50. Edinburgh University Press, 2019.

Baron, Marcia. *The Moral Status of Loyalty*. Dubuque, IO: Kendall/Hunt, 1984.

Barth, Frederick. "Political Leadership among Swat Pathans." In *Friends, Followers, and Factions: A Reader in Political Clientelism*, edited by Steffen W. Schmidt, James C. Scott, Carl Landé, and Laura Guasti, 207–17. Berkeley: University of California Press, 1977.

Bashir, Shahzad. *Messianic Hopes and Mystical Visions: The Nūrbakhshīya between Medieval and Modern Islam*. Columbia: University of South Carolina Press, 2003.

"Shah Ismaʿil and the Qizilbash: Cannibalism in the Religious History of Early Safavid Iran." *History of Religions* 45, no. 3 (2006): 234–56.

Sufi Bodies: Religion and Society in Medieval Islam. New York: Columbia University Press, 2011.

Bayānī, Khānbābā. *Tārīkh-i Niẓāmī-i Īrān: Dawrah-i Safaviyyah*. Tehran: Tulūʿ-i Qalam, 1379.

Blake, Stephen P. "Shah ʿAbbās and the Transfer of the Safavid Capital from Qazvin to Isfahan." In *Society and Culture in the Early Modern Middle East: Studies on Iran in the Safavid Period*, edited by Andrew J. Newman, 145–64. Leiden: Brill, 2003.

Shahjahanabad: The Sovereign City in Mughal India, 1639–1739. Cambridge University Press, 2002.

Böszörményi-Nagy, Iván, and Geraldine M. Spark. *Invisible Loyalties: Reciprocity in Intergenerational Family Therapy*. New York: Brunner-Mazel, 1973.

Buehler, Arthur F. *Sufi Heirs of the Prophet: The Indian Naqshbandiyya and the Rise of the Mediating Sufi Shaykh*. Columbia: University of South Carolina Press, 2008.

Bustikova, Lenka, and Cristina Corduneanu-HuCi. "Patronage, Trust, and State Capacity: The Historical trajectories of Clientelism." *World Politics* 69, no. 2 (2017): 277–326.

Calmard, Jean. "Naqshbandis and Safavids: A Contribution to the Religious History of Iran and Her Neighbors." In *Safavid Iran and Her Neighbors*, edited by Michel Mazzaoui, 7–48. Salt Lake City: University of Utah Press, 2003.

"Popular Literature under the Safavids." In *Society and Culture in the Early Modern Middle East: Studies on Iran in the Safavid Period*, edited by Andrew J. Newman, 315–39. Leiden: Brill, 2003.

Coleman, Stephen. "The Problems of Duty and Loyalty." *Journal of Military Ethics* 8, no. 2 (2009): 105–15.

Connor, James. *The Sociology of Loyalty*. Dordrecht: Springer, 2007.

Corstange, Daniel. *The Price of a Vote in the Middle East: Clientelism and Communal Politics in Lebanon and Yemen*. Cambridge University Press, 2017.

Creevey, Lucy E. "Ahmad Bambo 1850–1927." In *Studies in West African Islamic History*. Vol. 1, *The Cultivators of Islam*, edited by John Ralph Willis, 278–307. London: Frank Cass, 1979.

Dahl, Robert. "Power as the Control of Behavior." In *Power: Readings in Social and Political Theory*, edited by Steven Lukes, 37–58. New York University Press, 1986.

Dakake, David. "The Practice of *Dhikr* in the Early Islamic Community." In *Knowledge Is Light: Essays in Islamic Studies Presented to Seyyed Hossein Nasr by His Students in Honor of His Sixty-Sixth Birthday*, edited by Zailan Moris, 169–95. Chicago: ABC International Group, 1999.

Dale, Stephen. *The Orange Trees of Marrakesh: Ibn Khaldun and the Science of Man*. Cambridge, MA: Harvard University Press, 2015.

Dennerlein, Bettina. "Legitimate Bounds and Bound Legitimacy: The Act of Allegiance to the Ruler (*Bai'a*) in 19th Century Morocco." *Die Welt des Islams* 41, no. 3 (2001): 287–310.

DeWeese, Devin. "Spiritual Practice and Corporate Identity in Medieval Sufi Communities of Iran, Central Asia, and India: The Khalvatī/'Ishqī/Shattārī Continuum." In *Religion and Identity in South Asia and Beyond: Essays in Honor of Patrick Olivelle*, edited by Steven E. Lindquist, 251–300. London: Anthem Press, 2011.

Elias, James J. *The Throne Carrier of God: The Life and Thought of 'Alā' ad-Dawla as-Simnānī*. Albany: State University of New York Press, 1995.

Erkmen, Aslıhan. "The Visualization of Shaykh Ṣafī al-Dīn Isḥāq Ardabilī: A Unique Illustrated Copy of the *Ṣafvat al-Ṣafā* at the Aga Khan Museum Collection and Its Illustrations." *Iranian Studies* 50, no.1 (2017): 45–77.

Erwin, R. E. "Loyalty and Virtues." *Philosophical Quarterly* 42, no. 169 (1992): 403–19.

"Loyalties, and Why Loyalty Should Be Ignored." *Criminal Justice Ethics* 12, no. 1 (1993): 36–42.

Eyuboğlu, Sabahattin. *Pir Sultan Abdal*. Istanbul: Cem Yayınevi, 1977.

Faseh, Ramiz. *Seyyid İmadäddin Näsiminin Seçilmiş Bäzi Şeirlärinin Şärhi*. Bakı: Şärq-Qärb, 2007.

Felek, Özgen, and Alexander D. Knysh, eds. *Dreams and Visions in Islamic Societies*. Albany: State University of New York Press, 2013.

Felten, Eric. *Loyalty: The Vexing Virtue*. New York: Simon & Schuster, 2012.

Ferrer, José Cutillas. "War and Diplomacy: A Letter Describing Shah Tahmasb I and His Ministers." In *The Spanish Monarchy and Safavid Persia in the Early*

Modern Period: Politics, War and Religion, edited by Enrique García Hernán, Jose Cuttilas Ferrer, and Rudi Matthee, 29–41. Valencia: Albatros, 2016.
Fleischer, Cornell. "Alqās Mīrza." *Encyclopædia Iranica*. www.iranicaonline.org/articles/alqas-alqasb-alqas-mirza-safawi.
Fletcher, George P. *Loyalty: An Essay on the Morality of Relationships*. Oxford University Press, 1993.
Floor, Willem M. "The Khalifeh al-Kholafa of the Safavid Sufi Order." *Zeitschrift der Deutschen Morgenländischen Gesellschaft* 153, no. 1 (2003): 51–86.
Safavid Government Institutions. Costa Mesa: Mazda Publishers, 2001.
Fromherz, Allen. *Ibn Khaldun: Life and Times*. Edinburgh University Press, 2010.
Gallagher, Amelia. "Shah Isma'il's Poetry in the Silsilat al-Nasab-i Safawiyya." *Iranian Studies* 44, no. 6 (2011): 895–911.
Gellner, Ernest. "From Ibn Khaldūn to Karl Marx." *Political Quarterly* 32 (1961): 385–92.
Muslim Society. Cambridge University Press, 1981.
Nationalism. London: Phoenix, 1997.
Nations and Nationalism. Oxford: Blackwell, 1983.
Plough, Sword and the Book: The Structure of Human History. London: Collins Harvill, 1988.
Gewirth, Alan. "Ethical Universalism and Particularism." *Journal of Philosophy* 85, no. 6 (1988): 283–302.
Ghereghlou, Kioumars. "Ḥaydar Ṣafavi." *Encyclopædia Iranica*. www.iranicaonline.org/articles/haydar-safavi.
Gholami, Yadollah, Matthew Melvin-Koushki, and Faramarz Haj Manouchehri. "ʿAlī b. Abī Ṭālib." Encyclopaedia Islamica. http://dx.doi.org/10.1163/1875-9831_isla_COM_0252.
Goldman, Alvin I. "Toward a Theory of Social Power." In *Power: Readings in Social and Political Theory*, edited by Steven Lukes, 156–202. New York University Press, 1986.
Gölpınarlı, Abdülbâki. *Pir Sultan Abdal: Hayatı, Sanatı, Eserleri*. Istanbul: Varlık Yayınevi, 1963.
Gomez Licon, Adriana. "What They Said: Trump, Zelenskyy and Vance's Heated Argument in the Oval Office." *Associated Press*, February 28, 2025. https://shorturl.at/7YpD9.
Graham, Terry. "The Niʿmatu'llāhī Order under Safavid Suppression and in Indian Exile." In *The Heritage of Sufism*. Vol. 3, *Late Classical Persianate Sufism (1501–1750)*, edited by Leonard Lewisohn and David Morgan, 165–200. Oxford: Oneworld, 1999.
Grodzins, Morton. *The Loyal and the Disloyal: Social Boundaries of Patriotism and Treason*. University of Chicago Press, 1956.
Guetzkow, Harold. *Multiple Loyalties*. Princeton University Press, 1955.
Haneda, Masashi. *Le Châh et les Qizilbāš le Systeme Militaire Safavide*. Berlin: Schwarz, 1987.
"L'Évolution de la Garde Royale des Safavides." *Moyen Orient & Océan Indien* 1 (1984): 41–64.

Hanne, Eric J. "Ritual and Reality: The Bayʿa Process in Eleventh- and Twelfth-Century Islamic Courts." In *Court Ceremonies and Rituals of Power in Byzantium and the Medieval Mediterranean*, edited by Alexander Beihammer, Stavroula Constantinou, and Maria G. Parani, 141–57. Leiden: Brill, 2013.

Haqīqat Rafīʿ, ʿAbd al-Rafīʿ. *Tārīkh-i Junbish-i Sarbidārān va Dīgar Junbish'hā-yi Īrāniyān dar Qarn-i Hashtum-i Hijrī.* Tehran: Intishārāt-i Kūmish, 1374.

Hartmann, Angelika. *An-Nasir li-Din Allah (1180-1225): Politics, Religion, Culture in the Late Abbasid Period.* Berlin: De Gruyter, 1975.

Herrmann, Gottfried, and Gerhard Doerfer. "Ein Persisch-mongolischer Erlaß des Ǧalāyeriden Šeyḫ Oveys." *Central Asiatic Journal* 19 (1975): 1–84.

Hinz, Walther. *Irans Aufstieg Zum Nationalstaat im Fünfzehnten Jahrhundert.* Berlin: De Gruyter, 1936.

Hirschman, Albert O. *Exit, Voice, and Loyalty: Response to Decline in Firms, Organizations and States.* Cambridge, MA: Harvard University Press, 1970.

Hourani, Albert. "From Jabal 'Amil to Persia." *Bulletin of the School of Oriental and African Studies* 49 (1986): 133–40.

Hume, David. *Moral Philosophy.* Edited by Geoffrey Sayre-McCord. Indianapolis: Hackett, 2006.

Imber, Colin. *The Ottoman Empire, 1300–1650: The Structure of Power.* Basingstoke, Hampshire: Palgrave Macmillan, 2002.

Inalcik, Halil. *The Ottoman Empire: The Classical Age, 1300–1600.* Translated by Norman Itzkowitz and Colin Imber. London: Phoenix Press, 2000.

Islam, Riazul. *Indo-Persian Relations: A Study of the Political and Diplomatic Relations between the Mughul Empire and Iran.* Tehran: Iranian Culture Foundation, 1970.

Issawi, Charles. *An Arab Philosophy of History: Selections from the Prolegomena of Ibn Khaldūn of Tunis (1332–1406).* London: John Murray, 1950.

Izadi, Husayn, and Mahdi Ziraki. "Manāqib-khvānī dar Dawrah-yi Āl-i Būyah." *Tārīkh-i Islām* 33–34 (1387): 25–56.

Jaʿfariyān, Rasūl. *Kāvush'hā-yi Tāzah dar Bāb-i Rūzgār-i Safavī.* Qum: Nashr-i Adyān, 1384.

Safaviyyah dar ʿArsah-i Dīn, Farhang va Sīyāsat. Qum: Pizhūhishgāh-i Hawzah va Dānishgāh, 1379.

Sīyāsat va Farhang-i Rūzgār-i Safavī. Tehran: Nashr-i ʿIlm, 1388.

Tārīkh-i Qizilbashān-i Safavī dar Chand Matn-i Tārīkhī. Qum: Nashr-i Muvarrikh, 1396.

Tārīkh-i Tashayyuʿ dar Īrān: Az Āghāz tā Pāyān-i Qarn-i Nuhum-i Hijrī. 2 vols. Tehran: Nashr-i ʿIlm, 1395.

Tārīkh-i Tashayyuʿ dar Īrān: Az Āghāz tā Qarn-i Haftum-i Hijrī. 2 vols. Tehran: Shirkat-i Chāp va Nashr-i Sāzmān-i Tablīghāt-i Islāmī, 1388.

Jalālī, Hūshang. *Tārīkh-i Nizāmī-i Īrān az Dawrah-i Safavī tā Pāyān-i Difāʿ-i Muqaddas.* Tehran: Īrān-i Sabz, 1389.

Kant, Immanuel. *Lectures on Ethics.* Translated by Louis Infield. London: Methuen Press, 1979.

Karakaya-Stump, Ayfer. *The Kizilbash/Alevis in Ottoman Anatolia: Sufism, Politics and Community.* Edinburgh University Press, 2021.

"Who Really Were the Kizilbash? A Rethinking of the Kizilbash Movement in Light of New Sources and Research." In *The Safavid World*, edited by Rudi Matthee, 37–55. London: Routledge, 2021.

Karamustafa, Ahmet T. *God's Unruly Friends: Dervish Groups in the Islamic Later Middle Period, 1200–1550*. Salt Lake City: University of Utah Press, 1994.

Kasravī, Ahmad. *Shaykh Safī va Tabārash*. Tehran: Jār, 2535/1977.

Tārīkh-i Pānsad Sālah-i Khūzistān. Tehran, 1368.

Keller, Simon. *The Limits of Loyalty*. Cambridge University Press, 2007.

Kettering, Sharon. *Patrons, Brokers, and Clients*. Oxford University Press, 1986.

Keyvani, Mehdi. *Artisans and Guild Life in the Later Safavid Period: Contributions to the Social-Economic History of Persia*. Berlin: Klaus Schwarz, 1982.

Khafipour, Hani. "Beyond Charismatic Authority: The Crafting of a Monarch's Image in the Public Sphere." In *The Safavid World*, edited by Rudi Matthee, 111–25. London: Routledge, 2021.

"Echoes of the Safavid Past." In *In the Fields of Empty Days: The Intersection of Past and Present in Iranian Art*, edited by Linda Komaroff, 66–80. Los Angeles: Los Angeles County Museum of Art, 2018.

Khafipour, Hani, ed. *The Empires of the Near East and India: Source Studies of the Safavid, Ottoman, and Mughal Literate Communities*. New York: Columbia University Press, 2019.

Khafipour, Hani. "The Safavid Claim to Sovereignty according to a Court Bureaucrat." In *The Empires of the Near East and India: Source Studies of the Safavid, Ottoman, and Mughal Literate Communities*, edited by Hani Khafipour, 179–92. New York: Columbia University Press, 2019.

Khomeini, Ruhollah. *Sahīfah-yi Imām Khomeini*. Vol. 16. Tehran, 1360.

Kiyānī, Muhsin. *Tārīkh-i Khānqāh dar Īrān*. Tehran: Kitābkhānah-i Tahūrī, 1369.

Kleinig, John. "Loyalty." *Stanford Encyclopedia of Philosophy*. https://plato.stanford.edu/archives/sum2022/entries/loyalty/.

Loyalty and Loyalties: The Contours of a Problematic Virtue. Oxford University Press, 2014.

Lacoste, Yves. *Ibn Khaldūn: The Birth of History and the Past of the Third World*. Translated by David Macy. London: Verso, 1984.

Lakhassi, Abderrahmane. "Ibn Khaldūn." In *History of Islamic Philosophy*, edited by Seyyed Hossein Nasr and Oliver Leaman, 350–64. London: Routledge, 1996.

Landau-Tasseron, Ella. *The Religious Foundations of Political Allegiance: A Study of Bay'a in Pre-Modern Islam*. Washington, DC: Hudson Institute, 2010.

Lawson, B. Todd. "The Dawning Places of the Lights of Certainty in the Divine Secrets Connected with the Commander of the Faithful by Rajab Bursi (d. 1411)." In *The Heritage of Sufism*. Vol. 2, *The Legacy of Medieval Persian Sufism (1150–1500)*, edited by Leonard Lewisohn, 261–76. Oxford: Oneworld, 1999.

Lewisohn, Leonard. "'Ali ibn Abi Talib's Ethics of Mercy in the Mirror of the Persian Sufi Tradition." In *The Sacred Foundations of Justice in Islam: The Teachings of 'Ali ibn Abi Talib*, edited by M. Ali Lakhani, 109–45. Bloomington, IN: World Wisdom, 2006.

Lukes, Steven. *Power: A Radical View*. London: Palgrave Macmillan, 2005.

Lukes, Steven, ed. *Power: Readings in Social and Political Theory.* New York University Press, 1986.

MacIntyre, Alasdair. *Is Patriotism a Virtue?* Lawrence: University of Kansas Press, 1984.

Madelung, Wilferd. "Karakī." *EI*² IV. 1978.

Mahdi, Muhsin. *Ibn Khaldūn's Philosophy of History.* University of Chicago Press, 1971.

Malešević, Siniša. "Nationalism, War and Social Cohesion." *Ethnic and Racial Studies* 34, no. 1 (2011): 142–61.

The Rise of Organised Brutality: A Historical Sociology of Violence. Cambridge University Press, 2017.

The Sociology of War and Violence. Cambridge University Press, 2010.

"Where Does Group Solidarity Come From? Gellner and Ibn Khaldun Revisited." *Thesis Eleven* 128, no. 1 (2015): 85–99.

Malešević, Siniša, and Mark Haugaard, eds. *Ernest Gellner and Contemporary Social Thought.* Cambridge University Press, 2007.

Making Sense of Collectivity: Ethnicity Nationalism and Globalisation. London: Pluto Press, 2002.

Marlow, Louise, ed. *Dreaming across Boundaries: The Interpretations of Dreams in Islamic Lands.* Cambridge, MA: Harvard University Press, 2006.

Marsham, Andrew. "The Architecture of Allegiance in Early Islamic Late Antiquity: The Accession of Muʿāwiya in Jerusalem, ca. 661 CE." In *Court Ceremonies and Rituals of Power in Byzantium and the Medieval Mediterranean*, edited by Alexander Beihammer, Stavroula Constantinou, and Maria G. Parani, 87–112. Leiden: Brill, 2013.

Rituals of Islamic Monarchy: Accession and Succession in the First Muslim Empire. Edinburgh University Press, 2009.

Maryanski, Alexandra. "African Ape Social Networks: A Blueprint for Reconstructing Early Hominid Social Structure." In *The Archaeology of Human Ancestry: Power, Sex and Tradition*, edited by James Steele and Stephen Shennan, 67–90. London: Routledge, 1995.

Matthee, Rudi. "Loyalty, Betrayal, and Retribution: Biktash Khan, Yaʿqub Khan, and Shah ʿAbbas I's Strategy in Establishing Control over Kirman, Yazd and Fars." In *Ferdowsi, the Mongols and the History of Iran: Art, Literature and Culture from Early Islam to Qajar Persia*, edited by Robert Hillenbrand, A. C. S. Peacock, and Firuza Abdullaeva, 184–200. London: I.B. Tauris, 2013.

Persia in Crisis: Safavid Decline and the Fall of Isfahan. London: I.B. Tauris in Association with the Iran Heritage Foundation, 2012.

The Politics of Trade in Safavid Iran: Silk for Silver, 1600–1730. Cambridge University Press 1999.

Matthee, Rudi, ed. *The Safavid World.* London: Routledge, 2021.

Mazzaoui, Michel M. "From Tabriz to Qazvin to Isfahan: Three Phases of Safavid History." In *XIX. Deutscher Orientalistentag: Vom 28. Sept. bis 4. Okt. 1975 in Freiburg i. Br: Vorträge*, edited by Wolfgang Voigt, 514–22. Wiesbaden: Steiner, 1977.

"A 'New' Edition of the *Safvat al-Safā*." In *History and Historiography of Post-Mongol Central Asia and the Middle East: Studies in Honor of John E. Woods*, edited by Judith Pfeiffer and Sholeh A. Quinn, 303–31. Wiesbaden: Harrassowitz, 2006.

Meisami, Julie Scott. "History as Literature." *Iranian Studies 33*, no. 1–2 (2000): 15–30.

Persian Historiography to the End of the Twelfth Century. Edinburgh University Press, 1999.

Mélikoff, I. "Dj̲unayd." *EI*². http://dx.doi.org/10.1163/1573-3912_islam_SIM_2115.

Milani, Milad. *The Nature of Sufism: An Ontological Reading of the Mystical in Islam*. London: Routledge, 2021.

Sufism in the Secret History of Persia. London: Routledge, 2014.

Minorsky, Vladimir. "A Civil and Military Review in Fārs in 881/1476." *Bulletin of the School of Oriental and African Studies* 10, no. 1 (1939): 141–78.

"A Mongol Decree of 720/1320 to the Family of Shaykh Zāhid." *Bulletin of the School of Oriental and African Studies* 16, no. 3 (1954): 515–27.

Moin, Azfar. *The Millennial Sovereign: Sacred Kingship and Sainthood in Islam*. New York: Columbia University Press, 2012.

Monshi, Eskandar Beg. *History of Shah 'Abbas the Great*. Vol. 1. Translated by Roger M. Savory. Boulder, CO: Westview Press, 1978.

Morgan, David. *Medieval Persia, 1040–1797*. 2nd ed. London: Routledge, 2015.

Morimoto, Kazuo. "The Earliest ʿAlīd Genealogy for the Safavids: New Evidence for the Pre-Dynastic Claim to Sayyid Status." *Iranian Studies* 43, no. 4 (2010): 447–69.

Morton, Alexander H. "The Chub-i Tariq and Qizilbash Ritual in Safavid Persia." In *Etudes Safavides*, edited by Jean Calmard, 225–46. Paris: Paris Institut Français de Recherche en Iran, 1993.

Mottahedeh, Roy. *Loyalty and Leadership in an Early Islamic Society*. Princeton University Press, 1980.

Mudarrisī Chahārdahī, Murtazā. "Tashkīlāt-i Tarīqāt-i Safaviyyah." *Nashrīyah-i Anjuman-i Āsār-i Millī*, no. 2 (2535/1976).

al-Muhājir, Jaʿfar. *al-Hijra al-ʿĀmiliyya ilā Īrān fī al-ʿAsr al-Safawi*. Beirut: Dār al-Rawda, 1989.

Muruwwah, ʿAlī. *al Tashayyuʿ bayn Jabal ʿĀmil wa-Īrān*. London: Riad El-Rayyes Books, 1987.

Nafīsī, Saʿīd. *Sarchishmah-i Tasavvuf dar Īrān*. Tehran: Kitābfurūshī Furūghī, 1343.

Nasr, Seyyed Hossein. "Shiʿism and Sufism: Their Relationship in Essence and in History." *Religious Studies* 6, no. 3 (1970): 229–42.

Sufi Essays. Chicago: Kazi Publications, 1999.

Netton, Ian R. *Sufi Ritual: The Parallel Universe*. Richmond, UK: Curzon Press, 2000.

Newman, Andrew J. "The Myth of Clerical Migration to Safawid Iran: Arab Shiite Opposition to 'Ali al-Karaki and Safawid Shiism." *Die Welt des Islams* 33 (1993): 66–112.

Safavid Iran: Rebirth of a Persian Empire. London: I.B. Taruris, 2006.

"Sufism and Anti-Sufism in Safavid Iran: The Authorship of the Hadiqat al-Shi'a Revisited." *Iran* 37 (1999): 95–108.

"Sufism and the Safavids in Iran: A Further Challenge to 'Decline.'" In *Routledge Handbook on Sufism*, edited by Lloyd Ridgeon, 370–86. London: Routledge, 2020.

Nūrbakhsh, Javād. *In the Tavern of Ruin: Seven Essays on Sufism*. London: Khaniqah-i Nimatullahi Publications, 1978.

Nuyen, A. T. "The Value of Loyalty." *Philosophical Papers* 28, no. 1 (1999): 25–36.

Oldenquist, Andrew. "Loyalties." *Journal of Philosophy* 79, no. 4 (1982): 173–93.

Öztelli, Cahit. *Pir Sultan Abdal: Bütün Şiirleri*. Istanbul: Milliyet Yayinlari, 1971.

Parsons, Talcott. *Politics and Social Structure*. New York: The Free Press, 1969.

"Power and the Social System." In *Power: Readings in Social and Political Theory*, edited by Steven Lukes, 94–144. New York University Press, 1986.

Pierce, Mathew. *Twelve Infallible Men: The Imams and the Making of Shi'ism*. Cambridge, MA: Harvard University Press, 2016.

Podeh, Elie. "The *Bay'a*: Modern Political Uses of Islamic Ritual in the Arab World." *Die Welt des Islams* 50, no. 1 (2010): 117–52.

Posch, Walter. *Osmanisch-Safavidische Beziehungen 1545-1550: Der Fall Alkas Mirza*. 2 vols. Vienna, 2013.

Potter, Lawrence G. "Sufis and Sultans in Post-Mongol Iran." *Iranian Studies* 27, no. 1–4 (1994): 77–102.

Pūrjavādī, Nasr Allāh. *Sultān-i Tarīqat: Savānih-i Zindagī va Sharh-i Āṣār-i Khvājah Ahmad Ghazzālī*. Tehran: Mu'assasah-'i Intishārāt-i Āgāh, 1358.

Quinn, Sholeh A. "The Dreams of Shaykh Safi al-Dīn in Late Safavid Chronicles." In *Dreaming across Boundaries: The Interpretations of Dreams in Islamic Lands*, edited by Louise Marlow, 221–34. Cambridge, MA: Harvard University Press, 2006.

Historical Writings during the Reign of Shah 'Abbas: Ideology, Imitation, and Legitimacy in Safavid Chronicles. Salt Lake City: University of Utah Press, 2000.

Rabī', Muhammad Mahmoud. *The Political Theory of Ibn Khaldūn*. Leiden: Brill, 1967.

Rajabī, Amīr. *Sharh-i Safā: Zindagī va Ta'ālīm-i 'Irfānī-i Shaykh Safī al-Dīn Ardabīlī*. Tehran: Shirkat-i Intishārāt-i Sūrah-i Mihr, 1397.

Ranjbar, Muhammad 'Alī. "Mansab-i Khalīfat al-Khulafā dar Dawrah-i Safavī." *Ganjīnah-yi Asnād: Faslnāmah-yi Tahqīqāt-i Tārīkhī* 1–2, no. 33–34 (1378): 4–15.

Reemtsma, Jan Philipp. *Trust and Violence: An Essay on a Modern Relationship*. Princeton University Press, 2012.

Ridgeon, Lloyd. *Morals and Mysticism in Persian Sufism: A History of Sufi-Futuwwat in Iran*. London: Routledge, 2010.

Rizvi, Kishwar. "'Its Mortar Mixed with the Sweetness of Life': Architecture and Ceremonial at the Shrine of Safī al-Dīn Ishāq Ardabīlī during the Reign of Shāh Tahmāsb I." *The Muslim World* 90, no. 3 (2000): 323–51.

Royce, Josiah. *The Philosophy of Loyalty*. New York: Macmillan, 1908.

Ruiz de Elvira, Laura, Christoph Schwarz, and Irene Weipert-Fenner, eds. *Clientelism and Patronage in the Middle East and North Africa: Networks of Dependency.* London: Routledge, 2018.

Sakenfeld, Katharine Doob. *Faithfulness in Action: Loyalty in Biblical Perspective.* Philadelphia: Fortress Press, 1985.

Sanders, Paula. *Ritual, Politics and the City in Fatimid Cairo*. Albany: State University of New York Press, 1994.

Savory, Roger M. "The Office of Khalīfat Al-Khulafā under the Safawids." *Journal of the American Oriental Society* 85, no. 4 (1965): 497–502.

"The Principal Offices of the Safawid State during the Reign of Isma'īl I (907–30/1501–24)." *Bulletin of the School of Oriental and African Studies* 23, no. 1 (1960): 91–105.

"The Principal Offices of the Safawid State during the Reign of Tahmāsp I (930–84/1524–76)." *Bulletin of the School of Oriental and African Studies* 24, no. 1 (1961): 65–85.

"Some Notes on the Provincial Administration of the Early Safawid Empire." *Bulletin of the School of Oriental and African Studies* 27, no. 1 (1964): 114–28.

"Some Reflections on Totalitarian Tendencies in the Safavid State." *Der Islam* 53, no. 2 (1976): 226–41.

Schimmel, Annemarie. *Mystical Dimensions of Islam*. Chapel Hill: University of North Carolina Press, 1975.

Schrag, Brian. "The Moral Significance of Employee Loyalty." *Business Ethics Quarterly* 11, no. 1 (2001): 41–66.

Scott, James. "Patron-Client Politics and Political Change in Southeast Asia." *American Political Science Review* 66, no. 1 (1972): 91–113.

Shah-Kazemi, Reza. "Imam Ali." In *The Shi'i World: Pathways in Tradition and Modernity*, edited by Farhad Daftry, Shainool Jiwa, and Amyn B. Sajoo, 33–55. London: I.B. Tauris, 2015.

Justice and Remembrance: Introducing the Spirituality of Imam Ali. London: I.B. Taurus, 2011.

Sharīf al-Radī, Muhammad b. al-Husayn. *Nahj al-Balāgha*. Edited by Muhammad 'Abduh. Beirut, 1996.

Shaybī, Kāmil Mustafā. *Tashayyu' va Tasavvuf tā Āghāz-i Sadah-i Davāzdahum-i Hijrī.* Translated by 'Alī Rizā Zakāvatī Qarāgūzlū. Tehran: Amīr Kabīr, 1387.

Sifat'gul, Mansūr. *Sākhtār-i Nahād va Andīshah-i Dīnī dar Īrān-i 'Asr-i Safavī: Tārīkh-i Tahavvulāt-i Dīnī-i Īrān dar Sadah'hā-yi Dahum tā Davāzdahum-i Hijrī-i Qamarī.* Tehran: Mu'assasah Khadamāt-i Farhangī-i Rasā, 1381.

Simon, Róbert. *Ibn Khaldūn: History as Science and the Patrimonial Empire.* Translated by Klára Pogátsa. Budapest: Akadémiai Kiadó, 2002.

Simpson, Marianna Shreve, and Massumeh Farhad. *Sultan Ibrahim Mirza's Haft Awrang: A Princely Manuscript from Sixteenth-Century Iran*. New Haven, CT: Yale University Press, 1997.

Sirriyeh, Elizabeth. *Dreams and Visions in the World of Islam: A History of Muslim Dreaming and Foreknowing*. London: I.B. Tauris, 2018.

Sjoberg, Gideon. *The Preindustrial City: Past and Present*. Glencoe, IL: The Free Press, 1960.

Stewart, Devin J. "Notes on the Migration of 'Amuli Scholars to Safavid Iran." *Journal of Near Eastern Studies* 55, no. 2 (1996): 81–103.

Stone, Lawrence. *The Crisis of the Aristocracy, 1559–1641*. Oxford: Clarendon Press, 1965.

Subtelny, Maria E. *Timurids in Transition: Turko-Persian Politics and Acculturation in Medieval Iran*. Leiden: Brill, 2007.

Sümer, Faruk. *Naqsh-i Turkān-i Ānātulī dar Tashkīl va Tawsiʿah-i Dawlat-i Safavī (Safevi Devletinin Kurulusu ve Gelismesinde Anadolu Turklerinin Rolu)*. Translated by Ihsān Ishrāqī and Muhammad Taqī Imāmī. Tehran: Nashr-i Gustarah, 1371.

Safevî Devletinin Kuruluşu ve Gelişmesinde Anadolu Türklerinin Rolü. Ankara: Güven Matbaası, 1976.

Svanidze, Mikheil. "The Amasya Peace Treaty between the Ottoman Empire and Iran (June 1, 1555) and Georgia." *Bulletin of the Georgian National Academy of Sciences* 3, no. 1 (2009): 191–97.

Szuppe, Maria. "Kinship Ties between the Safavids and the Qizilbash Amirs in Late Sixteenth-Century Iran: A Case Study of the Political Career of Members of the Sharaf al-Dīn Oghli Tekelu Family." *In Safavid Persia: The History and Politics of an Islamic Society*, edited by Charles Melville, 79–104. London: I.B. Tauris, 1996.

Tabātabāʾī Majd, Ghulām Rizā. *Dard-i Talab: Zindagānī-i Shaykh Safī al-Dīn Ardabīlī*. Tabriz: Nashr-i Abū, 1376.

Taeschner, Fran. *Zünfte und Bruderschaften im Islam: Texte zur Geschichte der Futuwwa*. Zürich: Artemis Verlag, 1979.

Tilles, Daniel. "Wałęsa Condemns Trump Treatment of Zelensky, Likening It to Communist Interrogation." *Notes from Poland*, March 3, 2025. https://shorturl.at/0wFn8.

Togan, Zeki Velidi. "Sur l'origine des Safavides." In *Mélanges Louis Massignon*. Vol. 3, 345–57. Damascus: Institut Français de Damas, 1957.

Trimingham, J. Spencer. *The Sufi Orders in Islam*. Oxford: Clarendon Press, 1971.

Turner, Jonathan. *Face to Face: Toward a Sociological Theory of Interpersonal Behavior.* Stanford University Press, 2002.

Human Emotions: A Sociological Theory. London: Routledge, 2007.

Varelius, Jukka. "Is Whistle-Blowing Compatible with Employee Loyalty?" *Journal of Business Ethics* 85, no. 2 (2009): 263–75.

Vijdānī, Bihrūz. *Hazrat-i ʿAlī (ʿa.) dar Naghmah'hā-yi ʿĀmmiyānah-yi Īrān*. Tehran: Sāzmān-i Chāp va Intishārāt, Vizārat-i Farhang va Irshād-i Islāmī, 1380.

Walsh, John R. "The Revolt of Alqās Mīrzā." *Wiener Zeitschrift Für Die Kunde Des Morgenlandes* 68 (1976): 61–78.

Weingrod, Alex. "Power and Patronage." In *Patrons and Clients in Mediterranean Societies*, edited by Ernest Gellner and John Waterbury, 41–51. London: Duckworth, 1977.

Welch, Stuart Cary. *A King's Book of Kings: The Shahnameh of Shah Tahmasp*. New York: Metropolitan Museum of Art, 1972.

Woods, John E. *The Aqquyunlu: Clan, Confederation, Empire*. Salt Lake City: University of Utah Press, 1999.

Wrong, Dennis H. *Power: Its Forms, Bases, and Uses*. University of Chicago Press, 1988.

Yāhaqqī, Muhammad Jaʿfar. *Farhang-i Asātīr va Ishārāt-i Dāstānī dar Adabīyāt-i Fārsī*. Tehran: Surūsh, 1369.

Yıldırım, Rıza. "Beylikler Dünyasında Kerbela Kültürü ve Ehl-i Beyt Sevgisi: 1362 Yılında Kastamonu'da Yazılan Bir Maktel'in Düşündürdükleri." In *Kuzey Anadolu'da Beylikler Dönemi Sempozyumu: Bildiriler*, edited by Halil Çetin, 344–72. Çankırı: Çankırı Karatekin Üniversitesi Yayınları, 2012.

"The Commandment (*Buyruk*): An Introduction to the Sacred Texts of the Kizilbash-Alevi Community." In *Entangled Confessionalizations? Dialogic Perspectives on the Politics of Piety and Community Building in the Ottoman Empire, 15th–18th Centuries*, edited by Tijana Krstić and Derin Terzioğlu, 285–312. Piscataway, NJ: Gorgias Press, 2022.

"The Rise of the Safavids as a Political Dynasty: The Revolution of Shah Esmail, the Founder of the Safavid State." In *The Safavid World*, edited by Rudi Matthee, 56–76. London: Routledge, 2021.

"The Safavid Ecumene and the Formation of the Qizilbash-Alevi Community in the Ottoman Empire, c. 1500–c. 1700." *Iranian Studies* 52, no. 3–4 (2019): 449–83.

"Shīʾitisation of the Futuwwa Tradition in the Fifteenth Century." *British Journal of Middle Eastern Studies* 40, no. 1 (2013): 53–70.

Zakeri, Mohsen. *Sāsānid Soldiers in Early Muslim Society: The Origin of ʿAyyārān and Futuwwa*. Wiesbaden: Harrassowitz, 1995.

Zarinebaf-Shahr, Fariba. "Qizilbash 'Heresy' and Rebellion in Ottoman Anatolia during the Sixteenth Century." *Anatolia Moderna. Yeni Anadolu* 7 (1997): 1–15.

Zarrīn'kūb, ʿAbd al-Husayn. *Justujū dar Tasavvūf-i Īrān*. Tehran: Amīr Kabīr, 1385.

Zdaniuk, Bozena, and John M. Levine. "Group Loyalty: Impact of Members' Identification and Contributions." *Journal of Experimental Social Psychology* 37, no. 6 (2001): 502–9.

Index

Other Titles in the series

Agricultural Innovation in the Early Islamic World: The Diffusion of Crops and Farming Techniques, 700–1100, Andrew M. Watson

Muslim Tradition: Studies in Chronology, Provenance and Authorship of Early Hadith, G. H. A. Juynboll

Social History of Timbuktu: The Role of Muslim Scholars and Notables, 1400–1900, Elias N. Saad

Sex and Society in Islam: Birth Control before the Nineteenth Century, B. F. Musallam

Towns and Townsmen of Ottoman Anatolia: Trade, Crafts and Food Production in an Urban Setting, 1520–1650, Suraiya Faroqhi

Unlawful Gain and Legitimate Profit in Islamic Law: Riba, Gharar and Islamic Banking, Nabil A. Saleh

Men of Modest Substance: House Owners and House Property in Seventeenth-Century Ankara and Kayseri, Suraiya Faroqhi

Roman, Provincial and Islamic Law: The Origins of the Islamic Patronate, Patricia Crone

Economic Life in Ottoman Jerusalem, Amnon Cohen

Mannerism in Arabic Poetry: A Structural Analysis of Selected Texts (3rd Century AH/9th Century AD –5th Century AH/11th Century AD), Stefan Sperl

The Rise and Rule of Tamerlane, Beatrice Forbes Manz

Popular Culture in Medieval Cairo, Boaz Shoshan

Early Philosophical Shiism: The Ismaili Neoplatonism of Abū Ya'qūb al-Sijistānī, Paul E. Walker

Indian Merchants and Eurasian Trade, 1600–1750, Stephen Frederic Dale

Palestinian Peasants and Ottoman Officials: Rural Administration around Sixteenth-Century Jerusalem, Amy Singer

Arabic Historical Thought in the Classical Period, Tarif Khalidi

Mongols and Mamluks: The Mamluk–Īlkhānid War, 1260–1281, Reuven Amitai-Preiss

Knowledge and Social Practice in Medieval Damascus, 1190–1350, Michael Chamberlain

The Politics of Households in Ottoman Egypt: The Rise of the Qazdağlis, Jane Hathaway

Hierarchy and Egalitarianism in Islamic Thought, Louise Marlow

Commodity and Exchange in the Mongol Empire: A Cultural History of Islamic Textiles, Thomas T. Allsen

State and Provincial Society in the Ottoman Empire: Mosul, 1540–1834, Dina Rizk Khoury

The Mamluks in Egyptian Politics and Society, Thomas Philipp and Ulrich Haarmann (eds.)

The Delhi Sultanate: A Political and Military History, Peter Jackson

European and Islamic Trade in the Early Ottoman State: The Merchants of Genoa and Turkey, Kate Fleet

The Ottoman City between East and West: Aleppo, Izmir, and Istanbul, Edhem Eldem, Daniel Goffman, and Bruce Masters

The Politics of Trade in Safavid Iran: Silk for Silver, 1600–1730, Rudolph P. Matthee
The Idea of Idolatry and the Emergence of Islam: From Polemic to History, G. R. Hawting
A Monetary History of the Ottoman Empire, Şevket Pamuk
Classical Arabic Biography: The Heirs of the Prophets in the Age of al-Maʾmūn, Michael Cooperson
Empire and Elites after the Muslim Conquest: The Transformation of Northern Mesopotamia, Chase F. Robinson
Poverty and Charity in Medieval Islam: Mamluk Egypt, 1250–1517, Adam Sabra
Culture and Conquest in Mongol Eurasia, Thomas T. Allsen
Christians and Jews in the Ottoman Arab World: The Roots of Sectarianism, Bruce Masters
Arabic Administration in Norman Sicily: The Royal Diwan, Jeremy Johns
Law, Society and Culture in the Maghrib, 1300–1500, David S. Powers
Revival and Reform in Islam: The Legacy of Muhammad al-Shawkani, Bernard Haykel
Tolerance and Coercion in Islam: Interfaith Relations in the Muslim Tradition, Yohanan Friedmann
Guns for the Sultan: Military Power and the Weapons Industry in the Ottoman Empire, Gábor Ágoston
Marriage, Money and Divorce in Medieval Islamic Society, Yossef Rapoport
The Empire of the Qara Khitai in Eurasian History: Between China and the Islamic World, Michal Biran
Domesticity and Power in the Early Mughal World, Ruby Lal
Power, Politics and Religion in Timurid Iran, Beatrice Forbes Manz
Postal Systems in the Pre-Modern Islamic World, Adam J. Silverstein
Kingship and Ideology in the Islamic and Mongol Worlds, Anne F. Broadbridge
Justice, Punishment and the Medieval Muslim Imagination, Christian Lange
The Shiites of Lebanon under Ottoman Rule, 1516–1788, Stefan Winter
Women and Slavery in the Late Ottoman Empire, Madeline Zilfi
The Second Ottoman Empire: Political and Social Transformation in the Early Modern World, Baki Tezcan
The Legendary Biographies of Tamerlane: Islam and Heroic Apocrypha in Central Asia, Ron Sela
Non-Muslims in the Early Islamic Empire: From Surrender to Coexistence, Milka Levy-Rubin
The Origins of the Shīʿa: Identity, Ritual, and Sacred Space in Eighth-Century Kūfa, Najam Haider
Politics, Law, and Community in Islamic Thought: The Taymiyyan Moment, Ovamir Anjum
The Power of Oratory in the Medieval Muslim World, Linda G. Jones
Animals in the Qur'an, Sarra Tlili
The Logic of Law Making in Islam: Women and Prayer in the Legal Tradition, Behnam Sadeghi
Empire and Power in the Reign of Süleyman: Narrating the Sixteenth-Century Ottoman World, Kaya Şahin
Law and Piety in Medieval Islam, Megan H. Reid

Women and the Transmission of Religious Knowledge in Islam, Asma Sayeed
The New Muslims of Post-Conquest Iran: Tradition, Memory, and Conversion, Sarah Bowen Savant
The Mamluk City in the Middle East: History, Culture, and the Urban Landscape, Nimrod Luz
Disability in the Ottoman Arab World, 1500–1800, Sara Scalenghe
The Holy City of Medina: Sacred Space in Early Islamic Arabia, Harry Munt
Muslim Midwives: The Craft of Birthing in the Premodern Middle East, Avner Giladi
Doubt in Islamic Law: A History of Legal Maxims, Interpretation, and Islamic Criminal Law, Intisar A. Rabb
The Second Formation of Islamic Law: The Hanafi School in the Early Modern Ottoman Empire, Guy Burak
Sexual Violation in Islamic Law: Substance, Evidence, and Procedure, Hina Azam
Gender Hierarchy in the Qur'ān: Medieval Interpretations, Modern Responses, Karen Bauer
Intellectual Networks in Timurid Iran: Sharaf al-Dīn ʿAlī Yazdī and the Islamicate Republic of Letters, İlker Evrim Binbaş
Authority and Identity in Medieval Islamic Historiography: Persian Histories from the Peripheries, Mimi Hanaoka
The Economics of Ottoman Justice: Settlement and Trial in the Sharia Courts, Metin Coşgel and Boğaç Ergene
The Mystics of al-Andalus: Ibn Barrajān and Islamic Thought in the Twelfth Century, Yousef Casewit
Muhammad's Heirs: The Rise of Muslim Scholarly Communities, 622–950, Jonathan E. Brockopp
The First of the Modern Ottomans: The Intellectual History of Ahmed Vasif, Ethan Menchinger
Non-Muslim Provinces under Early Islam: Islamic Rule and Iranian Legitimacy in Armenia and Caucasian Albania, Alison Vacca
Women and the Making of the Mongol Empire, Anne F. Broadbridge
Slavery and Empire in Central Asia, Jeff Eden
Christianity in Fifteenth-Century Iraq, Thomas A. Carlson
Child Custody in Islamic Law: Theory and Practice in Egypt since the Sixteenth Century, Ahmed Fekry Ibrahim
Ibadi Muslims of North Africa: Manuscripts, Mobilization and the Making of a Written Tradition, Paul M. Love Jr.
Islamic Law of the Sea: Freedom of Navigation and Passage Rights in Islamic Thought, Hassan S. Khalilieh
Law and Politics under the Abassids: An Intellectual Portrait of al-Juwayni, Sohaira Z. M. Siddiqui
Friends of the Emir: Non-Muslim State Officials in Premodern Islamic Thought, Luke B. Yarbrough
The Crisis of Kingship in Late Medieval Islam: Persian Emigres and the Making of Ottoman Sovereignty, Christopher Markiewicz
Islam, Literature and Society in Mongol Anatolia, A. C. S. Peacock
Collective Liability in Islam: The ʿĀqila and Blood Money Payments, Nurit Tsafrir
Arabic Poetics: Aesthetic Experience in Classical Arabic Literature, Lara Harb

Persian Historiography across Empires: The Ottomans, Safavids, and Mughals, Sholeh A. Quinn

The Sufi Saint of Jam: History, Religion, and Politics of a Sunni Shrine in Shiʿi Iran, Shivan Mahendrarajah

Opposing the Imām: The Legacy of the Nawāṣib in Islamic Literature, Nebil Husayn

Revealed Sciences: The Natural Sciences in Islam in Seventeenth-Century Morocco, Justin K. Stearns

Agents of the Hidden Imam: Forging Twelver Shiʿism, 850–950 CE, Edmund Hayes

Islamic Law in Circulation: Shāfiʿī Texts across the Indian Ocean and the Mediterranean, Mahmood Kooria

Late Ottoman Origins of Modern Islamic Thought: Turkish and Egyptian Thinkers on the Disruption of Islamic Knowledge, Andrew Hammond

Female Religiosity in Central Asia: Sufi Leaders in the Persianate World, Aziza Shanazarova

The Science of Music: Knowledge Production in Medieval Baghdad and Beyond, Mohammad Sadegh Ansari

Universalism and Regionalism in the Early Islamic World: The Beginnings of Local History-Writing, Harry Munt

For EU product safety concerns, contact us at Calle de José Abascal, 56–1°,
28003 Madrid, Spain or eugpsr@cambridge.org.

www.ingramcontent.com/pod-product-compliance
Ingram Content Group UK Ltd.
Pitfield, Milton Keynes, MK11 3LW, UK
UKHW021842150226
468058UK00008B/112